Fundamentals of Financial Management

Fundamentals of Financial Management

Jake Collins

MURPHY & MOORE
www.murphy-moorepublishing.com

Published by Murphy & Moore Publishing,
1 Rockefeller Plaza,
New York City, NY 10020, USA

ISBN: 978-1-63987-245-9

Cataloging-in-Publication Data

Fundamentals of financial management / Jake Collins.
p. cm.
Includes bibliographical references and index.
ISBN 978-1-63987-245-9
1. Business enterprises--Finance. 2. Corporations--Finance. 3. Finance--Management.
I. Collins, Jake.

HG4011 .F86 2022
658.15--dc23

For information on all Murphy & Moore Publications
visit our website at www.murphy-moorepublishing.com

MURPHY & MOORE

Contents

Preface

Financial management is an area of business management which is devoted to the judicious use of capital and careful selection of the source of capital in order to enable a spending unit to reach the goals of the organization. It means applying general management principles to financial resources of the enterprise. The scope of financial management includes investment decisions, financial decisions and dividend decisions. Investment decisions include investment in fixed assets. Financial decisions are related to raising of finance from various resources. Dividend decisions are concerned with the finance manager who has to take decision with regards to the net profit distribution between shareholders and the enterprise. Basic objectives of financial management are maximization of profit, ensuring survival of company, minimizing capital cost, deliverance of significant returns, etc. This book explores all the important aspects of financial management in the present day scenario. The various sub-fields of financial management along with technological progress that have future implications are glanced at herein. Those in search of information to further their knowledge will be greatly assisted by this book.

Given below is the chapter wise description of the book:

Chapter 1- The strategic planning, directing, organizing and controlling of the financial activities of an organization or institute is referred to as financial management. It also entails the application of management principles to the financial assets of an organization. This is chapter will provide a brief introduction to all the significant aspects of financial management such as objectives of financial management and finance functions.

Chapter 2- Finance can be obtained from various sources such as retained earnings, lease financing, equity capital, preference shares and debentures. Retained earnings are the past profits earned by a company after subtracting the dividends it has paid in the past. This chapter discusses in detail these sources of finance for a complete understanding of the subject.

Chapter 3- The decisions made by investors as well as the top level management with regard to the amount of funds which have to be deployed in the investment opportunities are termed as investment decisions. This chapter closely examines the key concepts related to investment decisions, such as capital budgeting nature and process, to provide an extensive understanding of the subject.

Chapter 4- The decisions concerning the financing-mix of an organization taken by the financial manager are classified as financing decisions. They deal with the borrowing and dispensing of funds necessary for the investment decisions of an organization. The topics elaborated in this chapter will help in gaining a better perspective about financing decisions, cost of capital and capital structure.

Chapter 5- The important decisions taken by the finance manager with respect to the payout to the shareholders are called dividend decisions. A few of the models and theorems studied in relation to dividend decisions are Walter's model, Gordon's model and M&M hypothesis. This chapter discusses in detail these models and theorems connected to dividend decisions as well as dividend policies in practice.

Chapter 6- Working capital management is aimed at ensuring the efficient operation of a company by using the present liabilities and assets in an efficient manner. The working capital can be broadly categorized into gross working capital and net working capital. The diverse aspects of working capital management as well as these types of working capital have been thoroughly discussed in this chapter.

Chapter 7- The practice associated with the protection of economic value within a firm through the use of financial instruments in order to manage exposure to risk is termed as financial risk management. A few different types of risks considered within this field are operational risk, foreign exchange risk, credit risk and reputational risk. All these diverse types of risks and financial risk management have been carefully analyzed in this chapter.

At the end, I would like to thank all those who dedicated their time and efforts for the successful completion of this book. I also wish to convey my gratitude towards my friends and family who supported me at every step.

Jake Collins

1

Introduction to Financial Management

The strategic planning, directing, organizing and controlling of the financial activities of an organization or institute is referred to as financial management. It also entails the application of management principles to the financial assets of an organization. This is chapter will provide a brief introduction to all the significant aspects of financial management such as objectives of financial management and finance functions.

Meaning and Types of Finance

Finance is a term for matters regarding the management, creation, and study of money and investments. Finance can be broadly divided into three categories:

- Public finance
- Corporate finance
- Personal finance

There are many other specific categories, such as behavioral finance, which seeks to identify the cognitive (e.g., emotional, social, and psychological) reasons behind financial decisions.

Understanding Finance

"Finance" is typically broken down into three broad categories: Public finance includes tax systems, government expenditures, budget procedures, stabilization policy and instruments, debt issues, and other government concerns. Corporate finance involves managing assets, liabilities, revenues, and debts for a business. Personal finance defines all financial decisions and activities of an individual or household, including budgeting, insurance, mortgage planning, savings, and retirement planning.

Finance as a study of theory and practice distinct from the field of economics arose in the 1940s and 1950s with the works of Markowitz, Tobin, Sharpe, Treynor, Black, and Scholes, to name just a few. But particular realms of finance such as banking, lending, and investing, of course, money itself—have been around since the dawn of civilization in some form or another.

Around 3000 BC, banking seems to have originated in the Babylonian/Sumerian Empire where temples and palaces were used as safe places for the storage of financial assets grain, cattle, and silver or copper ingots. Grain was the currency of choice in the country, while silver was preferred in the city.

The financial transactions of the early Sumerians were formalized in the Babylonian Code of Hammurabi. This set of rules regulated ownership or rental of land, employment of agricultural labor, and credit. Yes, there were loans back then, and yes, interest was charged on them rates varied depending on whether you were borrowing grain or silver.

By 1200 BC, cowrie shells were used as a form of money in China. Coined money was introduced in the first millennium BC. King Croesus of Lydia (now Turkey) was one of the first to strike and circulate gold coins around 564 BC hence the expression, “rich as Croesus.”

Early Stocks, Bonds and Options

From the 6th century BC to the 1st century AD, the ancient Greeks enumerated six different types of loans; personal loans charged interest as high as 48% per month. There were also options contracts. According to Aristotle, a man named Thales went long on olive presses—buying the rights to use them, as he anticipated a big olive harvest. (He was right.)

Bills of exchange were developed during the middle ages as a means of transferring funds and making payments over long distances without physically moving large quantities of precious metals. Thirteenth-century merchants, bankers, and foreign exchange dealers used them in major European trading centers, like Genoa and Flanders.

The first financial exchange, dealing in commodities and, later, bonds and futures contacts, was the Antwerp Exchange, founded in 1460. During the 17th century, the action shifted to Amsterdam. 1602 saw the arrival of the first public company, the VOC (Vereenigde Oost-Indische Compagnie or United East India Company), which issued shares anyone could trade—on the newly created Amsterdam Exchange, the Western world’s first stock market.

Advances in Accounting

Compound interest interest calculated not just on principal but on previously accrued interest was known to ancient civilizations (the Babylonians had a phrase for “interest on interest,” which basically defines the concept). But it was not until medieval times that mathematicians started to analyze it in order to show how invested sums could mount up: One of the earliest and most important sources is the arithmetical manuscript written in 1202 by Leonardo Fibonacci of Pisa, known as Liber Abaci, which gives examples comparing compound and simple interest.

The first comprehensive treatise on book-keeping and accountancy, Luca Pacioli's Summa de arithmetica, geometria, proportioni et proportionalita, was published in Venice in 1494. A book on accountancy and arithmetic written by William Colson appeared in 1612, containing the earliest tables of compound interest written in English. A year later, Richard Witt published his Arithmeticall Questions in London in 1613, and compound interest was thoroughly accepted.

Towards the end of the 17th century, in England and the Netherlands, interest calculations were combined with age-dependent survival rates to create the first life annuities.

Public Finance

The federal government helps prevent market failure by overseeing the allocation of resources, distribution of income, and stabilization of the economy. Regular funding for these programs is secured mostly through taxation. Borrowing from banks, insurance companies, and other governments and earning dividends from its companies also help finance the federal government.

State and local governments also receive grants and aid from the federal government. Other sources of public finance include user charges from ports, airport services, and other facilities; fines resulting from breaking laws; revenues from licenses and fees, such as for driving; and sales of government securities and bond issues.

Corporate Finance

Businesses obtain financing through a variety of means, ranging from equity investments to credit arrangements. A firm might take out a loan from a bank or arrange for a line of credit. Acquiring and managing debt properly can help a company expand and become more profitable.

Startups may receive capital from angel investors or venture capitalists in exchange for a percentage of ownership. If a company thrives and goes public, it will issue shares on a stock exchange; such initial public offerings (IPO) bring a great influx of cash into a firm. Established companies may sell additional shares or issue corporate bonds to raise money. Businesses may purchase dividend-paying stocks, blue-chip bonds, or interest-bearing bank certificates of deposits (CD); they may also buy other companies in an effort to boost revenue.

Personal Finance

Personal financial planning generally involves analyzing an individual's or a family's current financial position, predicting short-term and long-term needs, and executing a plan to fulfill those needs within individual financial constraints. Personal finance depends largely on one's earnings, living requirements, and individual goals and desires.

Matters of personal finance include but are not limited to, the purchasing of financial products for personal reasons, like credit cards; life, health, and home insurance; mortgages; and retirement products. Personal banking is also considered a part of personal finance.

The most important aspects of personal finance include:

- Assessing the current financial status: expected cash flow, current savings, etc.
- Buying insurance to protect against risk and to ensure one's material standing is secure.
- Calculating and filing taxes.
- Savings and investments.
- Retirement planning.

As a specialized field, personal finance is a recent development, though forms of it have been taught in universities and schools as "home economics" or "consumer economics" since the early 20th century. The field was initially disregarded by male economists, as "home economics" appeared to be the purview of housewives. Recently, economists have repeatedly stressed widespread education in matters of personal finance as integral to the macro performance of the overall national economy.

Social Finance

Social finance typically refers to investments made in social enterprises including charitable organizations and some cooperatives. Rather than an outright donation, these investments take the form of equity or debt financing, in which the investor seeks both a financial reward as well as a social gain.

Modern forms of social finance also include some segments of microfinance, specifically loans to small business owners and entrepreneurs in less developed countries to enable their enterprises to grow. Lenders earn a return on their loans while simultaneously helping to improve individuals standard of living and to benefit the local society and economy.

Social impact bonds (also known as Pay for Success Bonds or social benefit bonds) are a specific type of instrument that acts as a contract with the public sector or local government. Repayment and return on investment are contingent upon the achievement of certain social outcomes and achievements.

Behavioral Finance

There was a time when theoretical and empirical evidence seemed to suggest that conventional financial theories were reasonably successful at predicting and explaining certain types of economic events. Nonetheless, as time went on, academics in the financial and economic realms detected anomalies and behaviors which occurred in the real world but could not be explained by any available theories.

It became increasingly clear that conventional theories could explain certain "idealized" events but that the real world was, in fact, a great deal more messy and disorganized, and that market participants frequently behave in ways that are irrational, and thus difficult to predict according to those models.

As a result, academics began to turn to cognitive psychology in order to account for irrational and illogical behaviors which are unexplained by modern financial theory. Behavioral science is the field that was born out of these efforts; it seeks to explain our actions, whereas modern finance seeks to explain the actions of the idealized "economic man" (Homo economicus).

Behavioral finance, a sub-field of behavioral economics, proposes psychology-based theories to explain financial anomalies, such as severe rises or falls in stock price. The purpose is to identify and understand why people make certain financial choices. Within behavioral finance, it is assumed the information structure and the characteristics of market participants systematically influence individuals' investment decisions as well as market outcomes.

Tenets of Behavioral Finance

Behavioral finance encompasses many concepts, but four are key: mental accounting, herd behavior, anchoring, and high self-rating and overconfidence. Mental accounting refers to the propensity for people to allocate money for specific purposes based on miscellaneous subjective criteria, including the source of the money and the intended use for each account. The theory of mental accounting suggests that individuals are likely to assign different functions to each asset group or account, the result of which can be an illogical, even detrimental, set of behaviors. For instance, some people keep a special "money jar" set aside for a vacation or a new home while at the same time carrying substantial credit card debt.

Herd behavior states that people tend to mimic the financial behaviors of the majority, or herd, whether those actions are rational or irrational. In many cases, herd behavior is a set of decisions and actions that an individual would not necessarily make on his or her own but which seem to have legitimacy because "everyone's doing it." Herd behavior often is considered a major cause of financial panics and stock market crashes.

Anchoring refers to attaching spending to a certain reference point or level, even though it may have no logical relevance to the decision at hand. One common example of "anchoring" is the conventional wisdom that a diamond engagement ring should cost about two months' worth of salary. Another might be buying a stock that briefly rose from trading around $65 to hit $80 and then fell back to $65, out of a sense that it's now a bargain (anchoring your strategy at that $80 price). While that could be true, it's more likely that the $80 figure was an anomaly, and $65 is the true value of the shares.

High self-rating refers to a person's tendency to rank him/herself better than others or higher than an average person. For example, an investor may think that he is an investment guru when his investments perform optimally, blocking out the investments that are performing poorly. High self-rating goes hand-in-hand with overconfidence, which reflects the tendency to overestimate or exaggerate one's ability to successfully perform a given task. Overconfidence can be harmful to an investor's ability to pick stocks.

What is Financial Management?

Financial Management means applying management principles to manage the financial resources of an organization. It simply involves planning, organizing, directing, and controlling financial operations to manage the finance of an organization efficiently. Financial Management is a methodology that a business implements to monitor and govern its revenue, expenses, and assets in order to maximize profitability and ensure sustainability.

Management of finance is a vital part of every business. Finance is termed as the backbone of every business and is required for carrying out each and every activity. Financial management is concerned with efficiently planning the procurement of funds and the utilization of these funds in the business. The finance manager is required to decide the proper capital structure of an organization deciding the optimum mix of debt and equity for raising required funds. Financial management concept ensures that an adequate amount of funds is always available in business from different sources and also it earns the best return on its investments.

Scope of Financial Management

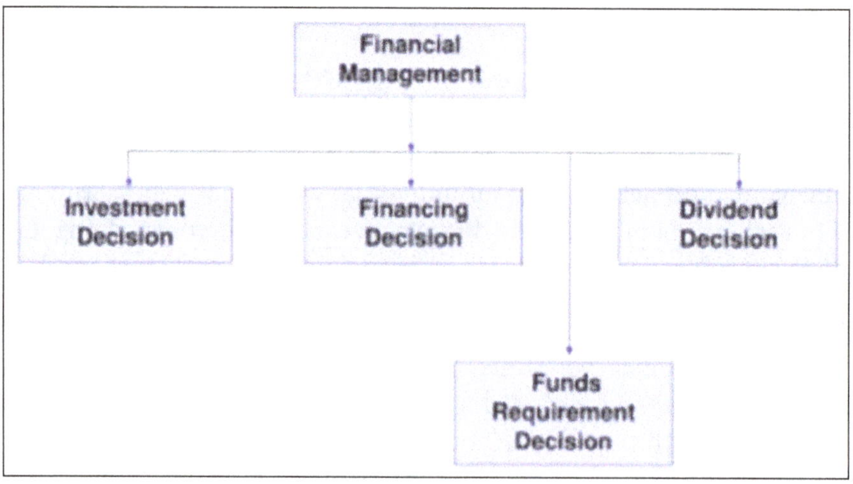

Investment Decision

Financial management is involved in managing all investment decisions of an organization. Investment decisions involve risk evaluation, measuring the cost of capital, and estimating benefits expected out of a particular project. Managers are responsible for deciding how available funds should be invested in fixed or current assets to earn optimum returns.

Working Capital Decision

Taking working capital decisions properly is another important scope of financial management. These decisions are concerned with investment in current assets or current liabilities. Working capital decisions revolve around working capital and short-term financing. Current assets include cash, inventories, receivables, short-term securities, etc. whereas current liabilities include creditors, bank overdraft, bills payable.

Financing Decision

Financing decisions involves deciding how the required funds should be raised from available long term or short term sources. A financial manager is required to form a proper finance mix or optimum capital structure of the company to raise its value. They are required to maintain a proper balance between equity and debt to provide maximum return to shareholders.

Dividend Decision

Financial management involves taking all dividend decisions of the company. These decisions involve developing a proper dividend policy regarding the distribution or retaining of company profits. The finance manager should decide an optimum dividend payout ratio out of available profit. He should consider all expansion and growth opportunities available to the organization and should avail them by retaining a proper amount of profit.

Ensures Liquidity

Maintaining proper liquidity in an organization is another important role played by financial management. The finance manager ensures that there is a regular supply of funds in an organization. He monitors all cash-inflows and cash-outflows and avoids any underflow or overflow like situations. Ensuring the optimum level of liquidity in an organization is one of the important scopes of financial management.

Profit Management

Financial management aims at increasing the profit of the company. It works towards reducing the cost of various activities through proper monitoring and setting up proper price policy. The finance manager measures the cost of capital and chooses cheap sources of capital by properly analyzing different sources available.

Nature of Financial Management

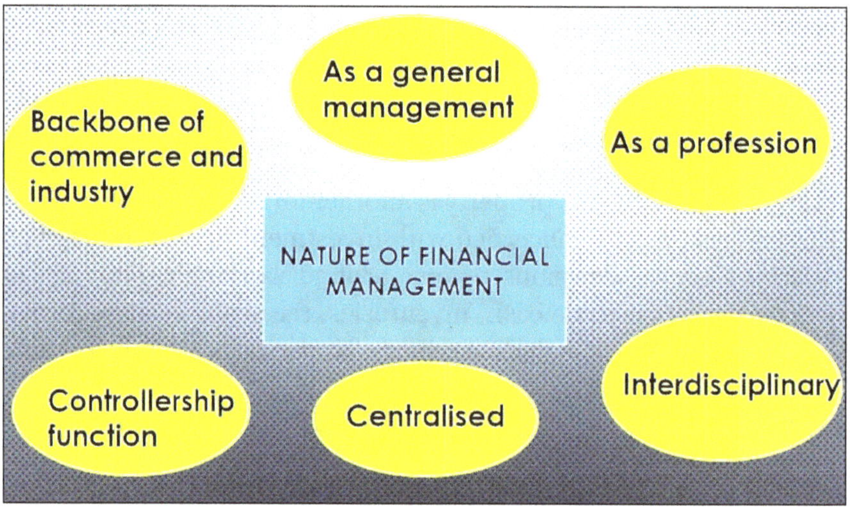

Estimates Capital Requirements

Financial management helps in anticipation of funds required for running the business. It estimates working and fixed capital requirements for carrying out all business activities. The finance manager prepares a budget of all expenses and revenues for a particular time period on the basis of which capital requirements are determined.

Decides Capital Structure

Deciding optimum capital structure for an organization is a must for attaining efficiency and earning better profits. It involves deciding the proper portion of different securities like common equity, preferred equity, and debt. The proper balance between debt and equity should be attained which minimizes the cost of capital.

Select Sources of Fund

Choosing the source of funds is one of the crucial decisions for every organization. There are various sources available for raising funds like shares, bonds, debentures, venture capital, financial institutions, retained earnings, owner investment, etc. Every business should properly analyze different sources of funds available and choose one which is cheapest and involves minimal risk.

Selects Investment Pattern

Once funds are procured it is important to allocate them among profitable investment avenues. The investment proposal should be properly analyzed regarding its safety, profitability, and liquidity. Before investing any amount in it all risk and return associated with it should be properly evaluated.

Raises Shareholders Value

Financial management works towards raising the overall value of shareholders. It aims at increasing the amount of return to shareholders by reducing the cost of operations and increasing the profits. The finance manager focuses on raising cheap funds from different sources and invest them in the most profitable avenues.

Management of Cash

Financial management monitors all funds movement in an organization. Finance managers supervise all cash movements through proper accounting of all cash inflows and outflows. They ensure that there is no situation like deficiency or surplus of cash in an organization.

Apply Financial Controls

Implying financial controls in business is a beneficial role played by financial management. It helps in keeping the company actual cost of operation within the limit and earning the expected profits. There are various processes involved in this like developing certain standards for business in advance, comparing the actual cost or performance with pre-established standards, and taking all required remedial measures.

Objectives of Financial Management

Profit Maximization as Objective of Financial Management

In the traditional phase, profit maximization was pointed out to be the important objective of financial management. Main motive of business concern is to earn profit. It can be said that most businesses function mainly for the purpose of earning profits. Profit is the yardstick by which efficiency of business operations can be measured. Profit maximization as objective of financial management means that all financial decisions in a firm are guided by the criteria of amount of profits that the financial decision generates or saves. Unprofitable projects and investment alternatives would be rejected. If sufficient funds are not available to finance all profitable investment projects then those with highest profits would be selected.

Arguments in Favor

Profit maximization as objective of financial management is justified on the following grounds:

- Main purpose of most businesses is to earn profits.
- Profit can be a suitable criterion for measuring success of business operations.
- Profit maximization ensures efficient utilization of scarce financial resources as these resources are allocated to uses which generate maximum profits.
- Profit maximization may lead to maximization of economic welfare of society. Since each individual component of society would seek maximum profitability, the economic welfare of society as a whole would be maximized.

Limitations

However, profit maximization as objective of financial management is severely criticised on following basis:

- It is a vague and ambiguous objective. The term profit is not specifically defined. It can mean Profit after tax or profit before tax, total profit or incremental profits.
- It does not consider the time value of money: Timing of receipt of benefits (cash inflows) is not considered. It does not make any difference between cash inflows occurring at different points of time.
- It ignores risk: Quality of benefits is also ignored. Profit maximization does not consider risk of not receiving or receiving less than expected cash inflows.
- The objective of a business enterprise is not just to maximize profit but also to create value for its owners.
- Based on Accounting Profit: Accounting profits can be easily affected by management through altering of accounting policies underlying the calculation of accounting profits.

Due to above drawbacks, profit maximization is regarded as an unrealistic and inappropriate objective of financial management.

Shareholder's Wealth Maximization as Objective of Financial Management

In the modern phase, the objective of financial management is considered to be Shareholder's Wealth Maximization. Since it is based on the concept of cash flows and considers timing of benefits, it overcomes the limitations of Profit Maximization objective and provides a realistic objective.

Shareholders' wealth includes market value of company's shares, reserves and surplus, accumulated profits. However, the main component is market value of shares. Market Value of Shares or Market Capitalization = Market price per Share x No. of Shares. Therefore, the finance manager should take all financial decisions in such a way that market value of firm's shares is maximized. Now since the no. of shares remain fixed over a given period of time. The focus of finance manager should be on maximization of market price per share so that shareholder's wealth is maximized. Finance manager may achieve higher share price quickly by selecting high risk-high return projects. But this may backfire which could result in a significant fall in share prices. If shareholders are not satisfied with the functioning of management or progress of the organization, they can communicate their displeasure by selling company's share which would end in a fall in share prices.

Other popular names for Wealth maximization are net present worth maximization or value maximization. This objective maximizes the net present value of a course of action to shareholders. This is based on the presumption that finance managers will seek to maximize the worth of shareholder's total investments. In this regard, finance managers would want to maximize the value of all investment projects which the firm selects and undertakes. For this, the net present value of a project is obtained based on its projected cash inflows and outflows and the cost of capital to the firm (discount rate). Net Present Value (NPV) can be obtained by subtracting present value of all cash outflows of the project from present value of all cash inflows received during the lifetime of the project.

$$NPV = \left[\frac{C_1}{(1+k)} + \frac{C_2}{(1+k)^2} + \frac{C_3}{(1+k)^3} + .. + \frac{C_n}{(1+k)^n}\right] - C_0$$

$$NPV = \sum_{t=1}^{n} \frac{C_t}{(1=k)^t} - C_0$$

Where: n = life of the project in years.

C_1, C_2, C_3, ... Cn are cash inflows of years 1,2,3, ... n.

C_0 is the initial cash outflow of the project.

k is the discount rate. It is the opportunity rate of return of investors or cost of capital of the firm.

Decision Rule:

- When the projects are not mutually exclusive: All projects with positive NPV i.e.,

NPV > 0 would be accepted because a positive NPV means that the project would increase shareholder's wealth. For example, if NPV of a project is + $ 50,000 it implies that undertaking the project would increase shareholder's wealth by $.50,000.

- When the projects are mutually exclusive: When the projects are mutually exclusive then the project with highest NPV should be selected. Further, in case there are several projects with positive NPV and there is a constraint of funds the projects may be ranked from highest NPV to lowest NPV and selected in that order so as to maximise shareholder's wealth.

Arguments in Favour

- Wealth maximization aims to maximise the value of investments or wealth of the shareholders. Hence is considered superior to profit maximization.
- It is based on the concept of Cash Flows, which is precise and unambiguous unlike profit. Here cash inflow is treated as benefit and cash outflow as cost associated with a particular decision.
- Wealth maximization considers the timing of occurrence of benefits (cash inflows) and costs (cash outflows). It thus takes into account the time value of money.
- Wealth maximization also considers the risk associated with occurrence of cash flows.
- Wealth maximization ensures that funds of a company are allocated to those uses which generate maximum value or worth to the shareholders.
- Shareholder's wealth maximization also upholds the economic welfare of the society as a whole by ensuring efficient allocation of society's scarce capital resources.

Criticism

- It is difficult to incorporate shareholder's wealth maximization as objective of financial management in day to day functioning of a modern business enterprise.
- Wealth maximization creates owners-management conflict and gives rise to agency problem.
- Wealth maximization is criticized on the grounds that it seeks to maximise only shareholder's wealth and is not concerned about welfare of other important stakeholders of the business such as management, creditors, employees, suppliers, distributors, customers.
- The criterion of wealth maximization is maximization of market price of a firm's shares. But in real life, share prices are affected by a large no. of reasons on which business has no control.

- Some argue that Wealth maximization is not much different than profit maximization. It is profit maximization in another form.

Profit Maximization vs. Shareholder's Wealth Maximization

Basis	Profit Maximization	Shareholder's Wealth Maximization.
Meaning	Goal of financial management is to maximise profits of the business organization.	Goal of financial management is to maximise wealth of the shareholders or owners of the business organization.
Vagueness	Objective is not clear and hence is vague and ambiguous.	Objective is clear and precise having no scope for vagueness and ambiguity.
Criteria	Maximization of Accounting Profits.	Maximization of Market Price per Share.
Time Value of Money	Ignores Time Value of Money.	Considers Time Value of Money.
Risk	Does not consider risk associated with cash flows.	Takes into account, the riskiness of cash flows.
Basis of Computation	Accounting Profits	Cash Flows
Acceptability	It is not widely accepted as objective of financial management.	It is widely accepted as objective of financial management.
Imperfect Markets	Makes assumption of perfect competition and hence is not applicable in imperfect markets.	Makes no such assumption and so can be universally applied to all market forms.
Manipulation	Can be easily manipulated by changing accounting policies.	Cannot be easily manipulated.

Other Objectives of Financial Management

Stakeholder's Welfare Maximization

Stakeholder in a company is anyone who has an interest in the company, can influence the fortunes of the company or is itself influenced by the happenings related to the company. Shareholders, management, creditors, employees and employee unions, suppliers, distributors, consumers and consumer groups, government and its agencies, local people living in close proximity to the business, environment groups and society at large are the main stakeholders of a company. Each of these groups are important for the functioning of the business. Thus, a finance manager cannot seek to maximise the interests of any one group and ignore the needs of others. Because the financial resources at the disposal of finance manager are limited he/she cannot maximise the benefits to every stakeholders. Also even if he/she had enough financial resources then also it would not have been possible because often the interests of various stakeholders are in conflict with each other.

For example:

- While shareholders would want more percentage of after tax profits to be distributed as dividends, the managers would want to retain more percentage of after tax profits in the business to meet future growth needs.

- Creditors would want firm to undertake lower risk projects so that their claims can be met but shareholders would want firm to undertake more risky projects so that they can earn more returns.
- Suppliers, distributors and employees would want higher payments, margins and salary respectively which would increase cost and hence price of the product but customers would want lower prices.

Thus, a finance manager has to indulge in a satisficing behaviour whereby the minimum requirements of all stakeholders are fulfilled. The extent to which a stakeholder's expectations are met will depend upon the degree of influence which that stakeholder possesses on the business in relation to other stakeholders. The shareholders wealth Maximization as the primary goal notwithstanding, there is a broader focus in financial management to include the interest of other stakeholders along with that of the shareholders. The goal should be to preserve the well-being of all stakeholders and not to maximise welfare of few of them.

However, it should not be inferred that stakeholder's welfare maximization is in conflict with the shareholder's wealth maximization objective. Protection of interest of various stakeholders and enhancement of their welfare is a corporation's responsibility. It in fact maximizes value to the shareholders in the long run by enabling a favorable relationship with various stakeholders and in turn minimizing stakeholder turnovers, clashes and lawsuits.

Maximization of Economic Value Added

The EVA can be obtained by deducting cost of funds used to finance an investment project from after-tax operating profits generated by the project.

EVA = Net Operating Profit after Tax – {Firm's Weighted Average Cost of Capital (%) * Total Capital Invested}.

If after tax operating profits are greater than cost of funds used for financing then EVA would be positive. If cost of funds are greater than after tax profits then EVA would be negative. A positive EVA would mean addition to shareholder's wealth by the amount of positive EVA and a negative EVA would cause shareholder's wealth to decline by the amount of negative EVA. Hence, only those investment projects which have positive EVA should be undertaken.

EVA is praised as objective of financial management because it is relatively simpler than other approaches and easy to understand; is theoretically sound and exhibits correlation with share prices, i.e., positive EVA can cause share prices to increase and vice versa. However, NPV is preferred over EVA as EVA does not account for size differences across projects, relies on financial accounting methods of revenue realization and expense recognition for computation and does not consider future cash flows by not computing their present value.

Maximization of Earning Per Share

EPS is obtained by deducting Preference share dividend from Net Income after tax and dividing by average outstanding equity shares. It gives earning per equity share.

$$\text{Earning Per Share (EPS)} = \frac{\text{Net Income after Tax} - \text{Dividend On Preference Shares}}{\text{Average Outstanding Equity Shares}}$$

In this approach, finance manager takes all actions with an aim to maximize earnings per share. Impact of all decision alternatives on EPS is seen. Only those investment projects are selected which increase EPS. All alternative courses of action which decrease EPS are not undertaken. This objective of financial management implies that all financial management decisions, viz., capital budgeting, capital structure, dividend and working capital management policy decisions of a firm are concerned with maximization of EPS. Maximizing EPS does not imply maximization of shareholder's wealth. The two concepts are different. Maximization of EPS ignores time value of money and risk associated with expected benefits. Also, market price of a company's share is not directly related to EPS. EPS can be one of the several factors influencing the market price of a company's share.

Maximization of Sales

In pursuance of this objective, the finance manager aims to maximise sales volume through cutting of prices, adding additional features and improving quality of the products, undertaking aggressive advertising and sales promotion campaigns, widening distribution networks and adding more intermediaries to penetrate deep in the market. However, this is not generally regarded as the objective of financial management because higher sales volume does not necessarily mean equal proportionate increase in profits of the enterprise or wealth of the shareholders or welfare of the stakeholders.

Maximization of Market Share

In this objective, focus is on establishing the firm as market leader by acquiring maximum percentage share of the overall market. Firm seeks to be the No.1 among companies operating in the market and wishes to create a brand, goodwill or image of the company to which everyone relates. It involves undertaking aggressive strategies to reach that position. But again like sales maximization, maximization of market share is also not considered as the objective of financial management because there does not exist a perfect correlation between higher market share and increased wealth of the shareholders or profitability of the business.

Finance Functions

The Finance Function is a part of financial management. Financial Management is the activity concerned with the control and planning of financial resources. In business, the finance function involves the acquiring and utilization of funds necessary for efficient operations. Finance is the lifeblood of business without it things wouldn't run smoothly. It is the source to run any organization, it provides the money, it acquires the money.

The Finance function has been classified into three:

- Long-Term Finance: This includes finance of investment 3 years or more. Sources of long-term finance include owner capital, share capital, long-term loans, debentures, internal funds and so on.
- Medium Term Finance: This is financing done between 1 to 3 years, this can be sourced from bank loans and financial institutions.
- Short Term Finance: This is finance needed below one year. Funds may be acquired from bank overdrafts, commercial paper, advances from customers, trade credit etc.

Objectives of Finance Functions

- Investment Decisions: This is where the finance manager decides where to put the company funds. Investment decisions relating to the management of working capital, capital budgeting decisions, management of mergers, buying or leasing of assets. Investment decisions should create revenue, profits and save costs.
- Financing Decisions: Here a company decides where to raise funds from. They are two main sources to consider mainly equity and borrowed. From the two a decision on the appropriate mix of short and long-term financing should be made. The sources of financing best at a given time should also be agreed upon.
- Dividend Decisions: These are decisions as to how much, how frequent and in what form to return cash to owners. A balance between profits retained and the amount paid out as dividends should be decided here.
- Liquidity Decisions: Liquidity means that a firm has enough money to pay its bills when they are due and have sufficient cash reserves to meet unforeseen emergencies. This decision involves the management of the current assets so you don't become insolvent or fail to make payments.

Why a Business Needs the Finance Functions

- Helps Establish a Business: Without money, you cannot get labor, land and so on with the finance function you can determine what is required to start your business and plan for it.

- Helps Run a Business: To remain in business you must cater to the day to day operating costs such as paying salaries, buying stationery, raw material, the finance function ensures you always have adequate funds to cater to this.
- To Expand, Modernize, Diversify: A business needs to grow otherwise it may become redundant in no time. With the finance function, you can determine and acquire the funds required to do so.
- Purchase Assets: You need money to purchase assets. This can be tangible assets like furniture, buildings or intangible like trademarks, patents, etc. to get this you need finances.

Importance of Finance Functions

- Identify Need of Finance: To starts a business you need to know how much is required to open it. So, the finance function helps you know how much the initial capital is, how much of it you have and how much you need to raise.
- Identify Sources of Finance: Once you know what needs to be raised you look at areas you can raise these funds from. You can borrow or get from various shareholders.
- Comparison of Various Sources of Finance: After identifying various fund sources compare the cost and risk involved. Then choose the best source of financing that suits your business needs.
- Investment: Once the funds are raised it is time to invest them. Investment decisions should be done in a manner that a business gets higher returns. Cost of funds procurement should be lower than the return on investment this will show a wise investment was made.

The Finance Function Involves

- Ensure enough funds at a reasonable cost.
- Ensure the safety of funds.
- Ensure efficient effective and profitable utilization of funds.
- Ensure that finance funds don't remain idle.

Time Value of Money - I

The time value of money (TVM) is the concept that money you have now is worth more than the identical sum in the future due to its potential earning capacity. This core principle of finance holds that provided money can earn interest, any amount of money is worth more the sooner it is received. TVM is also sometimes referred to as present discounted value.

The time value of money draws from the idea that rational investors prefer to receive money today rather than the same amount of money in the future because of money's potential to grow in value over a given period of time. For example, money deposited into a savings account earns a certain interest rate and is therefore said to be compounding in value.

Further illustrating the rational investor's preference assume you have the option to choose between receiving $10,000 now versus $10,000 in two years. It's reasonable to assume most people would choose the first option. Despite the equal value at the time of disbursement, receiving the $10,000 today has more value and utility to the beneficiary than receiving it in the future due to the opportunity costs associated with the wait. Such opportunity costs could include the potential gain on interest were that money received today and held in a savings account for two years.

Time Value of Money Formula

Depending on the exact situation in question, the time value of money formula may change slightly. For example, in the case of annuity or perpetuity payments, the generalized formula has additional or less factors. But in general, the most fundamental TVM formula takes into account the following variables:

- FV = Future value of money.
- PV = Present value of money.
- i = interest rate.
- n = number of compounding periods per year.
- t = number of years.

Based on these variables, the formula for TVM is:

$$FV = PV \times [1 + (i / n)]^{(n \times t)}$$

Time Value of Money Examples

Assume a sum of $10,000 is invested for one year at 10% interest. The future value of that money is:

FV = $10,000 x [1 + (10% / 1)] ^ (1 x 1) = $11,000

The formula can also be rearranged to find the value of the future sum in present day dollars. For example, the value of $5,000 one year from today, compounded at 7% interest, is:

PV = $5,000 / [1 + (7% / 1)] ^ (1 x 1) = $4,673

Effect of Compounding Periods on Future Value

The number of compounding periods can have a drastic effect on the TVM calculations. Taking the $10,000 example above, if the number of compounding periods is increased to quarterly, monthly, or daily, the ending future value calculations are:

- Quarterly Compounding: FV = $10,000 x [1 + (10% / 4)] ^ (4 x 1) = $11,038.
- Monthly Compounding: FV = $10,000 x [1 + (10% / 12)] ^ (12 x 1) = $11,047.
- Daily Compounding: FV = $10,000 x [1 + (10% / 365)] ^ (365 x 1) = $11,052.

This shows TVM depends not only on interest rate and time horizon, but also on how many times the compounding calculations are computed each year.

Time Value of Money - II

Congratulations!!! You have won a cash prize! You have two payment options:

- A: Receive $10,000 now

Or,

- B: Receive $10,000 in three years. Which option would you choose?

The answer depends on your understanding of the time value of money (TMV).

If you're like most people, you would choose to receive the $10,000 now. After all, three years is a long time to wait. Why would any rational person defer payment into the future when they could have the same amount of money now? For most of us, taking the money in the present is just plain instinctive. So at the most basic level, the time value of money demonstrates that all things being equal, it seems better to have money now rather than later.

But why is this? A $100 bill has the same value as a $100 bill one year from now, doesn't it? Actually, although the bill is the same, you can do much more with the money if you have it now because over time you can earn more interest on your money.

Back to our example: By receiving $10,000 today, you are poised to increase the future value of your money by investing and gaining interest over a period of time. For Option

B, you don't have time on your side, and the payment received in three years would be your future value.

If you are choosing Option A, your future value will be $10,000 plus any interest acquired over the three years. The future value for Option B, on the other hand, would only be $10,000. So how can you calculate exactly how much more Option A is worth, compared to Option B?

Future Value Basics

If you choose Option A and invest the total amount at a simple annual rate of 4.5%, the future value of your investment at the end of the first year is $10,450. We arrive at this sum by multiplying the principal amount of $10,000 by the interest rate of 4.5% and then adding the interest gained to the principal amount:

$$\$10{,}000 \times 0.045 = \$450$$

$$\$450 + \$10{,}000 = \$10{,}450$$

You can also calculate the total amount of a one-year investment with a simple manipulation:

$$OE = (\$10{,}000 \times 0.045) + \$10{,}000 = \$10{,}450$$

Where: OE=Original equation

$$\text{Manipulation} = \$10{,}000 \times [(1 \times 0.045) + 1] = \$10{,}450$$

$$\text{Final Equation} = \$10{,}000 \times (0.045 + 1) = \$10{,}450$$

The manipulated equation above is simply a removal of the like-variable $10,000 (the principal amount) by dividing the entire original equation by $10,000.

If the $10,450 left in your investment account at the end of the first year is left untouched and you invested it at 4.5% for another year, how much would you have? To calculate this, you would take the $10,450 and multiply it again by 1.045 (0.045 +1). At the end of two years, you would have $10,920.25.

Calculating Future Value

The above calculation, then, is equivalent to the following equation:

$$\text{Future Value} = \$10{,}000 \times (1 + 0.045) \times (1 + 0.045)$$

The rule of exponents, which states that the multiplication of like terms is equivalent to adding their exponents. In the above equation, the two like terms are (1+ 0.045), and the exponent on each is equal to 1. Therefore, the equation can be represented as the following:

$$\text{Future Value} = \$10{,}000 \times (1 + 0.045)^2$$

We can see that the exponent is equal to the number of years for which the money is earning interest in an investment. So, the equation for calculating the three-year future value of the investment would look like this:

$$\text{Future Value} = \$10{,}000 \times (1+0.045)^3$$

However, we don't need to keep on calculating the future value after the first year, then the second year, then the third year, and so on. You can figure it all at once, so to speak. If you know the present amount of money you have in an investment, its rate of return, and how many years you would like to hold that investment, you can calculate the future value (FV) of that amount. It's done with the equation:

$$FV = PV \times (1+i)^n$$

Where: FV=Future value

PV=Present value (original amount of money)

i=Interest rate per period

n=Number of periods

Present Value Basics

If you received $10,000 today, its present value would, of course, be $10,000 because the present value is what your investment gives you now if you were to spend it today. If you were to receive $10,000 in one year, the present value of the amount would not be $10,000 because you do not have it in your hand now, in the present.

To find the present value of the $10,000 you will receive in the future, you need to pretend that the $10,000 is the total future value of an amount that you invested today. In other words, to find the present value of the future $10,000, we need to find out how much we would have to invest today in order to receive that $10,000 in one year.

To calculate the present value, or the amount that we would have to invest today, you must subtract the (hypothetical) accumulated interest from the $10,000. To achieve this, we can discount the future payment amount ($10,000) by the interest rate for the period. In essence, all you are doing is rearranging the future value equation above so that you may solve for present value (PV). The above future value equation can be rewritten as follows:

$$PV = \frac{FV}{(1+i)^n}$$

An alternate equation would be:

$$PV = FV \times (1+i)^{-n}$$

Where: PV=Present value (original amount of money)

FV=Future value

i=Interest rate per period

n=Number of periods

Calculating Present Value

Let's walk backward from the $10,000 offered in Option B. Remember the $10,000 to be received in three years is really the same as the future value of an investment. If we had one year to go before getting the money, we would discount the payment back one year. Using our present value formula, at the current two-year mark, the present value of the $10,000 to be received in one year would be $\$10{,}000 \times (1 + .045)^{-1} = \$9569.38$.

Note that if today we were at the one-year mark, the above $9,569.38 would be considered the future value of our investment one year from now.

Continuing on, at the end of the first year we would be expecting to receive the payment of $10,000 in two years. At an interest rate of 4.5%, the calculation for the present value of a $10,000 payment expected in two years would be $\$10{,}000 \times (1 + .045)^{-2} = \$9157.30$.

Of course, because of the rule of exponents, we don't have to calculate the future value of the investment every year counting back from the $10,000 investment in the third year. We could put the equation more concisely and use the $10,000 as FV. So, here is how you can calculate today's present value of the $10,000 expected from a three-year investment earning 4.5%:

$$\$8{,}762.97=\$10{,}000\times(1+.045)^{-3}$$

So the present value of a future payment of $10,000 is worth $8,762.97 today if interest rates are 4.5% per year. In other words, choosing Option B is like taking $8,762.97 now and then investing it for three years. That Option A is better not only because it offers you money right now but because it offers you $1,237.03 ($10,000 - $8,762.97) more in cash. Furthermore, if you invest the $10,000 that you receive from Option A, your choice gives you a future value that is $1,411.66 ($11,411.66 - $10,000) greater than the future value of Option B.

Present Value of a Future Payment

Let's up the ante on our offer. What if the future payment is more than the amount you'd receive right away? Say you could receive either $15,000 today or $18,000 in four years. The decision is now more difficult. If you choose to receive $15,000 today and invest the entire amount, you may actually end up with an amount of cash in four years that is less than $18,000.

How to decide? You could find the future value of $15,000, but since we are always living in the present, let's find the present value of $18,000. This time, we'll assume interest rates are currently 4%. Remember that the equation for present value is the following:

$$PV=FV\times(1+i)^{-n}$$

In the equation above, all we are doing is discounting the future value of an investment. Using the numbers above, the present value of an $18,000 payment in four years would be calculated as $18,000 x (1 + 0.04)-4 = $15,386.48. From the above calculation, we now know our choice today is between opting for $15,000 or $15,386.48. Of course, we should choose to postpone payment for four years.

Financial Plan

A financial plan is a statement estimating the amount of capital and determining its composition. The quantum of funds needed will depend upon the assets requirements of the business. The time at which funds will be needed should be carefully decided so that finances are raised at a time when these are needed. The next aspect of a financial plan is to determine the pattern of financing. There are a number of ways for raising funds. The selection of various securities should be done carefully.

The funds may be raised by issuing of capital and debentures, rising of loans, etc. Which source of finance should be raised and up to what amount these should be raised is very important. Once a pattern of financing is selected then it becomes very difficult to modify it a financial plan also spells out the policies to be pursed for the floatation of various corporate securities, particular y regarding the time of their floatation.

Objectives of Financial Plan

- Adequate Funds: A financial plan would ensure the availability of sufficient funds to achieve enterprise goals.
- Balancing of Costs and Risks: There should be a balancing of costs and risks so as to protect the investors.
- Flexibility: A financial plan should ensure flexibility so as to adjust as per the requirements. It should be adjustable as per the changing conditions.
- Simplicity: The financial structure should not be complicated by issuing a variety of securities. The number of securities should be less so that it is easily understood.
- Long-term View: A financial plan should take a long-term view. The needs for funds in the near future and over a longer period should be considered while selecting the pattern of financing.

- Liquidity: The liquidity of funds should always be kept in mind while preparing a financial plan. During periods of depression it is the liquidity which can keep a concern going.
- Optimum use: A financial plan should ensure sufficient funds for genuine needs. Neither the plans should suffer due to shortage of funds nor there wasteful use of them. The funds should be put to their optimum use.
- Economy: The cost of raising the funds should be minimum. It should not impose disproportionate burden on the company. It can be ensured by a proper debt-equity mix.

Characteristics of a Sound Financial Plan

A Financial manager should consider the following factors while finalizing a financial plan:

- Simplicity: A financial plan should be so simple that it may be easily understood even by a layman. A complicated financial structure creates complications and confusion.
- Based on Clear-cut Objectives: Financial planning should be done by keeping in view the overall objectives of the company. It should aim to procure funds at the lowest cost so that profitability of the business is improved.
- Less Dependence on Outside Sources: A long-term financial planning should aim to reduce dependence on outside sources. This can be possible by retaining a part of profits for ploughing back. The generation of own funds is the way of financial operations. In the beginning, outside funds may be a necessity but financial planning should be such that dependence on such funds may be reduced in due course of time.
- Flexibility: The financial plan should not be rigid. It should allow a scope for adjustments as and when new situations emerge. There may be a scope for raising additional funds if fresh opportunities occur. Similarly, idle funds, if any, may be invested in short-term and low-risk bearing securities. Flexibility in a plan will be helpful in coping with the demands of the future.
- Solvency and Liquidity: Financial planning should ensure solvency and liquidity of the enterprise. Solvency requires that short-term and long-term payments should be made on dates when these are due. This will ensure credit worthiness and goodwill to the concern.
- Solvency will be possible when liquidity of assets is maintained. There should be sufficient funds whenever payments are to be made. Proper forecasting of future payments will be helpful in planning liquidity.

- Cost: The cost of raising capital is an important consideration in selecting a financial plan. The selection of various sources should be such that the cost burden should be mimimum. As and when possible interest bearing securities should be returned so that this burden is reduced.

- Profitability: A financial plan should adjust various securities in such a way that profitability of the enterprise is not adversely affected. The interest bearing securities and other liabilities should be so adjusted that business is able to improve its profitability.

	Characteristics of a Financial Plan
1.	Simplicity.
2.	Based on clear-cut objectives.
3.	Less Dependence on Outside Sources.
4.	Flexibility.
5.	Solvency and Liquidity.
6.	Cost.
7.	Profitability.

Considerations in Formulating Financial Plan

A financial plan should be carefully determined. It has long-term impact on the working of the enterprise. The following variables should be kept in mind while selecting a financial plan:

- Nature of the Industry: The needs for funds are different for various industries. The asset structure, element of seasonality, stability of earnings is not common factors for all industries. These variables will influence determining the size and structure of financial requirements.

- Standing of the Concern: The standing of a concern will influence a decision about financial plan. The goodwill of the concern, credit rating in the market, past performance, attitude of the management is some of the factors which will be considered in formulating a financial plan.

- Future Plans: The future plan of a concern should be considered while formulating a financial plan. The plans for expansion and diversification in near future will require a flexible financial plan. The sources of funds should be such which will facilitate required funds without any difficulty.

- Availability of Sources: There are a number of sources from which funds can be raised. The pros and cons of all available sources should be properly discussed for taking a final decision on the sources. The sources should be able to provide sufficient and regular funds to meet needs at various periods. A financial plan should be selected by keeping in view the reliability of various sources.

- General Economic Conditions: The prevailing economic conditions at the national level and international level will influence a decision about financial plan. These conditions should be considered before taking any decision about sources of funds. A favourable economic environment will help in raising funds without any difficulty. On the other hand, uncertain economic conditions may make it difficult for even a good concern to raise sufficient funds.
- Government Control: The government policies regarding issue of shares and debentures, payment of dividend and interest rate, entering into foreign collaborations, etc. will influence a financial plan. The legislative restrictions on using certain sources, limiting dividend and interest rates, etc.; will make it difficult to raise funds. So, government controls should be properly considered while selecting a financial plan.

Cash Management

Cash Management refers to the collection, handling, control and investment of the organizational cash and cash equivalents, to ensure optimum utilization of the firm's liquid resources. Money is the lifeline of the business, and therefore it is essential to maintain a sound cash flow position in the organization.

Receivables Cash Management

Any amount which the company has earned however not yet received, i.e. it's outstanding and is expected to be received in future, is known as receivables. An organization must manage its receivables to maintain the surplus cash inflow. It helps the firm to fulfill its immediate cash requirements. The cash receivables must be planned in such a way that the organization can realize its debts quickly and should allow a short credit period to the debtors.

Payables Cash Management

The payables refer to the payment which is unpaid by the organization and is to be paid off shortly. The organization should plan its cash outflow in such a manner that it can acquire an extended credit period from the creditors. This helps the firm to retain its cash resources for a longer duration to meet the short term requirements and sudden expenses. Even the organization can invest this cash in a profitable opportunity for that particular credit period to generate additional income.

Objectives of Cash Management

Why do we need to manage cash flow in the organization? What is the use of cash management in the business? Following purposes of cash management will resolve the above queries:

- Fulfill Working Capital Requirement: The organization needs to maintain ample liquid cash to meet its routine expenses which possible only through effective cash management.
- Planning Capital Expenditure: It helps in planning the capital expenditure and determining the ratio of debt and equity to acquire finance for this purpose.
- Handling Unorganized Costs: There are times when the company encounters unexpected circumstances like the breakdown of machinery. These are unforeseen expenses to cope up with; cash surplus is a lifesaver in such conditions.
- Initiates Investment: The other aim of cash management is to invest the idle funds in the right opportunity and the correct proportion.
- Better Utilization of Funds: It ensures the optimum utilization of the available funds by creating a proper balance between the cash in hand and investment.
- Avoiding Insolvency: If the business does not plan for efficient cash management, the situation of insolvency may arise. It is either due to lack of liquid cash or not making a profit out of the money available.

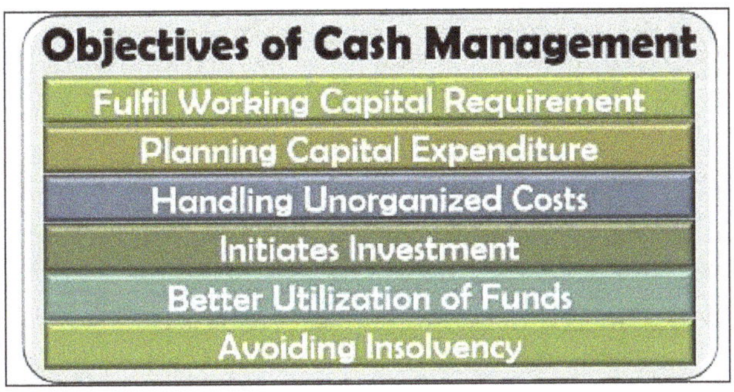

Cash Management Models

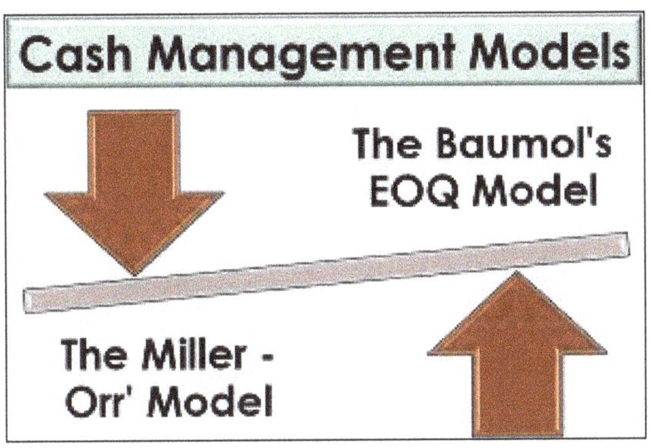

Cash management requires a practical approach and a strong base to determine the requirement of cash by the organization to meet its daily expenses. For this purpose, some models were designed to determine the level of money on different parameters. The two most important models are: The Baumol's EOQ Model and The Miller – Orr' Model.

The Baumol's EOQ Model

Based on the Economic Order Quantity (EOQ), William J. Baumol gave the Baumol's EOQ model, which influences the cash management of the company. This model emphasizes on maintaining the optimum cash balance in a year to meet the business expenses on the one hand and grab the profitable investment opportunities on the other side. The following formula of the Baumol's EOQ Model determines the level of cash which is to be maintained by the organization:

$$C = \sqrt{\frac{2FT}{i}}$$

Where,

- 'C' is the optimum cash balance,
- 'F' is the fixed transaction cost,
- 'T' is the total cash requirement for that period,
- 'i' is the rate of interest during the period.

The Miller – Orr' Model

Given below is the graphical representation of this model.

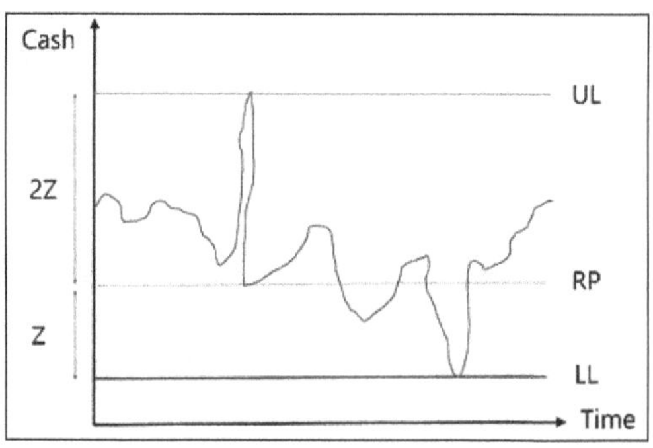

According to Merton H. Miller and Daniel Orr, Baumol's model only determines the cash withdrawal; however, cash is the most uncertain element of the business. There may be times when the organization will have surplus cash, thus discouraging withdrawals; instead, it may require making investments. Therefore, the company needs to decide the return point or the level of money to be maintained, instead of determining the withdrawal amount.

This model emphasizes on withdrawing the cash only if the available fund is below the return point of money whereas investing the surplus amount exceeding this level.

Where,

- 'Z' is the spread of cash,
- 'UL' is the upper limit or maximum level,
- 'LL' is the lower limit or the minimum level,
- 'RP' is the Return Point of cash.

We can see that the above graph indicates a lower limit which is the minimum cash a business requires to function. Adding up the spread of cash (Z) to this lower limit gives us the return point or the average cash requirement. However, the company should not invest the sum until it reaches the upper limit to ensure maximum return on investment. This upper limit is derived by adding the lower limit to the three times of spread (Z). The movement of cash is generally seen across the lower limit and the upper limit.

Let us now discuss the formula of the Miller – Orr' model to find out the return point of cash and the spread across the minimum level and the maximum level:

$$Z = \sqrt[3]{\frac{3TV}{4i}}$$

Where,

- 'Return Point' is the point at which money is to be invested or withdrawn.
- 'Minimum Level' is the minimum cash required for business sustainability.
- 'Z' is the spread across the minimum level and the maximum level.
- 'T' is the transaction cost per transfer.
- 'V' is the variance of daily cash flow per annum.
- 'i' is the daily interest rate.

Functions of Cash Management

Cash management is required by all kinds of organizations irrespective of their size, type and location. Following are the multiple managerial functions related to cash management:

- Investing Idle Cash: The Company needs to look for various short term investment alternatives to utilize surplus funds.

- Controlling Cash Flows: Restricting the cash outflow and accelerating the cash inflow is an essential function of the business.
- Planning of Cash: Cash management is all about planning and decision making in terms of maintaining sufficient cash in hand and making wise investments.
- Managing Cash Flows: Maintaining the proper flow of cash in the organization through cost-cutting and profit generation from investments is necessary to attain a positive cash flow.
- Optimizing Cash Level: The organization should continuously function to maintain the required level of liquidity and cash for business operations.

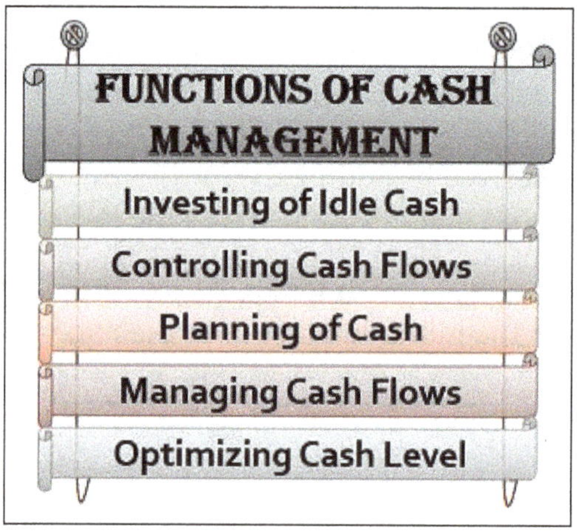

Cash Management Strategies

Cash management involves decision making at every step. It is not an immediate solution but a strategical approach to financial problems. Following are the strategies of cash management:

- Business Line of Credit: The organization should opt for a business line of credit at an initial stage to meet the urgent cash requirements and unexpected expenses.
- Money Market Fund: While carrying on a business, the surplus fund should be invested in the money market funds. These are readily convertible into cash whenever required and yield a considerable profit over the period.
- Lockbox Account: This facility provided by the banks enable the companies to get their payments mailed to its post office box. This lockbox is managed by the banks to avoid manual deposit of cash regularly.
- Sweep Account: The organizations should avail the facility of sweep accounts which is a mix of savings and fixed deposit account. Thus, the minimum balance

of the savings account is automatically maintained, and the excess sum is transferred to the fixed deposit account.

- Cash Deposits (CDs): If the company has a sound financial position and can predict the expenses well along with availing of a lengthy period, it can invest the surplus cash in the cash deposits. These CDs yield good interest, but early withdrawals are liable to penalties.

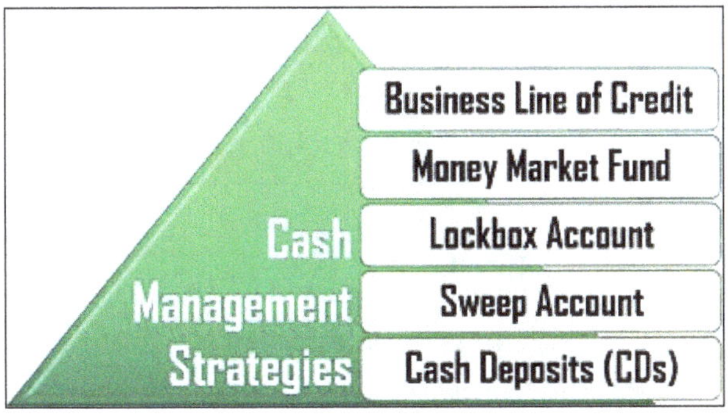

Cash Flow Management Techniques

Managing cash flow is a contemplative process and requires a lot of analytical thinking. The various techniques or tools used by the managers to practice cash flow management are as follows:

- Accelerating Collection of Accounts Receivable: One of the best ways to improve cash inflow and increase liquid cash by collecting the debts and dues from the debtors readily.
- Stretching of Accounts Payable: On the other hand, the company should try to extend the payment of dues by acquiring an extended credit period from the creditors.
- Cost Cutting: The Company must look for the ways of reducing its operating cost to main a good cash flow in the business and improve profitability.
- Regular Cash Flow Monitoring: Keeping an eye on the cash inflow and outflow, prioritizing the expenses and reducing the debts to be recovered, makes the organization's financial position sound.
- Wisely Using Banking Services: The services such as a business line of credit, cash deposits, lockbox account and sweep account should be used efficiently and intelligently.
- Upgrading with Technology: Digitalization makes it convenient for the organizations to maintain the financial database and spreadsheets to be assessed from anywhere anytime.

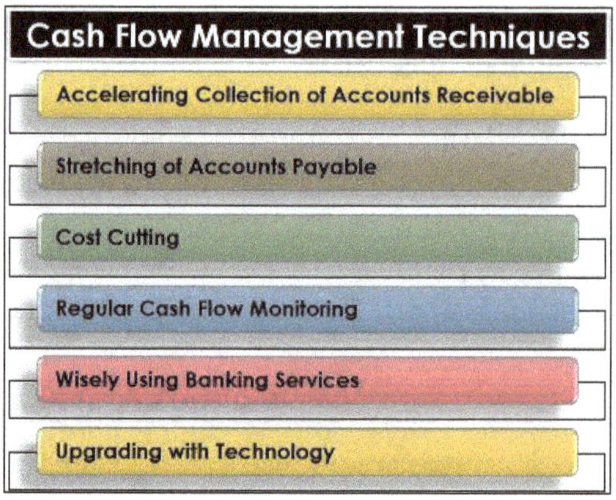

Limitations of Cash Management

Cash management is an inevitable part of business organizations. However, it has a few shortcomings which make it unsuitable for small organizations. These are as follows:

- Cash management is a very time consuming and skillful activity which is required to be performed regularly.
- As it requires financial expertise, the company may need to hire consultants or other experts to perform the task by paying administrative and consultation charges.
- Small business entities which are managed solely, face problems such as lack of skills, knowledge, time and risk-taking ability to practice cash management.

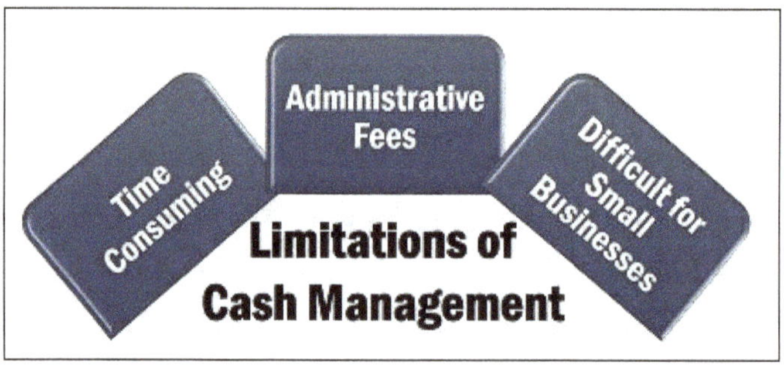

Nature and Scope of Financial Management

The nature and scope of financial management has evolved over period of time. It has expanded in its coverage and has seen a large number of new developments and innovations from academicians, researchers, practioners and regulators. Traditionally, Financial Management was a part of economics concerned with record keeping, arranging funds, managing cash etc. and thus was episodic in nature. It was viewed from outsider's (suppliers of funds) view point, was focused on long term financing and was more of descriptive in nature rather than analytical.

However, later on with increasing competition, globalization, growth and complexity in business activities, scope of financial management widened. It was no more an episodic activity but became as regular in nature as other areas like productions, marketing. Financial management emerged as a separate discipline. Focus was no more just on long term financing and record keeping but also on appraisal and comparative evaluation of long term investment proposals, management of funds required for running day to day business operations. As sole proprietorship and partnership gave way to corporations as preferred form of business, dividend policy and corporate governance rose in prominence. The nature of financial management in modern times is no more just theoretical or conceptual but is empirical based and analytical.

Today, almost every business decision and activity involve some financial implications and so financial management is required to evaluate their financial impact. Since decisions in virtually all areas of management (purchase, production, marketing, operations and logistic, human resource) have financial payoffs involved, they come within the scope and purview of financial management. Also, since financial decisions especially those relating to procurement and utilization of funds are necessary and have significant impact in every aspect of life, the scope of financial management covers all decision making entities of society viz. individuals, households, businesses, organizations and government.

Evolution of Financial Management

Financial management is evolutionary concept not a revolutionary concept. Its evolution may be divided broadly in three phases: the Traditional, the Transitional and the Modern phase. The time frame in demarcating these phases is not exact.

The Traditional Phase

The Traditional phase lasted for about four decades till early 1940's. In this phase, the focus of financial management was mostly on events of episodic nature like procurement of capital, engagement with major lenders like banks, issuance of securities, debt servicing, expansion, merger and compliance with legal aspects. The approach was mainly descriptive. Financial management was viewed mainly from the viewpoint of the investment bankers, lenders, and other outsiders.

The Transitional Phase

The Transitional phase began around the early 1940's continued till early 1950's. Financial management had almost similar nature and scope during this phase as during the traditional phase. However, there was an increasing emphasis on planning, procuring, managing and controlling funds to meet day to day financial needs of the business. Financial issues began to be analyzed in an analytical framework.

The Modern Phase

The mid 1950's marked the beginning of Modern phase in financial management owing to increasing competition, growth opportunities, globalization, breakthroughs in economic theories and development of quantitative methods of analysis. This led to development of a more analytical, empirical approach to decision making. Management or insider's view point became central to financial management. Development of Theory of Portfolio Management by Harry Markowitz in 1950, Theory of Leverage and Valuation of firm by Modigliani and Miller in 1958 and Option Valuation Model by Black and Scholes in 1970's are regarded as milestones in the evolutionary journey of modern financial management.

Since then, the fields of capital budgeting, capital structure , efficient market hypothesis, option pricing theory, agency theory, financial derivatives and risk management, valuation model, dividend policy, working capital management, financial modeling, financial engineering, international finance and behavioral finance to name a few, have seen fascinating developments. With the on-going endeavors of various academicians, researchers, practioners and regulators, we are poised to see many more significant advancements in these and upcoming areas, which would add further dimensions to financial management.

Interdisciplinary Aspects of Financial Management

Financial Management and Economics

Various economic theories provide guidelines to finance manager for decision making in real business situations. Finance manager must have understanding of microeconomic economic concepts like demand and supply analysis, behavior of costs, pricing theory, marginal analysis and profit optimization models under different market situations. These are of great relevance to finance manager in budgeting & forecasting, evaluating alternative investment proposals, profit planning. For fund raising, finance manager should have good understanding of functioning of financial institutions and market. Concepts of present value, economic income, opportunity cost, risk management, behavior of investors under different market situations and macroeconomic variables like inflation, employment, per capita income, aggregate demand, and aggregate supply have great implications for investment decisions.

Financial Management and Accounting

Financial managers have to take decisions about future. They make extensive use of historical accounting information for analyzing past performances and forecasting about future profitability, liquidity and solvency of the firm. So as one of the important users of accounting information they should be capable of understanding and interpreting financial information. Cost and Management accounting are specialized areas of accounting which provide accounting information in a form which facilitates efficient decision making. Finance manager also oversees preparation of financial statements as per legal & statutory requirements.

Financial Management and Statistics

In the modern phase, financial management has become more analytical and empirical. This requires application of large number of statistical tools and techniques such as measures of central tendency, measures of dispersion, correlation and regression, sampling and estimation, hypothesis testing on raw data to derive meaningful interpretation & conclusions. These tools and techniques are widely applied across all decision areas of financial management such as capital budgeting, capital structure, dividend and working capital.

Financial Management and Top Management

Top management formulates and implements strategy to maximize wealth of shareholders and achieve the stated goals & objective of business. All strategic decisions like strategic alliances, joint venture, mergers and acquisitions, demerger have significant financial impact on profitability, liquidity and solvency of firm in the long run. So top management along with chief finance officer assesses the impact of financial decisions and incorporates them in strategy formulation.

Financial Management and Production Management

Production department in a business organization is concerned with arrangement of raw materials, machinery, technology, manpower, tools and equipment to facilitate efficient and effective production of goods and services. They aim to complete production targets within time, minimise cost and ensure optimum utilization of production facilities. To achieve this, they incur expenditures on raw material, machinery, wages, operating expenses etc. These expenditures are estimated by production department and then sent for approval to the finance department. Finance manager after evaluating these estimates may suggest changes and thereafter allocates the required funds to the production department.

Financial Management and Marketing Management

Marketing managers make marketing plans, do demand forecasting, and take decisions regarding pricing, product promotion, product mix, market segmenting, targeting and positioning, choice & length of distributional channels. All of these involve payoffs between benefits generated and expenditures incurred. Finance managers work with their marketing colleagues to evaluate the profitability of alternative marketing proposals. Finance manager after due deliberation approves funding for selected proposals.

Financial Management and Human Resource Management

Human resource department of an organization takes several decisions that have financial implications such as manpower planning, recruitment, training and development programs, employee compensation and benefits which include wages, salary, bonus, commission, perquisites, and allowances. Financial manager discusses benefits and costs of these decisions with human resource manager and approves funds to implement them.

Concepts from fields of psychology and organizational behavior which earlier were used by human resource department are being today used by finance managers to understand the behavior of investors. This new area called behavioral finance has grown rapidly in past few decades by attracting interest of academicians and researchers in developing theory and conceptual framework for the field. Finance managers and practioners have also found it to be very practical and useful in their work.

Financial System

Financial system is the system that channelizes funds from funds surplus units or savers (like households) to funds deficit units like governments and business organizations. All decisions of financial management and entire functioning of finance department of any organization is directly affected by and linked to the surrounding financial system or environment. Financial Systems consists of closely interrelated financial assets or instruments, financial markets and financial institutions or intermediaries functioning within a regulatory framework.

Financial Assets or Instruments

Financial Assets are different from Real or Physical or Tangible assets such as land, buildings, machinery, and equipment's. Financial Assets or Instruments represent a financial claim of the holder or purchaser of the asset over the issuer or seller. It is liability for the issuer and asset for holder. Currencies, bank deposits, post office savings, shares, bonds, debentures, derivatives, mutual fund units are some commonly used financial assets.

Financial Markets

A financial market is a market in which financial assets like shares, bonds are traded. Financial markets facilitate:

- The raising of capital (in the capital markets).

- The transfer of risk (in the derivatives markets).
- Price discovery of financial assets.
- Global transactions with integration of financial markets.
- The transfer of liquidity (in the money markets).
- International trade (in the currency markets).

Types of Financial Markets

- Capital markets are markets for long term financial assets like shares, bonds. Capital markets can be further divided into primary and secondary markets. Newly formed (issued) securities are bought or sold in primary markets. Secondary markets allow investors to buy and sell existing securities.
- Money market is market for short term debt financing and investment.
- Foreign exchange markets facilitate the trading of foreign currencies.

Financial Institutions or Intermediaries

Financial intermediary are institutions which connect or establish linkages between fund surplus and fund deficit units allowing transfer of funds from savers to borrowers. Commercial banks, insurance companies, mutual funds, non-banking financial companies, investment bankers, merchant bankers, brokerage houses, central or state government established financial institutions are major financial intermediaries.

References

- Finance: investopedia.com, Retrieved 09, February 2020
- Nature-and-scope-of-financial-management: commercemates.com, Retrieved 21, May 2020
- Financial-function-types-importance-objectives: managementstudyhq.com, Retrieved 29, August 2020
- Time-value-of-money: investopedia.com, Retrieved 30, March 2020

2

Sources of Finance

Finance can be obtained from various sources such as retained earnings, lease financing, equity capital, preference shares and debentures. Retained earnings are the past profits earned by a company after subtracting the dividends it has paid in the past. This chapter discusses in detail these sources of finance for a complete understanding of the subject.

Retained Earnings

Retained Earnings (RE) are the accumulated portion of a business's profits that are not distributed as dividends to shareholders but instead are reserved for reinvestment back into the business. Normally, these funds are used for working capital and fixed asset purchases (capital expenditures) or allotted for paying off debt obligations.

Retained Earnings

	Historical Results				
FINANCIAL STATEMENTS	**2013**	**2014**	**2015**	**2016**	**2017**
Assets					
Cash	67,971	81,210	83,715	111,069	139,550
Accounts Receivable	5,100	5,904	6,567	7,117	7,539
Inventory	7,805	9,601	9,825	10,531	11,342
Property & Equipment	45,500	42,350	40,145	38,602	37,521
Total Assets	**126,376**	**139,065**	**140,252**	**167,319**	**195,951**
Liabilities					
Accounts Payable	3,902	4,800	4,912	5,265	5,671
Debt	50,000	50,000	30,000	30,000	30,000
Total Liabilities	**53,902**	**54,800**	**34,912**	**35,265**	**35,671**
Shareholder's Equity					
Equity Capital	70,000	70,000	70,000	70,000	70,000
Retained Earnings	2,474	14,265	35,340	62,053	90,280
Shareholder's Equity	**72,474**	**84,265**	**105,340**	**132,053**	**160,280**
Total Liabilities & Shareholder's Equity	**126,376**	**139,065**	**140,252**	**167,319**	**195,951**

Retained Earnings are reported on the balance sheet under the shareholder's equity section at the end of each accounting period. To calculate RE, the beginning RE balance is added to the net income or reduced by a net loss and then dividend payouts are subtracted. A summary report called a statement of retained earnings is also maintained, outlining the changes in RE for a specific period.

The Purpose of Retained Earnings

Retained earnings represent a useful link between the income statement and the balance sheet, as they are recorded under shareholders' equity, which connects the two statements. The purpose of retaining these earnings can be varied and includes buying new equipment and machines, spending on research and development, or other activities that could potentially generate growth for the company. This reinvestment into the company aims to achieve even more earnings in the future.

If a company does not believe it can earn a sufficient return on investment from those retained earnings (i.e., earn more than their cost of capital), then they will often distribute those earnings to shareholders as dividends or conduct a share buybacks.

What is the Retained Earnings Formula?

The RE formula is as follows:

RE = Beginning Period RE + Net Income/Loss – Cash Dividends – Stock Dividends

Where RE = Retained Earnings

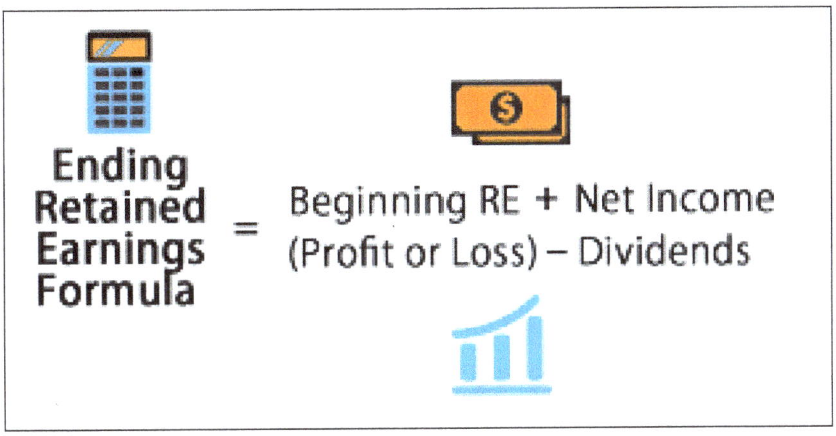

Beginning of Period Retained Earnings

At the end of each accounting period, retained earnings are reported on the balance sheet as the accumulated income from the prior year (including the current year's income), minus dividends paid to shareholders. In the next accounting cycle, the RE ending balance from the previous accounting period will now become the retained earnings beginning balance.

The RE balance may not always be a positive number, as it may reflect that the current period's net loss is greater than that of the RE beginning balance. Alternatively, a large distribution of dividends that exceed the retained earnings balance can cause it to go negative.

How Net Income Impacts Retained Earnings

Any changes or movement with net income will directly impact the RE balance. Factors such as an increase or decrease in net income and incurrence of net loss will pave the way to either business profitability or deficit. The Retained Earnings account can be negative due to large, cumulative net losses. Naturally, the same items that affect net income affect RE.

Examples of these items include sales revenue, cost of goods sold, depreciation, and other operating expenses. Non-cash items such as write-downs or impairments and stock-based compensation also affect the account.

	A B C	D	E	F	G	H	I	J	K	L	M
1		Historical Results					Forecast Period				
2	FINANCIAL STATEMENTS	2013	2014	2015	2016	2017	2018	2019	2020	2021	2022
3	Balance Sheet Check	OK	OK	OK	OK	OK	OK	OK	OK	OK	OK
24											
25	**Revenue**	102,007	118,086	131,345	142,341	150,772	165,849	182,434	200,678	220,745	242,820
26	Cost of Goods Sold (COGS)	39,023	48,004	49,123	52,654	56,710	69,657	85,744	100,339	79,468	84,987
27	**Gross Profit**	62,984	70,082	82,222	89,687	94,062	96,193	96,690	100,339	141,277	157,833
28	**Expenses**										
29	Salaries and Benefits	26,427	22,658	23,872	23,002	25,245	28,194	31,014	34,115	37,527	41,279
30	Rent and Overhead	10,963	10,125	10,087	11,020	11,412	15,000	15,000	15,000	15,000	15,000
31	Depreciation & Amortization	19,500	18,150	17,205	16,544	16,080	13,132	13,786	14,211	14,487	14,667
32	Interest	2,500	2,500	1,500	1,500	1,500	3,000	3,000	2,000	1,000	1,000
33	**Total Expenses**	59,390	53,433	52,664	52,066	54,237	59,327	62,800	65,326	68,014	71,946
34	**Earnings Before Tax**	3,594	16,649	29,558	37,622	39,825	36,866	33,890	35,013	73,263	85,887
35											
36	Taxes	1,120	4,858	8,483	10,908	11,598	10,322	9,489	9,804	20,514	24,048
37	**Net Earnings**	2,474	11,791	21,075	26,713	28,227	26,543	24,401	25,209	52,749	61,839
38											
39											
40	**Balance Sheet**										
41											
42	**Assets**										
43	Cash	67,971	81,210	83,715	111,069	139,550	161,050	179,175	177,827	232,676	292,140
44	Accounts Receivable	5,100	5,904	6,567	7,117	7,539	8,179	8,997	9,896	10,886	11,975
45	Inventory	7,805	9,601	9,825	10,531	11,342	15,267	21,142	27,490	21,772	23,284
46	Property & Equipment	45,500	42,350	40,145	38,602	37,521	39,389	40,603	41,392	41,905	42,238
47	**Total Assets**	126,376	139,065	140,252	167,319	195,951	223,885	249,916	256,605	307,239	369,637
48											
49	**Liabilities**										
50	Accounts Payable	3,902	4,800	4,912	5,265	5,671	7,061	8,692	10,171	8,056	8,615
51	Debt	50,000	50,000	30,000	30,000	30,000	30,000	30,000	10,000	10,000	10,000
52	**Total Liabilities**	53,902	54,800	34,912	35,265	35,671	37,061	38,692	20,171	18,056	18,615
53	**Shareholder's Equity**										
54	Equity Capital	70,000	70,000	70,000	70,000	70,000	70,000	70,000	70,000	70,000	70,000
55	Retained Earnings	2,474	14,265	35,340	62,053	90,280	116,824	141,225	166,434	219,183	281,022
56	**Shareholder's Equity**	72,474	84,265	105,340	132,053	160,280	186,824	211,225	236,434	289,183	351,022
57	**Total Liabilities & Shareholder's Equity**	126,376	139,065	140,252	167,319	195,951	223,885	249,916	256,605	307,239	369,637

How Dividends Impact Retained Earnings

Distribution of dividends to shareholders can be in the form of cash or stock. Both forms can reduce the value of RE for the business. Cash dividends represent a cash outflow and are recorded as reductions in the cash account. These reduce the size of a company's balance sheet and asset value as the company no longer owns part of its liquid assets.

Stock dividends, however, do not require a cash outflow. Instead, they reallocate a portion of the RE to common stock and additional paid-in capital accounts. This allocation does not impact the overall size of the company's balance sheet, but it does decrease the value of stocks per share.

End of Period Retained Earnings

At the end of the period, you can calculate your final Retained Earnings balance for the balance sheet by taking the beginning period, adding any net income or net loss, and subtracting any dividends.

Example Calculation

In this example, the amount of dividends paid by XYZ is unknown to us, so using the information from the Balance Sheet and the Income Statement, we can derive it remembering the formula Beginning RE – Ending RE + Net income (-loss) = Dividends.

Retained Earnings Example

Example 1. Extract from XYZ's Balance sheet (in millions except preferred stock and common stock)

	2016	2015
Shareholders' Equity		
Preferred stock	$ 5,200	$ 5,500
Common stock	$ 351	$ 351
Additional paid-in capital	$ 78,569	$ 77,283
Treasury stock	$ 3,211	$ 2,914
Retained earnings	**$ 78,732**	**$ 77,232**
Accumulated other comprehesive loss	-$ 3,271	$ 2,897
Total XYZ, Inc shareholders' equity	$ 162,792	$ 166,177
Equity attributable to non-controlling interests	$ 298	$ 313
Total Equity	$ 163,090	$ 166,490

XYZ Information from Consolidated Statements of Comprehensive Income.
For the years ended August 31, 2014 and 2013 (in million)

	2016	2015
Sales	$ 232,540	$ 227,506
Net Income	**$ 5,297**	**$ 4,769**

We already know:

Beginning RE: $77,232

Ending RE: $78,732

Net Income: $5,297

So, $77,232 – $78,732 + $5,297= $3,797

Dividends paid = $3,797

We can confirm this is correct by applying the formula of Beginning RE + Net income (loss) – dividends = Ending RE.

We have then \$77,232 + \$5,297 – \$3,797 = \$78,732, which is in fact our figure for Ending Retained Earnings.

Lease Financing

Lease financing is the source of payment which comes when the owner of assets (lesser) ready to provide their assets to another person in exchange of that lessor provides some agreed payment. In this way, the lessor leases the assets for a period of time on rent and lesser gets funds from the lessor. The periodical payment made by the lessee to the lessor is called the lease rental.

Under lease financing, the lessee is given the right to use the asset but the ownership lies with the lessor and at the end of the lease contract, the asset is returned to the lessor or an option is given to the lessee either to purchase the asset or to renew the lease agreement.

Types of Lease Financing

This is where the lessor transfers substantially all the risks and rewards of ownership to the lessee for rentals. In other words, it puts the lessee in the same condition where the lessee would have been if the lessee purchased the asset. Finance lease is classified into two phrases:

- Primary period: This is the non-cancellable period and in this period, the lessor recovers his total investment through lease rental and this period may last for an indefinite period of time.
- Secondary period: This period is also known as a peppercorn. It is almost the same as the primary period but in this period the lease rental is much smaller than that of primary period.

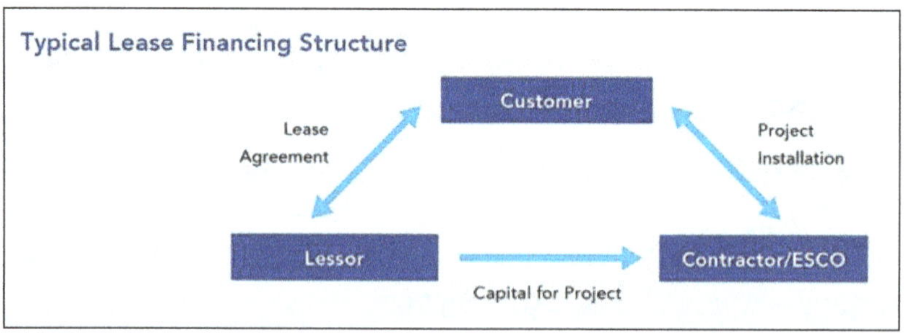

Features of Lease Finance

- A finance lease is a device that gives the lessee the right to use an asset.

- The money charged by the lessor on the primary period of lease is pretty much sufficient to recover his/her investment.
- The lessee is responsible for the maintenance of asset.

Operating Lease

This is also known as service lease, in this type of lease the risks and rewards incidental to the ownership of asset are not transferred by the lessor or the lessee. The term of such lease is much less than the economic life of the asset and thus the total investment of the lessor is not recovered through lease rental during the period of lease. In operating lease, the lessor usually provides advice to the lessee for repair, maintenance and technical know-how of the leased asset.

Features of Operating Lease

- The lessor provides the technical knowhow of the leased asset to the lessee.
- Risk and rewards incidental to the ownership of the asset are borne by the lessor.
- The lease term is much lower than the economic life of the asset.

Advantages of Lease Financing

To the Lessor:

- Assured regular income: The lessor get lease rental by leasing an asset during the period of the lease which is an assured regular income.
- The benefit of tax: As ownership lies with the lessor, the tax benefit is enjoyed by the lessor by way of depreciation of respect of the leased asset.

To the lessee:

- Tax benefits: A company is able to enjoy the tax advantage on lease payments as payments can be deducted as a business expense.
- Cheaper: Leasing is a source of financing which is cheaper than almost all sources of all the source of financing.

Disadvantages of Lease Financing

To the Lessor:

- Double taxation: Sales tax may be charged twice; first at the time of purchase of assets and second at the time of leasing the asset.
- Unprofitable in case of inflation: Lessor gets a fixed amount of lease rental every year and they cannot increase this even if the cost of the asset goes up.

To the Lessee:

- Ownership: The lessee will not become the owner of the asset at the end of lease agreement unless he decides to purchase it.
- Compulsion: Finance lease is non-cancellable and even if a company does not want to use the asset, the lessee is required to pay the lease rentals.

Finance Lease

A Finance Lease, also known as capital lease, is a type of lease in which a finance company is seen as the legal owner of the asset for the time period of the lease, while the lease has control over the operation of the assets and will enjoy part of returns from asset and at the same time suffer economic risk from the use of the asset.

A financial lease is the method employed by business for the equipment purchase with a payment structure which would last for an agreed time period. It can be properly defined as an agreement in which the lessor receives lease payments to cover costs of ownership. The lessor will however be responsible for costs of maintenance, taxes and insurance.

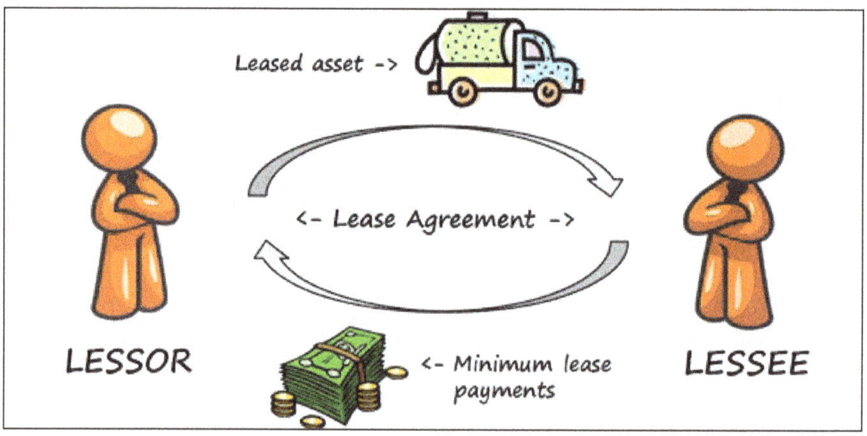

A Finance Lease IFRS is similar in structure to a normal purchase agreement which is financed by making use of a term loan due to the fact that the payments are paid monthly. In contrast to a normal purchase agreement, the lessee doesn't present the outstanding balance as debt, but indicates payments as expenses and retains the ownership title of the equipment. For the duration of the lease period, The finance company is seen as the rightful owner of the asset.

Types of Lease Financing

Types of Lease Financing are majorly characterized by:

- The lessee (customer or borrower) selecting an asset (equipment, vehicle, software).
- The lessor (finance company) purchasing the asset.

- The lessee will make use of the asset during the period of the lease.
- The lessee will make installment payments on the use of the asset.
- The lessor will gain a large part of the cost of the asset including interest from the installment payment made by the lessee.
- The lessee can obtain full ownership of the asset if he wants (e.g. By paying the last installment, or bargain option purchase price).

The terms of a finance lease agreement are similar to that of a hire purchase agreement and closed-end leasing due to the fact that the normal outcome is that the lessee will gain ownership of the asset after the lease has been settled. The difference between them is that, there have different methods of treating accounting variables and tax implications. There may be tax benefits for the lessee to lease an asset instead of purchasing it and it may be the sole reason for engaging in a finance lease.

Finance Lease on Accounting Entries

Due to the fact that a finance lease is capitalized, it causes an increase of both assets and liabilities in the balance sheet. Due to this, there is a reduction in working capital but am increment in debt/equity ratio, which leads to the formation of leverage.

Expenses of finance leases are assigned between interest expense and principal value in similar ways to a bond or loan, this mean that in a statement indicating cash flows, portions of lease payments are recorded as part of operating cash flow and under financing cash flow. This will lead to an increment in operating cash flows.

The IFRS criterion for Finance Lease is: If the ownership is transferred to the lessee by large amounts of risks and rewards, it can be said to be a finance lease. If it doesn't fulfill this condition to be called a finance lease, then it is an operating lease. The transfer of risk to the lessee may be indicated by conditions which may include an option for the lessee to purchase the asset at a low price after the lease agreement has been fulfilled. The type of asset, the duration of the lease and the value of lease payment can also be considered as factors.

Equity Capital

Equity, typically referred to as shareholders' equity (or owners' equity for privately held companies), represents the amount of money that would be returned to a company's shareholders if all of the assets were liquidated and all of the company's debt was paid off in the case of liquidation. In the case of acquisition, it is the value of company sale minus any liabilities owed by the company not transferred with the sale.

In addition, shareholder equity can represent the book value of a company. Equity can sometimes be offered as payment-in-kind. It also represents the pro-rata ownership of a company's shares. Equity can be found on a company's balance sheet and is one of the most common pieces of data employed by analysts to assess the financial health of a company.

Formula and Calculation for Shareholder Equity

The following formula and calculation can be used to determine the equity of a firm, which is derived from the accounting equation:

Shareholders' Equity=Total Assets−Total Liabilities

This information can be found on the balance sheet, where these four steps should be followed:

- Locate the company's total assets on the balance sheet for the period.
- Locate total liabilities, which should be listed separately on the balance sheet.
- Subtract total liabilities from total assets to arrive at shareholder equity.
- Note that total assets will equal the sum of liabilities and total equity.

Shareholder equity can also be expressed as a company's share capital and retained earnings less the value of treasury shares. This method, however, is less common. Though both methods yield the same figure, the use of total assets and total liabilities is more illustrative of a company's financial health.

By comparing concrete numbers reflecting everything the company owns and everything it owes, the "assets-minus-liabilities" shareholder equity equation paints a clear picture of a company's finances, which can be easily interpreted by investors and analysts. Equity is used as capital raised by a company, which is then used to purchase assets, invest in projects, and fund operations. A firm typically can raise capital by issuing debt (in the form of a loan or via bonds) or equity (by selling stock). Investors typically seek out equity investments as it provides greater opportunity to share in the profits and growth of a firm.

Equity is important because it represents the value of an investor's stake in a company, represented by their proportion of the company's shares. Owning stock in a company gives shareholders the potential for capital gains as well as dividends. Owning equity will also give shareholders the right to vote on corporate actions and in any elections for the board of directors. These equity ownership benefits promote shareholders' ongoing interest in the company.

Shareholder equity can be either negative or positive. If positive, the company has enough assets to cover its liabilities. If negative, the company's liabilities exceed its assets; if prolonged, this is considered balance sheet insolvency. Typically, investors view companies with negative shareholder equity as risky or unsafe investments. Shareholder equity alone is not a definitive indicator of a company's financial health; used in conjunction with other tools and metrics, the investor can accurately analyze the health of an organization.

Components of Shareholder Equity

Retained earnings are part of shareholder equity and are the percentage of net earnings that were not paid to shareholders as dividends. Think of retained earnings as savings since it represents a cumulative total of profits that have been saved and put aside or retained for future use. Retained earnings grow larger over time as the company continues to reinvest a portion of its income.

At some point, the amount of accumulated retained earnings can exceed the amount of equity capital contributed by stockholders. Retained earnings are usually the largest component of stockholders' equity for companies that have been operating for many years.

Treasury shares or stock represent stock that the company has bought back from existing shareholders. Companies may do a repurchase when management cannot deploy all the available equity capital in ways that might deliver the best returns. Shares bought back by companies become treasury shares, and their dollar value is noted in an account called treasury stock, a contra account to the accounts of investor capital and retained earnings. Companies can reissue treasury shares back to stockholders when companies need to raise money.

Many view stockholders' equity as representing a company's net assets its net value, so to speak, would be the amount shareholders would receive if the company liquidated all its assets and repaid all its debts.

Example of Shareholder Equity

Using a historical example, below is a portion of Exxon Mobil Corporation's (XOM) balance sheet as of September 30, 2018:

- Total assets were $354,628 (highlighted in green).
- Total liabilities were $157,797 (1st highlighted red area).
- Total equity was $196,831 (2nd highlighted red area).

The accounting equation whereby assets = liabilities + shareholder equity is calculated as follows:

Shareholder equity = $354,628, (total assets) - $157,797 (total liabilities) = $196,831

Exxon Mobil Corporation
Condensed Consolidated Balance Sheet
(million of dollars)

	Sept. 30, 2018
Assets	
Current assets	
Cash and cash equivalents	5,669
Notes and accounts receivable – net	27,880
Inventories	
Crude oil, products and merchandise	14,617
Materials and supplies	4,144
Other current assets	1,665
Total current assets	53,975
Investments, advances and long-term receivables	40,427
Property, plant and equipment – net	249,153
Other assets, including intangibles – net	11,073
Total assets	354,628
Liabilities	
Current liabilities	
Notes and loans payable	19,413
Accounts payable and accrued liabilities	41,714
Income taxes payable	4,161
Total current liabilities	65,288
Long-term debt	20,624
Postretirement benefits reserves	21,448
Deferred income tax liabilities	27,084
Long-term obligations to equity companies	4,625
Other long-term obligations	18,728
Total liabilities	157,797
Commitments and contingencies (Note 3)	
Equity	
Common stock without par value (9,000 million shares authorized, 8,019 million shares issued)	15,254
Earnings reinvested	419,155
Accumulated other comprehensive income	(18,370)
Common stock held in treasury (3,785 million shares at September 30, 2018 and 3,780 million shares at December 31, 2017)	(225,674)
ExxonMobil share of equity	(190,365)
Noncontrolling interests	6,466
Total equity	196,831
Total liabilities and equity	354,628

Other Forms of Equity

The concept of equity has applications beyond just evaluating companies. We can more generally think of equity as a degree of ownership in any asset after subtracting all debts associated with that asset. Below are several common variations on equity:

- A stock or any other security representing an ownership interest in a company.
- On a company's balance sheet, the amount of the funds contributed by the owners or shareholders plus the retained earnings (or losses). One may also call this stockholders' equity or shareholders' equity.
- In margin trading, the value of securities in a margin account minus what the account holder borrowed from the brokerage.
- In real estate, the difference between the property's current fair market value and the amount the owner still owes on the mortgage. It is the amount that the owner would receive after selling a property and paying any liens. Also referred to as "real property value."

- When a business goes bankrupt and has to liquidate, equity is the amount of money remaining after the business repays its creditors. This is most often called "ownership equity," also known as risk capital or "liable capital."

Private Equity

When an investment is publicly traded, the market value of equity is readily available by looking at the company's share price and its market capitalization. For private entitles, the market mechanism does not exist and so other forms of valuation must be done to estimate value.

Private equity generally refers to such an evaluation of companies that are not publicly traded. The accounting equation still applies where stated equity on the balance sheet is what is left over when subtracting liabilities from assets, arriving at an estimate of book value. Privately held companies can then seek investors by selling off shares directly in private placements. These private equity investors can include institutions like pension funds, university endowments, and insurance companies, or accredited individuals.

Private equity is often sold to funds and investors that specialize in direct investments in private companies or that engage in leveraged buyouts (LBOs) of public companies. In an LBO transaction, a company receives a loan from a private equity firm to fund the acquisition of a division or another company. Cash flows or the assets of the company being acquired usually secure the loan. Mezzanine debt is a private loan, usually provided by a commercial bank or a mezzanine venture capital firm. Mezzanine transactions often involve a mix of debt and equity in the form of a subordinated loan or warrants, common stock, or preferred stock.

Private equity comes into play at different points along a company's life cycle. Typically, a young company with no revenue or earnings can't afford to borrow, so it must get capital from friends and family or individual "angel investors." Venture capitalists enter the picture when the company has finally created its product or service and is ready to bring it to market. Some of the largest, most successful corporations in the tech sector, like Google, Apple, Facebook, and Amazon—or what is referred to as BigTechs or GAFAM—all began with venture capital funding.

Venture capitalists (VCs) provide most private equity financing in return for an early minority stake. Sometimes, a venture capitalist will take a seat on the board of directors for its portfolio companies, ensuring an active role in guiding the company. Venture capitalists look to hit big early on and exit investments within five to seven years. An LBO is one of the most common types of private equity financing and might occur as a company matures.

A final type of private equity is a Private Investment in a Public Company (PIPE). A PIPE is a private investment firm's, a mutual fund's, or another qualified investors' purchase, of stock in a company at a discount to the current market value (CMV) per share, to raise capital.

Unlike shareholder equity, private equity is not accessible for the average individual. Only "accredited" investors, those with a net worth of at least $1 million, can take part in private equity or venture capital partnerships. For investors who have don't meet this marker, there is the option of exchange-traded funds (ETFs) that focus on investing in private companies.

Equity Begins at Home

Home equity is roughly comparable to the value contained in home ownership. The amount of equity one has in their residence represents how much of the home that they own outright by subtracting from it the mortgage debt owed. Equity on a property or home stems from payments made against a mortgage, including a down payment, and from increases in property value.

Home equity is often an individual's greatest source of collateral, and the owner can use it to get a home-equity loan, which some call a second mortgage or a home-equity line of credit. Taking money out of a property or borrowing money against it is an equity takeout.

For example, let's say Sam owns a home with a mortgage on it. The house has a current market value of $175,000 and the mortgage owed totals $100,000. Sam has $75,000 worth of equity in the home or $175,000 (asset total) - $100,000 (liability total).

Brand Equity

When determining an asset's equity, particularly for larger corporations, it is important to note these assets may include both tangible assets, like property, and intangible assets, like the company's reputation and brand identity. Through years of advertising and development of a customer base, a company's brand can come to have an inherent value. Some call this value "brand equity," which measures the value of a brand relative to a generic or store-brand version of a product.

For example, many soft-drink lovers will reach for a Coke before buying a store-brand cola because they prefer the taste, or are more familiar with the flavor. If a 2-liter bottle of store-brand cola costs $1 and a 2-liter bottle of Coke costs $2, then the Coca-Cola has brand equity of $1.

There is also such a thing as negative brand equity, which is when people will pay more for a generic or store-brand product than they will for a particular brand name. Negative brand equity is rare and can occur because of bad publicity, such as a product recall or a disaster.

Equity vs. Return on Equity

Return on equity (ROE) is a measure of financial performance calculated by dividing net income by shareholder equity. Because shareholder equity is equal to a company's assets minus its debt, ROE could be thought of as the return on net assets. ROE is considered a measure of how effectively management is using a company's assets to create profits.

Equity has various meanings but usually represents ownership in an asset or a company such as stockholders owning equity in a company. ROE is a financial metric that measures how much profit is generated from a company's shareholder equity.

Preference Shares

Preference shares also commonly known as preferred stock, is a special type of share where dividends are paid to shareholders prior to the issuance of common stock dividends. Ergo, preference shareholders hold preferential rights over common shareholders when it comes to sharing profits. Consequently, if a company lands into bankruptcy, preference shareholders are issued dividends first or have the first right to the company's assets before common stock investors. For preference shareholders, the dividend is fixed however they don't hold voting rights as opposed to common shareholders.

Investors who have been in the stock market for longer than most go after preference share types. The dividends earned on these shares are significantly higher than ordinary shares. Their popularity can be established by the fact that many preference shareholders do not own any other stock except for this variety.

It has been observed that more and more companies are coming out with different types of preference shares. In essence, they have traces of both equity and debt shares. From this angle, these shares are also categorised as hybrid financing instruments. Over the last few years, as the bear market run continues globally, more investors are looking towards preference shares as a viable means of gaining significant returns in the long run.

Features of Preference Shares?

Several features have made these financial instruments the chosen vessels for investors. Most of these characteristics have made them superior earners even during low economic growth phases. The most attractive features are:

- Preference shareholders have significantly more heft than standard shareholders of any company. They have the first rights to all dividends paid by the companies whose shares they own.
- Holders of these shares do not have any voting rights in any business proceedings. The features, thus, also falls among the major disadvantages of preference shares. It might seem like a major handicap for any investor; however, it

is precisely the reason why so many companies offer these shares. The aspect is also similar to debenture owners.

- One feature which is under-advertised is that the dividends are paid to the shareholders on specific dates. It is not entirely dissimilar to a monthly income.
- If an investor decides to buy a special type of these shares, they should look for irredeemable preference shares. These shares allow the holder to have a certain say on their maturity dates.
- One of the advantages of preference shares is that they are identical to PAT for most corporations. The taxation element is decided on the dividends that are payable on every pre-arranged dividend fund.

Different Types of Preference Shares

There are many types of preference shares enumerated below:

- Cumulative Preference Share: Cumulative shares have a provision that allows investors to be paid dividends in arrears. It so happens that a company doesn't have the financial capacity to pay dividends to its shareholders. Unless dividends are not paid to preference shareholders, they cannot be paid to common shareholders. In such a scenario, the company decides to pay cumulative dividends in the next year. Sometimes, interest earned by the shareholders on arrear dividends is also given to the cumulative preferred stock holders. The calculation is as follows:

  Quarterly Dividend = [Rate of dividend * Par Value] divided by 4

  Cumulative dividends paid per share = Quarterly dividend * Total Number of payments missed.

- Non-Cumulative Preference Shares: Non-cumulative preferred shareholders are eligible to be paid dividends only from a year's profit. So a non-cumulative preferred stock does not issue unpaid dividends to the shareholders neither can holders of such stock claim unpaid dividends in the future.
- Redeemable Preference Shares: In case of redeemable shares, a company has the right to buy back the shares for its own use from shareholders at a fixed date or by giving prior notice after a period of time.
- Irredeemable Preference Shares: These shares can only be redeemed by the company at the time of liquidation or when the company winds up operations.
  - Participating preference shares: Participating preference shares is where the company issuing the dividends pays increased dividends to the shareholders along with the preference dividend. This is done at a fixed rate.

Additionally, participating preference shareholders have rights on the surplus asset of the company at the time of its liquidation.

- Non-Participating Preference Shares: In case of non-participating preference shares the shareholders are entitled only to the dividends at a fixed rate and not to the surplus profit. The extra profit is distributed among the common shareholders.
- Convertible Preference Shares: Shareholders of such shares have the option to convert the common shares to preferred shared. These shares are opted by investors who wish to receive preferred share dividend as well as want to benefit from an increase in the common shares. So the benefits are two fold- fixed returns by means of preferred dividends as well as the opportunity to earn higher returns as the common stock price increases. This conversion can happen within a certain period as per prior agreement, stated in the memorandum.
- Non-Convertible Preference Shares: Shareholders of these shares do not hold the rights to convert to issuer's common shares.
- Preference shares with a callable option: For shareholders having preference shares with a callable option, the issuing company holds the right to call in or buy back the stocks at a predetermined price after a set date. The call price, date post which the shares can be called and the call premium are mentioned in the prospectus.
- Adjustable Rate Preference Shares: For such shareholders, the dividend rates depends on the prevailing interest rates in the market and hence are not fixed.

Several reasons exist as to why these shares are preferred over other types. If you are an investor, opting for these shares is the way to future-proofing your investments, thus helping you reap the advantages of preference shares. For example, if by chance the corporation announces bankruptcy; all holders of preferential stocks will get the first and privileged access to the assets going under the hammer.

Such advantages are bound to attract those who have low-risk appetites when it comes to investments in uncertain times. Besides, if the company's ordinary shares start performing extraordinarily well, the preferred shareholders can easily transfer some of the shares into standard ones and benefit therein.

One great feature which companies offer is callable preference shares. The nomenclature means that the investor has a right to repurchase the shares whenever he or she likes. In short, can only benefit from.

Risks Associated with these Shares?

Like all other financial instruments, these shares have certain inherent risks as well, highlighting the disadvantages of preference shares. During significant market fluctuations, there are doubts about how much dividends the shares will yield. Thus, those with slightly lower risk appetite may not prefer taking too many chances in this specific investment option.

Moreover, some types of preference shares which may initially guarantee greater returns as they are associated with PAT. However, the risks associated with the same may also be very high. Lastly, these shares are issued primarily by companies that have a substantial market capitalization and can provide substantial dividends to a very large subscriber base for a sustained period. It might seem a risk-mitigating factor but may or may succeed in the real world.

Debentures

When it comes to corporate finance, company debentures are loan instruments for medium to a long term of period. These are offered by both large companies and the government. Debentures mainly work on the reputation of the issuing authorities and at a fixed interest rate. Authority bodies issue debentures when they seek to borrow money from the public at a predetermined rate of interest.

Types of Debentures

There are several types of debentures available in the market.

1. Secured debentures: When company debentures are secured against assets of the concerned company, these are called secured or mortgage debenture. If the security is on assets of the issuing company, then it is called fixed charge debentures. Contrarily, if the security is not specific but generic assets of the organisation, it is called a floating charge debenture.

Secured debentures examples are such as company or factory building. If the company gets insolvent, the loan amount needs to be cleared before selling the property. These are divided into two further categories:

- First mortgage or preferred debenture: First mortgages or preferred debentures' obligations are justified first with preference in time of realisation of the assets.
- Second mortgage or ordinary debenture: After fulfilling the first mortgage debentures debt, second mortgage or ordinary company debentures will be serviced in the event of realisation.

2. Unsecured debentures: Unsecured debentures are created only out of the credibility of the company, and they don't carry securities against any assets of the concerned

company. Therefore, the relevant organisation doesn't offer any protection on the rate of paying interest or on paying off the loan amount to the holders.

3. Convertible debentures: Convertible debentures are mixed financial tools carrying the benefits of both debt and equity shares. Individuals who hold company debentures like convertible debenture are allowed to convert their assets into stocks. This conversion will be done with a specific ratio and after a certain period depending on the terms and conditions of the contract.

- Furthermore, convertible debentures have two types – partly convertible and fully convertible. As the name suggests, fully convertible debentures are allowed to be converted entirely into equities. However, with party convertibles, only a limited part can be converted into stocks as per the norms of the contract. Here is a convertible debenture example:
- A company authorizes convertible debentures with a 15:1 rate, and the conversion can be done after 2 years. Now, after 2 years, the stock price of the company goes up from $ 40 to $ 100.
- Now, the convertible debenture holders can convert their debenture into stock at the ratio of 15:1. Here, one debenture will convert into the stock worth of $ 100 X 15 = $. 1500.

4. Non-convertible debentures: Debentures that don't allow the holders to opt for the conversation of debt to stock are called non-convertible debentures. This type of debenture endures as debt only.

5. Redeemable debentures: If the company debentures issuing authorities are legally mandated to redeem the debenture certificate on a particular date and pay the return to the investors, then those are called redeemable debentures.

6. Irredeemable debentures: Contrary to the previous one, irredeemable debentures don't carry along a redemption date with it. Therefore, these debentures can be redeemed either when the company will liquefy its assets or as per the terms and condition of the debenture contract. Another name of these debt instruments is a perpetual debenture.

7. Registered debentures: Registered debentures are those debt tools where the credentials of the holders such as their name, bank details, residential address, etc. are legally enrolled with the issuing authority. Hence, the investors must notify the organisation if the company debentures have already been transferred to another individual. Or else, the accumulated return will be credited to the previous holder.

8. Bearer debenture: Differently, bearer debentures don't carry any registration with any specific investor's details. With a mere delivery process, the debentures are transferred to any new holders. Moreover, the accumulated interest is paid at the exchange of coupon attached to the debenture certificate.

Features of Debentures

As an investment avenue, debentures carry some lucrative features. Few features of debenture include:

- As the return is determined with a fixed rate of income and the investment is secured with the charge of the company's assets, this is a preferred investment option. Fixed return at lower risk is the preferred investment avenue for all.
- Holding company debentures don't imply any ownership of the company. Therefore, debenture holders don't possess the right to vote or control the management of the issuing authority. Yet, in case of default return, they can avail legal steps against the organisation.
- With a higher face value, debentures come with a better return than share investment.
- In the event of liquefying the company, debenture holders get preferences in terms of repaying the borrowing amount.
- Irrespective of having profit or loss, the concerned company is bound to return the obligations at a predetermined rate of interest to the debenture holders.

Differences Between Shares and Debentures

Even though both debenture shares can raise capital for a company, they are different from each other in every other aspect. Here are some differences between them in a nutshell:

Particulars	Debenture	Share
Definition	Company debentures are the loan contract by that company borrow fund from the public.	The fund raised by share selling is the company's assets.
Status of the holders	Investors who buy debentures from a company are entitled as debenture holders, and they are creditors to the company.	Individuals who own shares of a company are determined as shareholders, and they are owners of the concerned organisation.
Payment security	Debenture carries security on return.	Shares don't carry any security on return.
Return	Companies repay the borrowings at a fixed rate of interest to the debenture holders.	Shareholders get a return by dividend payment.
Operation method	In case of debentures, the holders get interest regardless of the profit of the company.	Shareholders' payments are made from the profit earned by the concerned company.
Controlling rights	Company debenture holders are not allowed to vote or control the management.	As owners, shareholders carry the power to vote and control the management to some extent.
Conversion option	Debentures can be converted into shares.	Shares don't carry the option to be converted into debentures.

Trust deed	At the time of issuing debentures, a trust deed is mandated to be circulated as well. This is to protect the investment as there is no collateral against the loan.	Shares don't carry any trust deed.

Debenture Stock

Often, debenture and debenture stocks are treated similarly. However, they are not similar. Companies and government bodies issue debt instruments or securities to accumulate funds at times via debentures. On the other hand, debenture stocks are loan contracts between a company and the holders. Here, the holders are paid dividends from the profit earned by the company, at predetermined intervals.

As per the operation of debenture stock, it works similar to the way preferred stocks operate. Also, when it comes to the risk factor of an investment, debenture stocks carry a similar risk of any other kind of equities. However, these are backed by the trust deed. Hence, the trust acts as a protector to the shareholders. And, the stockholders can appoint receivers who will help them to realize the assets to keep the holder's money safe.

To sum up, debentures are safe investment avenues where the money will be protected. Also, the return is determined at a fixed rate of interest regardless of the loss and profit of the issuing company. Furthermore, in the event of realization of the assets of the concerned organisation, debentures holders are preferred to receive the return. However, issuing company debentures regularly can lead the company to disable the balance sheet, which leads to the company gradually losing its creditworthiness.

Commercial Banks

A commercial bank is a financial institution that grants loans, accepts deposits, and offers basic financial products such as savings accounts and certificates of deposit to individuals and businesses. It makes money primarily by providing different types of loans to customers and charging interest.

The bank's funds come from money deposited by the bank customers in saving accounts, checking accounts, money market accounts, and certificates of deposit (CDs). The depositors earn interest on their deposits with the bank. However, the interest paid to depositors is less than the interest rate charged to borrowers. Some of the loans offered by a commercial bank include motor vehicle loans, mortgages, business loans, and personal loans.

Functions of Commercial Banks

The basic role of a commercial bank is to provide financial services to the general public, businesses, and companies. Banks also ensure economic stability and sustainable growth of a country's economy. A commercial bank performs the following functions:

1. Accepting Deposits: Accepting deposits is one of the oldest functions of a commercial bank. When banks started, they charged a commission for keeping money on behalf of the public. With the changes in the banking industry over the years and the profitability of the business, banks now pay a small amount of interest to the depositors who keep money with them. However, depositors also incur administrative fees to maintain their accounts.

Banks accept three types of deposits. The first one is the savings deposit for small savers who are paid interest on their accounts. They can withdraw their money up to a limited amount by writing a cheque. The second type of deposit is the current account for people in business who can withdraw their money at any time without notice. Banks do not typically pay interest on deposits held in current accounts. Instead, the account holders are charged a nominal fee for the services rendered.

The last type of deposit is the term or fixed deposit. Customers who have money that they do not need for the next six months or more can save in the fixed account. The rate of interest paid increases with the length of the fixed deposit. Customers can only withdraw the money at the end of the agreed period by writing to the bank.

2. Advancing Credit Facilities: Advancing loans is an essential function of banks since it accounts for the highest percentage of revenue earned annually. Banks mostly offer short-term and medium-term loans from a percentage of the cash deposits at a high interest rate. They do not provide long-term financing due to the need to maintain liquidity of assets. Before advancing loans to customers, banks consider the borrower's financial status, business profitability, nature and size of the business, and ability to repay the loan without default.

3. Credit Creation: While granting loans to customers, banks do not provide the loan in cash to the borrower. Instead, the bank creates a deposit account from which the borrower can draw funds. This allows the borrower to withdraw money by cheque according to his needs. By creating a demand deposit in the borrower's account without printing additional money, the bank increases the amount of money in circulation.

4. Agency Functions: Commercial banks serve as agents of their customers by helping them in collecting and paying cheques, dividends, interest warrants, and bills of exchange. Also, they pay insurance premiums, utility bills, rent, and other charges on behalf of their clients.

Banks also trade shares, securities, and debentures, and they provide advisory services for customers that want to buy or sell these investments. In property administration, commercial banks act as trustees and executors of the estate on behalf of their customers. Banks charge a nominal fee for the agency functions performed on behalf of their clients.

Other Functions

Apart from the above primary functions, banks also perform several other functions. They provide foreign exchange to clients who are in the import and export business, by buying and selling foreign currency. However, banks must get permission from the regulatory body, mainly the central bank, before dealing with foreign exchange.

A commercial bank also acts as a custodian of precious stones and other valuables. They provide customers with lockers where they can put their jewelry, precious metals, and crucial documents. Such items are more secure when stored at the bank than keeping them at home where they may be stolen or damaged.

Types of Loans Offered by Commercial Banks

There are several types of loans advanced by commercial banks to their clients. These loans include:

1. Bank Loan: A bank loan is an amount of money offered by a bank to a borrower at a defined interest rate for a fixed period. Before granting a bank loan to a client, a bank must obtain several important documents to verify that the borrower will pay back the loan. These documents may include copies of identity, proof of income, and audited financial statements in the case of corporate clients.

The loan is granted against collateral that, if the customer defaults, the bank can sell them to recover the money. The collateral may be equipment, machinery, real estate property, inventory, documents of ownership, and other items.

2. Cash Credit: Cash credit is an arrangement between the bank and a client, and it allows the client to withdraw money beyond their account limit. The cash credit is advanced for a period of one year, but it may extend to even three years in special circumstances.

The amount is deposited in the current account of the borrower and can be withdrawn through a cheque. The interest charged on the cash credit depends on the amount of money and the duration for which the money has been withdrawn.

3. Bank Overdraft: A bank overdraft is a form of financing that allows the current account holders to overdraw their account up to a specified limit. It does not require any written formalities and clients use the overdraft to meet urgent needs. Interest is charged on the amount that the current account has been overdrawn with and not the full amount of overdraft allowed by the bank.

4. Discounted Bills of Exchange: A bank discounts a bill of exchange by providing money immediately to the holder of the bill. The bank deposits the money in the holder's current account, after deducting an interest rate for the loan period. Once the bill of exchange matures, the bank gets its payment from the banker of the bill holder.

Regulation by Central Banks

Commercial banks are regulated by the central banks in their respective countries. Central banks act as the supervisor of commercial banks, and they impose certain regulations to ensure banks operate within the stipulated rules.

For example, central banks make it mandatory for commercial banks to maintain bank reserves with them. Some central banks set the minimum bank reserves, requiring banks to keep a particular percentage of their customer deposits at the central bank. The reserves help to cushion banks against unexpected events like bank runs and bankruptcy.

References

- Retained-earnings-guide, accounting, knowledge: corporatefinanceinstitute.com, Retrieved 02, July 2020
- Lease-financing: how-to-finance.online, Retrieved 14, January 2020
- Finance-lease: how-to-finance.online, Retrieved 09, March 2020
- Company-debentures: groww.in, Retrieved 29, May 2020
- Commercial-bank, finance, knowledge: corporatefinanceinstitute.com, Retrieved 11, February 2020

3

Investment Decisions

The decisions made by investors as well as the top level management with regard to the amount of funds which have to be deployed in the investment opportunities are termed as investment decisions. This chapter closely examines the key concepts related to investment decisions, such as capital budgeting nature and process, to provide an extensive understanding of the subject.

Nature and Process of Capital Budgeting

Capital Budgeting refers to the investment decisions in capital expenditure incurred by which the benefits are received after one year. Capital expenditure is the expenditure which is occurred in the present time but the benefits of this expenditure or investment are received in future.

Capital expenditure is incurred on the fixed assets to acquire them or to improve them which gives benefits over a period of time. Capital Budgeting involves the planning and controlling of investment of funds which are to be invested in the capital assets as capital expenditure. It is a process of deciding whether to invest or not in a long-term investment whose returns are realized after five or ten years or more.

Nature of Capital Budgeting

- Long Term Effect: Capital budgeting is a long-term process, the long-term investment can give favourable returns or negative returns over a period of time. Future of the company is based on the investment. The future of the company depends on the return on the short-term investment, it can help in the growth of the firm and the wrong decision can endanger the survival of the firm.
- High Degree of Risk: There is a high degree of risk in long-term investment as the decision is based on the estimated returns in the future. In the modern era fashion, taste and preference lead to high risk as the customers can switch from the product in this long-term. The company has to think about the future needs and wants of the customers to obtain gains.
- Huge Funds: Huge funds are to be invested in the capital budgeting, long-term assets are purchased for a longer period of time. Large amount of funds is required and there is a high risk in taking decision that where the funds are to be

invested as mentioned above the capital budgeting can lead to growth of company and can also become the reason of downfall of the company that's why the decision should be taken after proper analysis.

- Irreversible Decision: The long-term decision making is irreversible in most of the cases, it is a long-term process and the decision once taken has a huge investment invested in it as capital expenditure. The company cannot reverse it back easily because of high investment of funds. The sale of high-value assets is not easy there is a problem in selling assets of high value in the market.
- Impact Competitive Strength: The future competitive strength of the firm is also based on the future decisions. The future profit of the firm is determined by the decision which has been taken in the present and the cost of the product is also defined by the decisions. If the decision is in favour then the firm can sell the product at a higher price than the competition in the market and vice-Versa.
- Impact on Cost Structure: Cost structure is affected by the vital decisions the firm has to fix the costs of the supervision, insurance, interest etc. If the investment does not generate returns then the profitability of the firm is affected. Future profitability of the company totally depends on the cost structure.

Scope of Capital Budgeting

- Use of Machinery: Due to advancements in technology Human are replaced by the machinery in production. These types of machinery can produce products at a cheaper rate. Capital budgeting helps in finding out the cost to acquire the machinery.
- Decision Making: Capital budgeting helps in deciding whether to buy or lease a Machinery for production and Decision to replace old machinery with new. Other decisions are also made with information through capital budgeting.
- Increase Profits: Capital Budgeting directly influences the profitability of the business. It Help in reducing the cost of operations to business by taking decision for long term capital. It helps to provide proper information about current expenditure and future benefit that saves the unnecessary expenses.
- Improves Performance: Capital Budgeting has an effective role in accelerating the overall performance of business organizations. By providing the long term assets by acquiring Plant and machinery that Improves the Performance of the production department.
- Selection of Machinery: Various types of machines are available in the market for production. The cost of the machine is different based on their capacity. Capital Budgeting helps in deciding which one to buy for our organization.

Cash Flow for Investment Analysis

The data for the computation of cash flow is provided by the research and development, marketing and accounting department. The data is further processed to compute the cash flow. The cost and benefits of the project can be estimated on the basis of profit or cash flows.

Estimation of Cost and Benefits of the Project using Profits

Computation

The amount of profit is calculated on the basis of accounting methods. The objective of financial management is to maximize the wealth of shareholders therefore the appropriate amount is the profit after tax. PAT can be easily computed from readily available accounting data in books of the firm.

	Revenue	xxx
Less:	Expense	xxx
	Earnings before depreciation, interest and tax (EBDIT)	xxx
Less:	Depreciation	xxx
	Earnings before interest and tax (EBIT)	xxx
Less:	Taxes	xxx
	Profit after tax (PAT)	xxx

Table: The simplest way to compute the amount of profit after tax.

Limitations

There are several reasons as to why PAT is not the appropriate measure of cash flow in order to estimate the wealth of the shareholders:

- The accounting profit is calculated on the principle of accrual concept so the revenues and expenditure are recognized at the time of incurring these amounts rather than when cash is received and paid. It fails to reflect the true cash position of the company.
- The amount of PAT includes non-cash expenses like depreciation which does not involve any cash outflow.
- Amount of PAT will differ and can be manipulated depending using different accounting methods. This distortion in information is a limitation to correctly assess the wealth of the company and thereby the shareholders.

- The total amount of capital expenditure is not charged to the profits in the same year. It understates the cash outflow of the company.

The profit does not show the true picture of financial position of the firm.

Estimation of Cost and Benefits of the Project using Cash Flows

The relevant measure of estimating the cost and benefits of an investment proposal is to compute the cash flows. The amount of cash flows is computed on the basis of all cash revenues and expenses ignoring all non-cash expenses. An investment proposal involves cash flow at three points in time:

- The first cash flow is at the time of making investment which involves cash outflow in terms of purchase price of machine and other equipment.
- The proposal will result in subsequent generation of revenue for the firm. Thus, it will involve the computation for annual cash flows for the life of the project.
- The final cash flow is terminal cash flow which occurs at the end of the life of the project. The terminal cash flow may involve the winding up of the project and realization of salvage value. These cash flows will make it different from the normal cash flows which occur at the end of year.

Initial Investment

When a firm takes up new project, it needs to incur some expenses to start the work. The usual capital budgeting decisions are replacement, modernization and purchase of equipment. The first type of cash outflow which takes place at the beginning is the purchase price of the machine (or any other asset). The other expenses in form of installation of the machine and transportation cost are also added to the cost of machine.

Additional working capital: In addition, in case of taking up new project, it is also possible that the company now needs more cash; it is required to have more inventories etc. which can be clubbed together and termed as net working capital. This additional requirement of funds becomes the part of cost or the funds which are required to start the project.

Salvage value of existing machine (if any): This cash inflow arising due to sale of old machine will provide the funds to the company and its cash outflow requirement will decline. The book value of the machine is arrived at by deducting the amount of depreciation from the purchase price of old machine. The book value of old machine is compared with the salvage value of the machine. When the salvage value is more than the book value, it will result in capital gain. The appropriate tax rate is used to the tax on capital gain. This tax is then deducted from the salvage value amount to compute the net cash inflow due to sale of old machine.

Table: The process of computing initial investment can be shown as:

Cost or purchase price of the asset		xxx
Add, installation expenses		xxx
Add, transportation cost		xxx
Add, other incidental expenses		xxx
Total cost of asset (A)		xxx
Add, increase in working capital		xxx
Funds required (B)		xxx
Subtract (F) as computed below		
Salvage value of old machine (C)	xxx	
Less book value of old machine (D)	xxx	
Capital gain/ loss	xxx	
Tax on capital gain (E)	xxx	
Net salvage value (F = C-E)	xxx	xxx
Initial investment amount (B-F)		xxx

This cost is compared with the benefits of the project which occur over a period of time. Therefore, once the amount of initial investment is known, the next step is to compute the subsequent annual cash flows associated with the project.

Annual Net Cash Flows

The cash flows rather than accounting profit is used for investment decision process. The simple way of computing the cash flow is to subtract the cash expenditure from the cash revenues.

Depreciation: Although the depreciation is the non-cash expenditure and as it should not be part of cash outflow. However this approach will provide the incorrect amount of cash flows when earnings of the firm are subject to tax. When a company is liable to pay taxes, the amount of depreciation is deducted to arrive at the taxable income figure. It reduces the amount of tax liability of the company. This reduction in taxes due to the presence of depreciation is called depreciation tax shield. The amount of depreciation tax shield is equal to the amount of depreciation (DEP) multiplied by the tax rate (T) i.e. Dep (T).

Table: Net Cash Flow after incorporating depreciation can be computed as below.

Revenue	xxx
Less expense	xxx
Earnings before depreciation, interest and tax (EBDIT)	xxx
Less, depreciation	xxx
Earnings before interest and tax (EBIT)	xxx

Less, tax	xxx
Profit after tax (PAT)	xxx
Add, Depreciation	xxx
Net cash flow	xxx

The amount of net cash flow is arrived at by deducting all cash expenses from the cash revenue and further taking into account the impact of depreciation and the depreciation tax shield.

Impact of Increase in Working Capital

Thus, the net working capital is computed by deducting the amount of current liabilities from the current assets. The increase in working capital due to new project in any of the year should be deducted from the cash flow of that year to arrive at the amount of relevant cash flow.

NCF = PAT + DEP - change in working capital

Future Capital Expenditure

If any further capital expenditure is made in order to preserve or increase the productive capacity of the assets, it should be deducted from the cash flows of that year to derive the amount of net cash flow for that particular year.

NCF = PAT + DEP - change in working capital – capital expenditure

Example: The following information is available with respect to the revenue and expenditure of X Ltd.

Revenue	30,00,000
Less expense	10,00,000
Earnings before depreciation, interest and tax (EBDIT)	20,00,000
Less, depreciation	12,50,000
Earnings before interest and tax (EBIT)	7,50,000
Taxes (40%)	3,00,000
Compute net cash flows.	

Solution: NCF = PAT + DEP- change in working capital – capital expenditure.

Table: The net cash flow.

Revenue	30,00,000
Less expense	10,00,000
Earnings before depreciation, interest and tax (EBDIT)	20,00,000
Less, depreciation	12,50,000

Earnings before interest and tax (EBIT)	7,50,000
Taxes (40%)	3,00,000
PAT = EBIT (1-T)	4,50,000
Add, Depreciation	12,50,000
NCF	17,00,000

This cash flow is the amount which is generated every year from the operations of the firm. This amount is computed in a way that it is unaffected by the accounting policies and procedures. This is the net addition to the wealth of the shareholders every year.

Terminal Net Cash Flow

There are some additional cash flows which form the part of terminal cash flow:

- Salvage value: When the productive capacity of the new machine is over, at the end of this its productive life, the asset is disposed off and the amount generated is added to the cash flow amount. The tax on capital gain is computed by comparing the salvage value with the book value. This amount of tax is then deducted from the salvage value to arrive at the net salvage value. This net salvage value is added to the cash flow of the last year to compute net cash flow of terminal year.
- Release of working capital: It is assumed that the amount of additional working capital which is required at the beginning of the project or as increased in any subsequent year is released at the terminal year. This amount is added to the cash flow to compute NCF. Terminal net cash flow: NCF + Salvage value + Release of working capital

Example: Calculate the incremental net cash flow from the following data.

Purchase price of the new asset	$10, 00,000
Installation costs	2, 00,000
Increase in working capital in year zero	2, 50,000
Salvage value of new machine after 4 years	3, 50,000
Revenues from new asset (annual)	21, 50,000
Cash expenses on new asset (annual)	9, 50,000
Current book value (old asset)	4, 00,000
Present scrap value (old asset)	5, 00,000
Revenue from old asset (annual)	19, 25,000
Cash expenses on old asset (annual)	11, 25,000
Planning period, 4 years	

Depreciation on new asset: 92% of the cost is to be depreciated in the ratio of 5:8:6:4 over 4 years Existing asset is depreciated at a rate of $1,00,000 p.a. Tax rate is 40 %.

Solution: This question provides information regarding two machines, new and old. In order to make investment decisions, it is necessary to figure out the incremental cash flows from the new machine. We start with computing the cash flows associated with these two machines.

A: New Machine

Initial Cash Outflow

Cost or purchase price of the asset	10,00,000
Add, installation expenses	2, 00,000
Total cost of asset (A)	12,00,000
Add, increase in working capital	2,50,000
Funds required (B)	14,50,000

Subtract net salvage value as computed below,		
Salvage value of old machine (C)	5,00,000	
Less book value of old machine (D)	4,00,000	
Capital gain/ loss	1,00,000	
Less Tax on capital gain @ 40% (E)	40,000	
Net salvage value (F = C-E)		4,60,000
Initial investment amount (B-F)		9,90,000

Annual Cash Flows

New Machine	Year 1	Year 2	Year 3	Year 4
Annual Revenue	21,50,000	21,50,000	21,50,000	21,50,000
Less, Cash Expenses	9,50,000	9,50,000	9,50,000	9,50,000
EBDIT	12,00,000	12,00,000	12,00,000	12,00,000
Less Depreciation (WN 1)	2,40,000	3,84,000	2,88,000	1,92,000
PBT	9,60,000	8,16,000	9,12,000	10,08,000
Less, Tax (40%)	3,84,000	3,26,400	3,64,800	4,03,200
PAT	5,76,000	4,89,600	5,47,200	6,04,800
Add, Depreciation	2,40,000	3,84,000	2,88,000	1,92,000
Net Cash Flow	8,16,000	8,73,600	8,35,200	7,96,800

WN1: Computation of Depreciation

The problem states that 92% of the cost will be depreciated. 92% of the cost is 92% of

(10,00,000 +2,00,000) which is $ 11,04,000. This value is to be depreciated over a period of 4 years in the ratio of 5:8:6:4. The amount of depreciation is $ 2,40,000, $ 3,84,000, $ 2,88,000 and $ 1,92,000 for the four years respectively.

Terminal Cash Flow

The fourth year is the terminal year. It will involve the following cash flows.

Salvage value of new machine (A)	3,50,000	
Less Book value (8% of 12,00,000) (B)	96,000	
Capital gain	2,54,000	
Tax on capital gain @ 40% (C)	1,01,600	
Net salvage value (D = A-C)	2,48,400	2,48,400
Add working capital released		2,50,000
Terminal Cash Flow		4,98,400

In addition to it, there will also be normal annual net cash flow arising in year 4.

B: Old Machine

In case old machine, the depreciation is charged on the basis of straight line method. Thus, we can compute the annual net cash flow for one year and it will remain the same for other years as well.

Annual Revenue	19,25,000
Less Cash expenses	11,25,000
PBDIT	8,00,000
Less Depreciation (given)	1,00,000
PBT	7,00,000
Less Tax (40%)	2,80,000
PAT	4,20,000
Add Depreciation	1,00,000
NCF	5,20,000

Analysis of incremental cash flows of new machine over old machine:

- Initial investment = $9, 90,000.
- Annual incremental NCF.

Machine	Net Cash Flows			
	Year 1	Year 2	Year 3	Year 4
New Machine	8,16,000	8,73,600	8,35,200	7,96,800
Old Machine	5,20,000	5,20,000	5,20,000	5,20,000
Incremental NCF	2,96,000	3,53,600	3,15,200	2,76,800

Total Terminal Year Cash Flow

Incremental NCF	2,76,800
Terminal cash flow of machine	4,98,400
7,75,200	

Additional Aspect of Capital Budgeting Decisions

These additional factors can be easily incorporated into the computation of cash flows associated with the investment proposals.

- Sunk costs: Sunk cost is the cost which is incurred in the past and cannot be changed now. It is the historical expenses which has already taken place. Suppose a firm purchased a land ten years ago and the land is not used for any purpose and lying vacant. The cost of the land should not form the part of the new project, when the land is used for that project because cost has already incurred and if we deduct this cost from the new project, it may make the project unnecessarily less profitable.
- Opportunity costs: It is the benefit from the next best alternative. Suppose this land has alternate use that it can be given on rent. This amount of rent is the loss in revenue which results when we use the land for the new project and this rent is not earned. As this loss in revenue is the result of taking up the new project, it should be deducted from the revenues generated by the new project. Thus all opportunity costs should be the part of cash flow estimation analysis.
- Allocated overheads: A business concern usually has some fixed costs which cannot be assigned to any specific business unit. These are the costs which will be incurred irrespective of the production process. When a new machine is purchased or a new project is undertaken, these should be ignored and not be the part of cash flow analysis. For example, suppose the allocated overheads are of $ 90,000 and company has nine machines. This cost is allocated to these costs equally and each machine is charged $ 10,000. Suppose now firm purchases a new machine and the number of machines increases to ten. Further it is stated that the amount of $ 9000 (90,000/10) would be charged to each machine. Now the question before us is whether this amount of $ 9,000 should be taken into consideration while computing cash flows of new machine? These allocated overheads would be incurred whether we purchase new machine or not. Hence, it should not be taken into consideration while estimating the cash flows of the new machine. However, if it is stated that if we take up new machine, the amount of overheads will increase to, let's say, $ 1,05,000. Under this situation, this additional amount of $ 15,000 (1,05,000-90,000) is taken as the cash outflow due to new machine.
- Marketing survey: When a firm undertakes a market survey before launching a new product, it involves time and cost. At the time of assessing the cash flows of the new project, this marketing survey expense should not be the part of

cash flow analysis. This expense is incurred in the past and cannot be changed whether we take up the new project or not.

- Financing aspect of Investment Decisions: In terms of computation of net cash flows, it means that we should not take into consideration the payment of interest on debentures and dividend while estimating cash flows. When profit after tax is given after considering the interest payment, the net cash flows are computed by making appropriate adjustments for interest payments. The actual mechanism can be explained with the help of following example. Example: Suppose the following information is given:

Revenue	1,00,000
Less expense	40,000
Earnings before depreciation, interest and tax (EBDIT)	60,000
Less, depreciation	10,000
Earnings before interest and tax (EBIT)	50,000
Less, interest	20,000
Earnings Before Tax	30,000
Less, taxes (40%)	12,000
Profit after tax	18,000

Compute the net cash flow from the above data.

Solution:

Profit after tax	18,000
Add, Interest expenses	20,000
Add, Depreciation	10,000
	48,000
Less, Interest tax shield (interest × tax rate)	8,000
NCF	40,000

The tax benefit which arises due to tax deductibility of interest payment is called interest tax shield which is equal to interest multiplied by the tax rate. The amount of PAT is arrived at by taking into account the interest tax shield. We can write the net cash flows as:

$$NCF = PAT + Interest - interest \times tax\ rate + Depreciation.$$

ARR and Payback Period Method

There are mainly two techniques covered under traditional approach to capital budgeting:

- Accounting Rate of Return
- Payback Period

Accounting Rate of Return Method

This is the simplest way of calculating the return from any project. It is based on accounting profits rather than the cash flows. Accounting rate of return, also known as the Average rate of return or ARR calculates the return, generated from net income of the proposed capital investment. Accounting rate of return is calculated by dividing the average profit by the initial investment in order to get the ratio or return that can be expected.

Computation

It is computed by dividing the average annual profits after tax by the average investment.

As we can notice, this formula depends on two factors, namely average annual profits and average investments. Now, we proceed to define the process of computing these two variables.

Average Annual Profits After Taxes

There are two situations for which we need to compute the average profits after taxes.

- Equal Annual profits: when the amount of annual profits is same for all the years, the average annual profit will be equal to the annual profit after taxes. Suppose there is a project which is expected to generate an equal, amount of annual profit of $ 5000 for the next five years, the average annual profit for this project will be equal to $ 5000.
- Unequal amount of annual profits: When the amount of annual profits after taxes is different for various years, we can compute its average by using arithmetic mean method as shown in the following example.

Example: There is a project which will generate the following annual profit after taxes for the next five years. Compute the average annual profit of the project.

Year	Annual profit after taxes
1	10,000
2	30,000
3	45,000
4	20,000
5	30,000

Solution: The sum of all profits is $ 1,35,000 and its average is 1,35,000/5 which comes out to be $27,000. The next task which is involved in computing accounting rate of return is to calculate the amount of average investment.

Average Investment

- Original cost: When no information is given regarding the deprecation method and its computation, the original investment cost can be taken as the average investment. In addition to the original investment, suppose there are installation expenses also, the same should also be the part of average investment. For example, there is machine costing $ 50,000 and has installation expenses of $ 10,000. The average investment amount for this machine would be $ 60,000.
- Average investment after charging depreciation.

When the investments are subject to depreciation, the following steps are taken to calculate the amount of average investment.

1. First step is to compute the opening and closing book value of the investment after charging depreciation for various years.

2. The next step involves identifying the average book value of investment for each year. It is computed by adding the opening and closing book value for each year and then dividing the sum by two.

3. The final step is to compute the average of the 'average of book values' for each year. The amount so obtained is called average investment and it is used to compute the accounting rate of return.

All these steps can be shown by using the following example. Example: There is a project which will generate an annual profit of $ 3000 for the next 5 yea$ The cost of the project is $ 60,000 and its salvage value is expected to be $ 10,000 at the end of fifth year. The machine is subject to straight line depreciation method. Compute its accounting rate of return.

Solution: The first factor which is required is average annual profits after taxes. As the amount of annual profits after taxes is equal thus it will also be the average annual profit after tax that is $ 3000.

The next task is to compute the average investment. The investment is subject to straight line depreciation, thus the amount of depreciation for each year is equal to:

$$= \frac{60{,}000 \times 10{,}000}{5}$$

The amount of depreciation is $ 10,000 for each year. The following table shows the computation of average investment:

Year	Opening BV	Closing BV	Average BV
1	60,000	50,000	55,000
2	50,000	40,000	45,000

3	40,000	30,000	35,000
4	30,000	20,000	25,000
5	20,000	10,000	15,000
		Total	1,75,000

The average investment is 1,75,000/5 which is equal to $35,000.

Further, it may be noted that when the investment is subject to straight line depreciation method, we can use the following short cut method to compute average investment.

Average Investment = ½ (original cost + installation expenses-salvage value) + salvage value

Average investment = ½ (60,000-10,000) + 10,000

= 25,000 +10,000

= 35,000

The amount is same as computed above, however, it requires less computation to reach to the value of average investment. Now, we have all the necessary input to compute the accounting rate of return. The accounting rate of return is compute as:

$$= \frac{3{,}000}{35{,}000} \times 100$$

Thus the ARR is equal to 8.5%. The firm is expected to earn 8.5% rate of return from this project. If the project involves any additional working capital, the same must also be added to the amount of average investment computed above.

Decision Making Criteria

The firms make their investment decision on the basis of accounting rate of return. The rule is to compare the computed value of accounting rate of return with some predetermined rate of return. When the accounting rate of return is greater than the benchmark or some predetermined rate of return, the project is accepted. On the other hand, when the accounting rate of return is less than the predetermined rate of return, the project is not accepted. In case of mutually exclusive projects, ranks can be formed on the basis of accounting rate of return and then the project with highest rank may be accepted.

Merits

This method has the merits which can be explained as follows:

- It is simple to calculate and understand.
- Its basis is on accounting data which can be simply accessed from accounts of company.

- It measures the benefits in percentage which makes it easily comparable and provides an easy rule to make investment decision.

Demerits

Having stated its benefits, there are quite serious limitations which put a doubt on its usage. These are stated below:

- The first problem with this method is that it is based on account profit rather than cash flows. We discussed in earlier section that the objective of financial management is to maximize the wealth of the shareholde$ To attain this goal, the focus must be on the cash flows rather than on the accounting profits.
- The other major shortcoming of this method is that it does not take into account the time value of money. This method treats all cash flows on equal footing; it does not pay attention to the timing of the cash flow. The amount of cash flow whether received early or late is given equal importance which is contrary to the concept of time value of money.
- This method ignores the size of the investment. Sometimes, the accounting rate of return may be same for various projects but some may involve huge cash flows. Given the size of investment, the decision cannot simply be taken on the basis of accounting rate of return.

Let's consider the example given below:

Machine	Average Annual profits	Average Investment	ARR
A	10,000	1,00,000	10%
B	1000	10,000	10%
C	1500	15,000	10%

Thus for all three machines A, B and C, the accounting rate of return is same however, machine A requires huge cash outlay and the decision cannot be taken solely on the basis of ARR. The availability of funds is also another concern which should be taken into consideration while making investment decision.

We should not out rightly reject or accept any method, rather an informed view must be taken and overall all these merits and demerits should be properly weighed by the decision maker before making any investment commitment.

Payback Period Method

This is the simplest and most commonly used non discounting technique of capital budgeting. The payback period is the time period which is required to recover the original investment. Using this method, the firm aims to figure out the time period under which the investment will be recovered.

Computation

Payback period may be computed by:

- The first type of project is one which involves equal amount of cash flows for various year.

Cost Benefit Analysis

Profitability Index

Profitability index (PI), also known as profit investment ratio (PIR) and value investment ratio (VIR), is the ratio of payoff to investment of a proposed project. It is a useful tool for ranking projects because it allows you to quantify the amount of value created per unit of investment. Profitability index is an investment appraisal technique calculated by dividing the present value of future cash flows of a project by the initial investment required for the project. Formula:

$$\text{Profitability Index} = \frac{\text{Present Value of Future Cash Flows}}{\text{Initial Investment Required}}$$

$$= 1 + \frac{\text{Net Present Value}}{\text{Initial Investment Required}}$$

Explanation: Profitability index is actually a modification of the net present value method. While present value is an absolute measure (i.e. it gives as the total dollar figure for a project), the profibality index is a relative measure (i.e. it gives as the figure as a ratio).

Decision Rule

Rules for selection or rejection of a project:

- If PI > 1 then accept the project
- If PI < 1 then reject the project

Profitability index is sometimes called benefit-cost ratio too and is useful in capital rationing since it helps in ranking projects based on their per dollar return.

Example: Company C is undertaking a project at a cost of $ 50 million which is expected to generate future net cash flows with a present value of $ 65 million. Calculate the profitability index.

Solution: Profitability Index = PV of Future Net Cash Flows / Initial Investment Required

Profitability Index = $ 65M / $ 50M = 1.3

Net Present Value = PV of Net Future Cash Flows – Initial Investment Required

Net Present Value = $ 65M - $ 50M = $ 15M.

The information about NPV and initial investment can be used to calculate profitability index as follows:

Profitability Index = 1 + (Net Present Value / Initial Investment Required)

Profitability Index = 1 + $ 15M/ $ 50M = 1.3

Advantages of Profitability Index

The advantages of profitability index for a firm are listed below:

- The profitability index tells about an investment increasing or decreasing the firm's value.
- The profitability index takes into consideration all cash flows of the project.
- The profitability index takes the time value of money into consideration.
- The profitability index also considers the risk involved in future cash flows with the help of cost of capital.
- The profitability index is also helpful in ranking and picking projects while rationing of capital.

Disadvantages of Profitability Index

In addition to the aforesaid advantages, there are also certain disadvantages featured by the profitability index. These include:

- An estimate about the cost of capital is required so as to calculate the profitability index of a firm.
- The profitability index of a firm might not, sometimes, provide the correct decision while being used to compare mutually exclusive projects under consideration.

Net Present Value

In simple terms, it is the current value of the money that you may be spending or earning in the future. Today's $ 1.00 can be equivalent to $1.10 one year from now in terms of the standard interest rate that you can get in the market. If so:

- The NPV of $1.10 on July 30, 2012 is $ 1.00.

- The rate that we took as example above is called the "discount rate".

In order to evaluate a project's worthiness, in terms of the investment and returns over the next few years, we would apply a standard "discount rate" per market interest rates for the degree of risk we are undertaking on that project. We will then sum up the cash inflows (returns) and cash outflows (investments) for each year of evaluation, and take the resultant amount and apply the discount rate for the number of years we are looking ahead, from today.

We would do that for each year of evaluation (investment, returns considered) similarly and arrive at the actual earnings in today's value for all those future earnings and investments.

- If the resultant number is negative, it would mean negative returns on investment with respect to NPV.
- If the resultant number is positive, it would mean positive returns on investment with respect to NPV.
- If we compare two projects for such NPV, then the higher the NPV the better it is (considering the same amount of initial investments on both projects).
- It is also common to consider variable discount rates across years for more realistic evaluation of the project's value in today's terms.

Formula

Each cash inflow/outflow is discounted back to its present value (PV). Then they are summed. Therefore NPV is the sum of all terms,

$$\frac{R_t}{(1+i)^t}$$

Where,

t - the time of the cash flow.

i - the discount rate (the rate of return that could be earned on an investment in the financial markets with similar risk); the opportunity cost of capital.

R_t - the net cash flow (the amount of cash, inflow minus outflow) at time t.

If	It Means	Then
NPV > 0	the investment would add value to the firm.	the project may be accepted.
NPV < 0	the investment would subtract value from the firm.	the project should be rejected.
NPV = 0	the investment would neither gain nor lose value for the firm.	We should be indifferent in the decision whether to accept or reject the project. This project adds no monetary value. Decision should be based on other criteria, e.g. strategic position.

Example of NPV

A corporation must decide whether to introduce a new product line. The new product will have startup costs, operational costs, and incoming cash flows over six yea$ This project will have an immediate (t=0) cash outflow of $100,000 (which might include machinery, and employee training costs). Other cash outflows for years 1–6 are expected to be $5,000 per year. Cash inflows are expected to be $30,000 each for years 1–6. All cash flows are after-tax, and there are no cash flows expected after year 6. The required rate of return is 10%. The present value (PV) can be calculated for each year.

Year	Cash flow	Present value
$T=0$	$\frac{-100,000}{(1+0.10)^0}$	-$100,000
$T=1$	$\frac{30,000-5,000}{(1+0.10)^1}$	$22,727
$T=2$	$\frac{30,000-5,000}{(1+0.10)^2}$	$20,661
$T=3$	$\frac{30,000-5,000}{(1+0.10)^3}$	$18,783
$T=4$	$\frac{30,000-5,000}{(1+0.10)^4}$	$17,075
$T=5$	$\frac{30,000-5,000}{(1+0.10)^5}$	$15,523
$T=6$	$\frac{30,000-5,000}{(1+0.10)^6}$	$14,112

The sum of all these present values is the net present value, which equals $8,881.52. Since the NPV is greater than zero, it would be better to invest in the project than to do nothing, and the corporation should invest in this project if there is no mutually exclusive alternative with a higher NPV.

NPV does not consider Risk or Inflation in the calculation. In other words, we consider a standard rate for inflation across a project, which is OK, but considering the same rate for risk is not. It should be considered in addition to NPV.

Internal Rate of Return

The internal rate of return (IRR) is a rate of return used in capital budgeting to measure and compare the profitability of investments. It is also called the discounted cash flow rate of return (DCFROR) or the rate of return (ROR). In the context of savings and loans the IRR is also called the effective interest rate. The term internal refers to the fact that its calculation does not incorporate environmental factors (e.g., the interest rate or inflation).

The internal rate of return on an investment or project is the "annualized effective compounded return rate" or "rate of return" that makes the net present value (NPV as NET of all cash flows (both positive and negative) from a particular investment equal to zero.

In more specific terms, the IRR of an investment is the discount rate at which the net present value of costs (negative cash flows) of the investment equals the net present value of the benefits (positive cash flows) of the investment.

Internal rates of return are commonly used to evaluate the desirability of investments or projects. The higher a project's internal rate of return, the more desirable it is to undertake the project. Assuming all projects require the same amount of up-front investment, the project with the highest IRR would be considered the best and undertaken first. A firm (or individual) should, in theory, undertake all projects or investments available with IRRs that exceed the cost of capital. Investment may be limited by availability of funds to the firm and/or by the firm's capacity or ability to manage numerous projects.

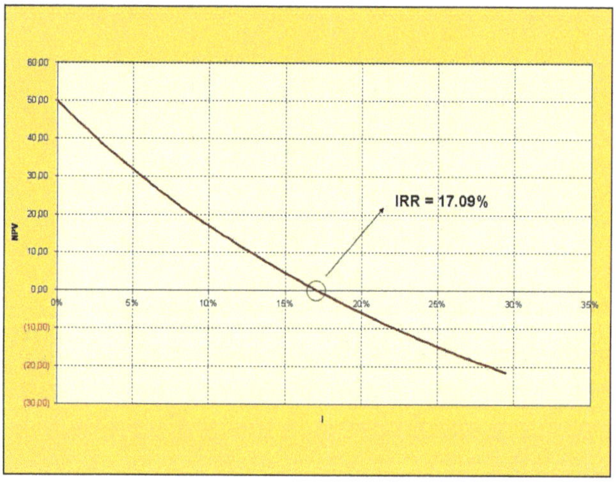

Showing the position of the IRR on the graph of NPV(r)⟨r (is labelled 'i' in the graph).

Uses

Because the internal rate of return is a rate quantity, it is an indicator of the efficiency, quality, or yield of an investment. This is in contrast with the net present value, which is an indicator of the value or magnitude of an investment.

An investment is considered acceptable if its internal rate of return is greater than an established minimum acceptable rate of return or cost of capital. In a scenario where an investment is considered by a firm that has equity holders, this minimum rate is the cost of capital of the investment (which may be determined by the risk-adjusted cost of capital of alternative investments). This ensures that the investment is supported by equity holders since, in general, an investment whose IRR exceeds its cost of capital adds value for the company (i.e., it is economically profitable).

Calculation

Given a collection of pairs (time, cash flow) involved in a project, the internal rate of return follows from the net present value as a function of the rate of return. A rate of return for which this function is zero is an internal rate of return.

Given the (period, cash flow) pairs (n, C_n) where n is a positive integer, the total number of periods N and the net present value NPV , the internal rate of return is given by r in:

$$NPV = \sum_{n=0}^{N} \frac{C_n}{(1+r)^n}$$

The period is usually given in years, but the calculation may be made simpler if r is calculated using the period in which the majority of the problem is defined (e.g., using months if most of the cash flows occur at monthly intervals) and converted to a yearly period thereafter. Any fixed time can be used in place of the present (e.g., the end of one interval of an annuity); the value obtained is zero if and only if the NPV is zero. In the case that the cash flows are random variables, such as in the case of a life annuity, the expected values are put into the above formula. Often, the value of r cannot be found analytically. In this case, numerical methods or graphical methods must be used.

Example: If an investment may be given by the sequence of cash flows,

Year (n)	Cash flow (C_n)
0	4000
1	1200
2	1410
3	1875
4	1050

then the IRR r is given by,

$$NPV = -4000 + \frac{1200}{(1+r)^1} + \frac{1410}{(1+r)^2} + \frac{1875}{(1+r)^3} + \frac{1050}{(1+r)^4} = 0$$

In this case, the answer is 14.3%.

Numerical Solution

Since the above is a manifestation of the general problem of finding the roots of the equation $NPV(r)$, there are many numerical methods that can be used to estimate r. For example, using the secant method, r is given by:

$$r_{n+1} = r_n - NPV_n \left(\frac{r_n - r_{n-1}}{NPV_n - NPV_{n-1}} \right)$$

Where r_n is considered the the approximation of the IRR.

This r can be found to an arbitrary degree of accuracy.

The convergence behaviour of the sequence is governed by the following:

- If the function $NPV(i)$ has a single real root r, then the sequence will converge reproducibly towards r.
- If the function $NPV(i)$ has n real roots $r_1 r_2 \ldots\ldots\ldots\ldots r_n$, then the sequence will converge to one of the roots and changing the values of the initial pairs may change the root to which it converges.
- If function $NPV(i)$ has no real roots, then the sequence will tend towards $+\infty$.

Having $r_1 > r_0$ when $NPV_0 > 0$ or $r_1 < r_0$ when $NPV_0 < 0$ may speed up convergence of r_n to r.

Numerical Solution for Single Outflow and Multiple Inflows

Of particular interest is the case where the stream of payments consists of a single outflow, followed by multiple inflows occurring at equal periods. In the above notation, this corresponds to:

$$C_0 < 0,\ C_n \geq 0 \text{ for } n \geq 1.$$

In this case the NPV of the payment stream is a convex, strictly decreasing function of interest rate. There is always a single unique solution for IRR. Given two estimates r_1 and r_2 for IRR, the secant method equation with $n = 2$ will always produce an improved estimate r_3. This is sometimes referred to as the Hit and Trial (or Trial and Error) method. More accurate interpolation formulas can also be obtained: for instance the secant formula with correction.

$$r_{n+1} = r_n - NPV_n \left(\frac{r_n - r_{n-1}}{NPV_n - NPV_{n-1}} \right) \left(1 - 1.4 \frac{NPV_{n-1}}{NPV_{n-1} - 3NPV_n + 2C_0} \right)$$

(Which is most accurate when $0 > NPV_n > NPV_{n-1}$) has been shown to be almost 10 times more accurate than the secant formula for a wide range of interest rates and initial guesses. For example, using the stream of payments {−4000, 1200, 1410, 1875, 1050} and initial guesses $r_1 = 0.25$ and $r_2 = 0.2$ the secant formula with correction gives an IRR estimate of 14.2% (0.7% error) as compared to IRR = 13.2% (7% error) from the secant method.

If applied iteratively, either the secant method or the improved formula will always converge to the correct solution. Both the secant method and the improved formula rely on initial guesses for IRR. The following initial guesses may be used:

$$r_1 = \left(A/|C_0|\right)^{2/(N+1)} - 1$$

$$r_2 = \left(1 + r_1\right)^p - 1$$

Where,

$$A = \text{Sum of Inflows} = C_1 + ... + C_N$$

$$p = \frac{\log\left(A/|C_0|\right)}{\log\left(A/NPV_{1,in}\right)}$$

Decision Criterion

- If the IRR is greater than the cost of capital, accept the project.
- If the IRR is less than the cost of capital, reject the project.

Problems with Using Internal Rate of Return

As an investment decision tool, the calculated IRR should not be used to rate mutually exclusive projects, but only to decide whether a single project is worth investing in.

In cases where one project has a higher initial investment than a second mutually exclusive project, the first project may have a lower IRR (expected return), but a higher NPV (increase in shareholders' wealth) and should thus be accepted over the second project (assuming no capital constraints).

IRR assumes reinvestment of interim cash flows in projects with equal rates of return (the reinvestment can be the same project or a different project). Therefore, IRR overstates the annual equivalent rate of return for a project whose interim cash flows are reinvested at a rate lower than the calculated IRR. This presents a problem, especially for high IRR projects, since there is frequently not another project available in the interim that can earn the same rate of return as the first project.

When the calculated IRR is higher than the true reinvestment rate for interim cash flows, the measure will overestimate – sometimes very significantly – the annual equivalent return from the project. The formula assumes that the company has additional projects, with equally attractive prospects, in which to invest the interim cash flows.

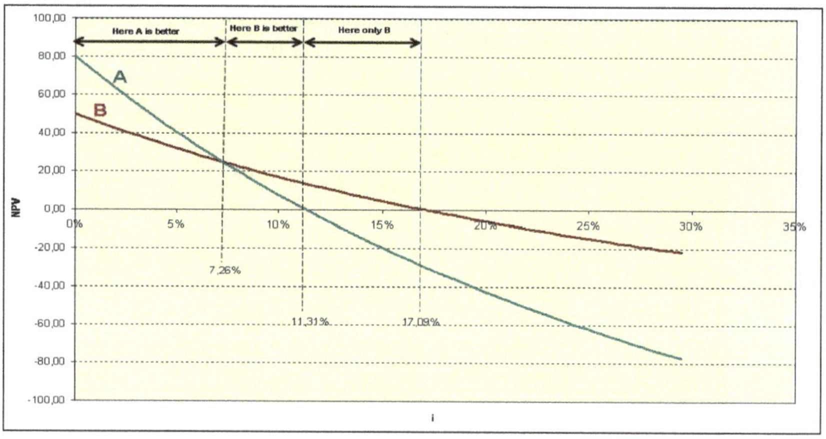

NPV vs discount rate comparison for two mutually exclusive projects. Project 'A' has a higher NPV (for certain discount rates), even though its IRR (= x-axis intercept) is lower than for project 'B'.

This makes IRR a suitable (and popular) choice for analyzing venture capital and other private equity investments, as these strategies usually require several cash investments throughout the project, but only see one cash outflow at the end of the project (e.g., via IPO or M&A).

Since IRR does not consider cost of capital, it should not be used to compare projects of different duration. Modified Internal Rate of Return (MIRR) does consider cost of capital and provides a better indication of a project's efficiency in contributing to the firm's discounted cash flow.

In the case of positive cash flows followed by negative ones and then by positive ones (for example, + + – – – +) the IRR may have multiple values. In this case a discount rate may be used for the borrowing cash flow and the IRR calculated for the investment cash flow. This applies for example when a customer makes a deposit before a specific machine is built.

In a series of cash flows like (–10, 21, –11), one initially invests money, so a high rate of return is best, but then receives more than one possesses, so then one owes money, so now a low rate of return is best. In this case it is not even clear whether a high or a low IRR is better. There may even be multiple IRRs for a single project, like in the example 0% as well as 10%. Examples of this type of project are strip mines and nuclear power plants, where there is usually a large cash outflow at the end of the project. In general, the IRR can be calculated by solving a polynomial equation. Sturm's theorem can be used to determine if that equation has a unique real solution. In general the IRR equation cannot be solved analytically but only iteratively.

When a project has multiple IRRs it may be more convenient to compute the IRR of the project with the benefits reinvested. Accordingly, MIRR is used, which has an assumed reinvestment rate, usually equal to the project's cost of capital. With multiple internal rates of return, the IRR approach can still be interpreted in a way that is consistent with the present value approach provided that the underlying investment stream is correctly identified as net investment or net borrowing.

NPV vs IRR

The underlying cause of the NPV and IRR conflict is the nature of cash flows (normal vs non-normal), nature of project (independent vs mutually-exclusive) and size of the project.

Independent projects are projects in which decision about acceptance of one project does not affect decision regarding othe$ Since we can accept all independent projects if they add value, NPV and IRR conflict does not arise. The company can accept all projects with positive NPV.

However, in case of mutually-exclusive projects, an NPV and IRR conflict may arise in which one project has a higher NPV but the other has higher IRR. Mutually exclusive projects are projects in which acceptance of one project excludes the others from consideration. The conflict either arises due to relative size of the project or due to the different cash flow distribution of the projects. Since NPV is an absolute measure, it will rank a project adding more dollar value higher regardless of the initial investment required. IRR is a relative measure, and it will rank projects offering best investment return higher regardless of the total value added.

NPV: The Preferred Technique

Whenever an NPV and IRR conflict arises, always accept the project with higher NPV. It is because IRR inherently assumes that any cash flows can be reinvested at the internal rate of return. This assumption is problematic because there is no guarantee that equally profitable opportunities will be available as soon as cash flows occur. The risk of receiving cash flows and not having good enough opportunities for reinvestment is called reinvestment risk. NPV, on the other hand, does not suffer from such a problematic assumption because it assumes that reinvestment occurs at the cost of capital, which is conservative and realistic.

Example: Conflict due to size of a project.

Project A needs $10 million investment and generates $10 million each in year 1 and year

2. It has NPV of $7.4 million at a discount rate of 10% and IRR of 61.8%. Project B needs $1 million investment and generates $2 million in Year 1 and $1 million in Year 2. Its NPV at a discount rate of 10% and IRR turn out to be $1.6 million and 141.4% respectively.

Based on NPV one would conclude that Project A is better, but IRR offers a contradictory view. This conflict arose due to the size of the project. In the end, we should go with the NPV recommendation.

Example: Conflict due to unconventional cash flows.

Let us consider two projects: C and D, both need $10 million investment each. Project C generates $15 million in Year 1 and $10 million in Year 2. Project D generates 0 in Year 1 and $30 million in Year 2. You can verify that Project C has NPV of $11.9 million at 10% discount rate and IRR of 100%. Project D has NPV of $14.8 million and IRR of 73.2%.

Despite both having the same initial investment, Project C has a higher NPV but Project D has a higher IRR. This is because in case of Project C more cash flows are in Year 1 resulting in longer reinvestment periods at higher reinvestment assumption and hence it has a higher IRR. As the NPV is not skewed by the overstated reinvestment rate assumption, hence it is the preferred method.

Similarities and Differences Between NPV and IRR

NPV is theoretically sound because it has realistic reinvestment assumption. It considers the cost of capital and provides a dollar value estimate of value added, which is easier to understand. Another particularly important feature of NPV analysis is its ability to notch the discount rate up and down to allow for different risk level of projects.

However, NPV is dependent on the size of the project. Without careful analysis, an investor might select a high NPV project ignoring the fact that many smaller NPV projects could be completed with the same investment resulting in higher aggregate NPV. It requires careful analysis in capital rationing. The size of project is irrelevant for IRR. It will rank a project requiring initial investment of $1 million and generating $1 million each in Year 1 and Year 2 equal to a project generating $1 in Year 1 and Year 2 each with initial investment of $1. This feature makes it a good complement to NPV.

IRR is also easier to calculate because it does not need estimation of cost of capital or hurdle rate. It just requires the initial investment and cash flows. However, this same convenience can become a disadvantage if we accept projects without comparison to cost of capital.

However, IRR's assumption of reinvestment at IRR is unrealistic and could result in inaccurate ranking of projects. Another, quite serious weakness is the multiple IRR problem. In case of non-normal cash flows, i.e. where a project has positive cash flows followed by negative cash flows, IRR has multiple values.

Capital Rationing

Capital rationing is a strategy used by companies or investors to limit the number of projects they take on at a time. If there is a pool of available investments that are all expected to be profitable, capital rationing helps the investor or business owner choose the most profitable ones to pursue.

Companies that employ a capital rationing strategy typically produce a relatively higher return on investment (ROI). This is simply because the company invests its resources where it identifies the highest profit potential.

Example: Capital rationing is about putting restrictions on investments and projects taken on by a business. To illustrate this better, let's consider the following example.

VV Construction is looking at five possible projects to invest in, as shown below:

Project	Investment Capital	Net Present Value (NPV)
1	$2 billion	$2 billion
2	$4 billion	$4 billion
3	$5 billion	$3 billion
4	$4 billion	$2 billion
5	$6 billion	$5 billion

To determine which project offers the greatest potential profitability, we compute each project using the following formula:

Profitability = NPV / Investment Capital

Project	NPV / Investment Capital	Profitability
1	$2 billion / $2 billion	1
2	$4 billion / $4 billion	1
3	$3 billion / $5 billion	0.6
4	$2 billion / $4 billion	0.5
5	$5 billion / $6 billion	.83

Based on the table above, we can conclude that projects 1 and 2 offer the greatest potential profit. Therefore, VV Construction will likely invest in those two projects.

Types of Capital Rationing

There are two types of capital rationing – hard and soft rationing.

- Hard capital rationing: Hard capital rationing represents rationing that is being imposed on a company by circumstances beyond its control. For example, a company may be restricted from borrowing money to finance new projects because it has suffered a downgrade in its credit rating. Thus, it may be difficult or effectively impossible for the company to secure financing, or it may only be able to do so at exorbitant interest rates.

- Soft capital rationing: In contrast, soft capital rationing refers to a situation where a company has freely chosen to impose some restrictions on its capital expenditures, even though it may have the ability to make much higher capital investments than it chooses to. The company may choose from any of a number of methods for imposing investment restrictions on itself. For example, it may temporarily require that a project offer a higher rate of return than is usually required in order for the company to consider pursuing it. Or the company may simply impose a limit on the number of new projects that it will take on during the next 12 months.

Benefits of Capital Rationing

Capital rationing is used by many investors and companies in order to ensure that only the most feasible investments are made. It helps ensure that businesses will invest only in those projects that offer the highest returns. It may appear that all investments with high projected returns should be taken. However, there are times when funds are low or when a company or an individual investor merely wants to improve their cash flows before making any more investments. It may also be the case that the investor has reason to believe that they can make the investment under more favorable terms by waiting a bit longer before pursuing it. For example, the company's management may expect a significant drop in interest rates within the next six months, which would make for less expensive financing costs.

Limited Numbers of Projects are Easier to Manage

When a company invests in a large number of projects simultaneously, the sharing of funds means less capital available for each individual project. This typically translates to more time and effort being required to monitor and manage each project. Also, allocating limited resources across several projects may actually threaten the success of the projects, if, for example, the projected budget for one or more projects turns out to have significantly underestimated costs. Wise capital rationing can help a company avoid such problems.

Capital Rationing Offers Increased Investment Flexibility

Investment opportunities are constantly changing. Portfolio managers usually keep a significant portion of available investment funds in the form of cash. Maintaining a ready supply of excess cash, first of all, provides greater financial stability and makes it easier for investors to adjust to sudden adverse circumstances that may arise.

Keeping some excess cash in reserve accomplishes something else as well. It ensures that if a particularly attractive unseen golden opportunity should suddenly arise, the investor has funds available to take immediate advantage of the situation. The ability to act quickly may be the difference between a good investment opportunity and a great one.

Potential Disadvantages of Capital Rationing

Capital rationing also comes with its own set of potential disadvantages, including the following:

- High capital requirements: Because only the most profitable investments are taken on under a capital rationing scenario, rationing can also spell high capital requirements.
- Goes against the efficient capital markets theory: Instead of investing in all projects that offer high profits, capital rationing only allows for selecting the projects with the highest estimated returns on investment. But the efficient markets theory holds that it is virtually impossible, over time, to continually select superior investments that significantly outperform others. Capital rationing may, in fact, expose an investor to greater risk by failing to hold a diversified investment portfolio.

Risk Analysis

Financial risks create the possibility of losses arising from the failure to achieve a financial objective. The risk reflects uncertainty about foreign exchange rates, interest rates, commodity prices, equity prices, credit quality, liquidity, and an organization's access to financing. These financial risks are not necessarily independent of each other. For instance, exchange rates and interest rates are often strongly linked, and this interdependence should be recognized when managers are designing risk management systems. Financial risks can be subdivided into distinct categories; a convenient classification is indicated in figure.

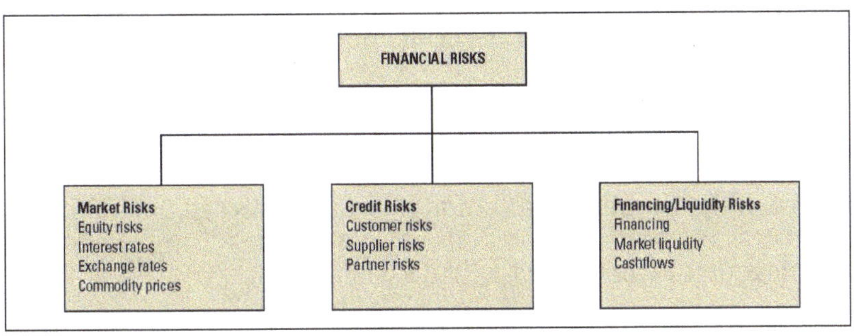

Figure: Categories of Financial Risk.

- Market risks: These are the financial risks that arise because of possible losses due to changes in future market prices or rates. The price changes will often relate to interest or foreign exchange rate movements, but also include the price of basic commodities that are vital to the business.

- Credit risks: Financial risks associated with the possibility of default by a counter-party. Credit risks typically arise because customers fail to pay for goods supplied on credit. Credit risk exposure increases substantially when a firm depends heavily upon a small number of large customers who have been granted access to a significant amount of credit. The significance of credit risk varies between sectors, and is high in the area of financial services, where short- and long-term lending are fundamental to the business. A firm can also be exposed to the credit risks of other firms with which it is heavily connected. For example, a firm may suffer losses if a key supplier or partner in a joint venture has difficulty accessing credit to continue trading.
- Financing, liquidity and cash flow risks: Financing risks affect an organization's ability to obtain ongoing financing. An obvious example is the dependence of a firm on its access to credit from its bank. Liquidity risk refers to uncertainty regarding the ability of a firm to unwind a position at little or no cost, and also relates to the availability of sufficient funds to meet financial commitments when they fall due. Cashflow risks relate to the volatility of the firm's day-to-day operating cash flow.

Why Manage Financial Risks?

Firms can benefit from financial risk management in many different ways, but perhaps the most important benefit is to protect the firm's ability to attend to its core business and achieve its strategic objectives. By making stakeholders more secure, a good risk management policy helps encourage equity investors, creditors, managers, workers, suppliers, and customers to remain loyal to the business. In short, the firm's goodwill is strengthened in all manner of diverse and mutually reinforcing ways. This leads to a wide variety of ancillary benefits:

- The firm's reputation or 'brand' is enhanced, as the firm is seen as successful and its management is viewed as both competent and credible.
- Risk management can reduce earnings volatility, which helps to make financial statements and dividend announcements more relevant and reliable.
- Greater earnings stability also tends to reduce average tax liabilities.
- Risk management can protect a firm's cash flows.
- Some commentators suggest that risk management may reduce the cost of capital, therefore raising the potential economic value added for a business.

- The firm is better placed to exploit opportunities (such as opportunities to invest) through an improved credit rating and more secure access to financing.
- The firm is in a stronger position to deal with merger and acquisitions issues. It is also in a stronger position to take over other firms and to fight off hostile takeover bids.
- The firm has a better managed supply chain, and a more stable customer base.

These benefits show that it is difficult to separate the effects of financial risk management from the broader activities of the business. It is therefore important to ensure that all parties within the organization recognize and understand how they might create or control financial risks. For example, staff in the marketing department might be trained on how to reduce financial risks through their approach to pricing and customer vetting. Similarly, buying policies can create financial risks by, for example, creating an exposure to exchange rate movements. Consequently, it is important to establish an integrated framework for managing all financial risks.

A Risk Management Framework

Organizations face many different types of risks, but they can all be managed using a common framework. The framework therefore directly applies to financial risk management, and provides a context that (a) outline the different types of financial risks, and (b) explain how financial risks may be identified and assessed before implementing appropriate strategies and control systems.

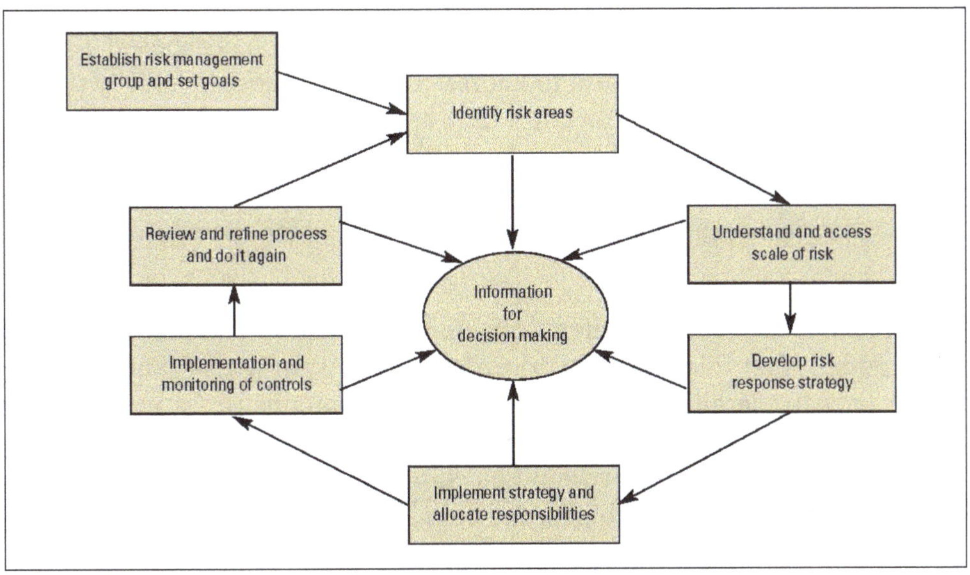

Figure: The Risk Management Cycle.

Risk management cycle, illustrated in Figure, shows that risk management forms a control loop that starts with defining risks by reference to organizational goals, then progressing through a series of stages to a reassessment of risk exposures following the implementation of controls.

At the organizational level, the stages of the risk cycle are set against the background of a clearly articulated risk policy. Drafted by senior management, the policy indicates the types of risks senior management wants the organization to take or avoid, and establishes the organization's overall appetite for risk taking. The starting point is therefore a general understanding of (a) the range and type of risks that an organization may face in pursuing its specific strategic objectives, and (b) the scale and nature of any interdependencies between these risks. This overview can then be used as the basis for constructing a more detailed risk management strategy for each risk category – in this case, financial risks.

Based on the cycle illustrated in figure, the core elements of a financial risk management system are:

- Risk identification and assessment.
- Development of a risk response.
- Implementation of a risk control strategy and the associated control mechanisms.
- Review of risk exposures (via internal reports) and repetition of the cycle.

Risk Identification and Assessment

The first stage is to identify the risks to which the organization is exposed. Risk identification needs to be methodical, and to address the organization's main activities and their associated risks. Risk identification may be carried out via questionnaires, surveys, brainstorming sessions, or a range of other techniques such as incident investigation, auditing, root cause analysis, or interviews. The aim is to use staff expertise to identify and describe all the potential financial risks to which the organization may be exposed.

The scale of each identified risk is then estimated, using a mix of qualitative and quantitative techniques. After this, risks are prioritized. The resulting risk ranking should relate directly back to overall corporate objectives. A commonly used approach is to map the estimated risks against a likelihood/impact matrix, such as that illustrated below. Often, both likelihood and impact would be classified into high, medium, or low. The more likely the outcome, and the bigger the impact, the more significant the risk would become. And it is especially important to identify and assess those risks that have the potential to severely jeopardize the organization's ability to achieve its objectives, or even to threaten its very survival.

The estimated risks can then be prioritized using a likelihood/impact matrix, such as that illustrated in figure.

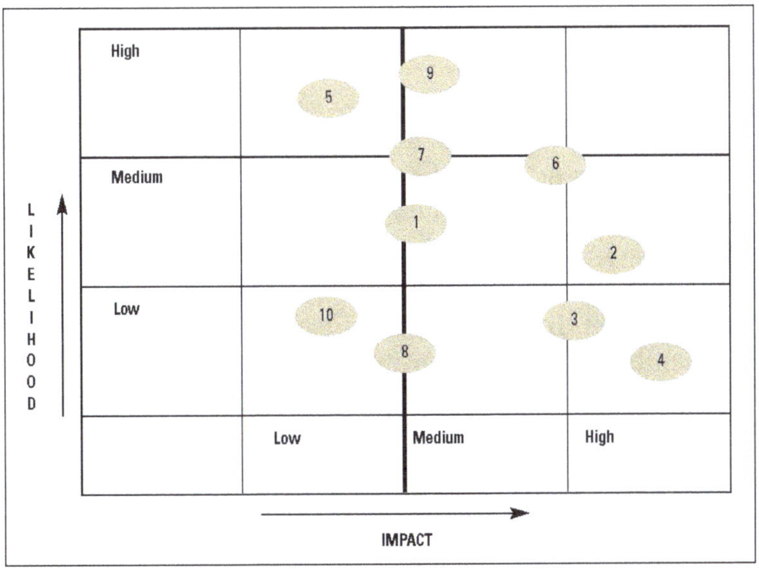

Figure: A Likelihood/Impact Matrix.

The numbers relate to individually identified risks, and risk impact may be expressed in either financial (quantitative) or nonfinancial (qualitative) terms. A private sector business may express impact in terms of forecast income, profit, or cash flow. On the other hand a public sector organization may measure impact in terms of its ability to provide services to a prescribed level.

Let us suppose that risk number five in the grid relates to the likelihood and risk of the impact on bad debts of a rise in interest rates. For a company retailing small-ticket consumer goods, the anticipated likelihood is shown as high – probably because of prevailing economic conditions – but the impact is relatively low. The accompanying risk register will include more specific details of the risk, such as specific interest rate forecasts, as well as the estimated monetary impact and the assumptions underlying its calculation. In the case of a mortgage provider operating under the same economic conditions, this same risk may be identified as having a much higher impact because of the size of the potential defaults and the fact that lending is its core business. In other words, the component risks and also the resulting matrix of likelihood and consequences will vary from business to business, and are subject to a degree of subjective judgment. As long as this subjectivity is recognized, the grid provides a useful tool for ranking risks and determining the appropriate levels of monitoring and control.

Many firms find it useful to record their risk information in a risk register. Such a register would include information on the type of risk, its likelihood of occurrence, its likely consequence, its potential monetary impact, and its relationship (if any) with other identified risks. The risk register, which would also include information such as forecasts of key variables, the assumptions on which calculations are based, and the institution's response to each risk, would be regularly updated.

Risk Response

The organization then needs to respond to the risks it has identified. An example would include setting out a policy defining the organization's response to a particular risk, and explain how that policy fits in with its broader objectives. It would also (a) set out the management processes to be used to manage that risk, (b) assign responsibility for handling it, and (c) set out the key performance measures that would enable senior management to monitor it. In more serious cases, it might also include contingency plans to be implemented if a projected event actually occurred.

The organization should take account of the effectiveness of alternative possible responses. This requires that it be possible to identify the level of "gross" risk prior to a response, and the level of "net" risk left after it. The organization should also take account of the costs and prospective benefits of alternative responses, as well as take account of how any response would relate to its risk appetite and its ability to achieve its strategic objective.

The possible responses can be categorized into three categories, as illustrated in figure. Internal strategies imply a willingness to accept the risk and manage it internally within the framework of normal business operations. An example would be a decision to use the customer's currency for pricing of all exports, and using internal netting processes to manage currency exposures. Risk sharing strategies relate to strategies that mitigate or share risks with an outside party. An example would be a forward contract, which 'locks in' a particular future price or rate. This prevents losses from unfavourable currency movements, but locks the buyer into a fixed future exchange rate. Another example is a joint venture.

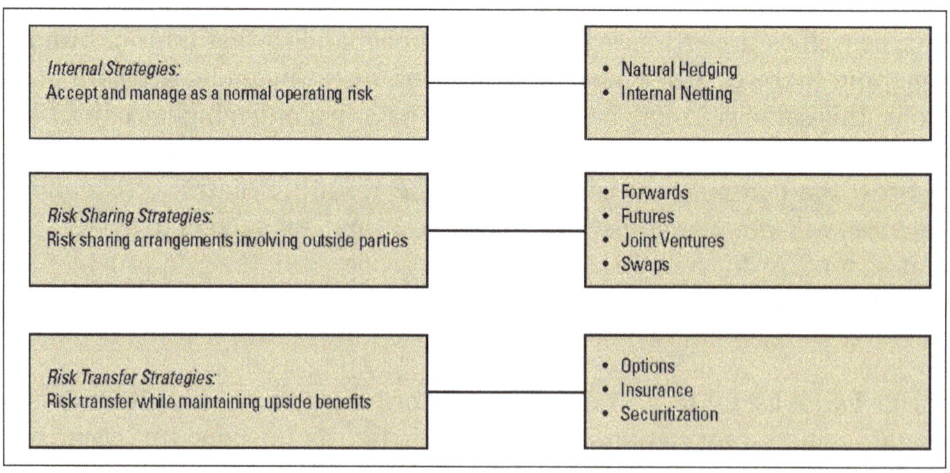

Figure: Risk Strategies and Tools.

Risk transfer involves paying a third party to take over the downside risk, while retaining the possibility of taking advantage of the upside risk. An option, for example, creates the opportunity to exchange currency at a preagreed rate, known as the strike price. If the subsequent exchange rate turns out to be favorable, the holder will exercise the option, but if the subsequent exchange rate is unfavourable, the holder will let it lapse. Thus, the option protects the holder from downside risk while retaining the possible benefits of upside risk. Note, by the way, that the greater flexibility of risk transfer tools is usually accompanied by greater cost.

Risk Control Implementation

Having selected a risk response, the next stage is to implement it and monitor its effectiveness in relation to the specified objectives. Implementation includes allocating responsibility for managing specific risks and, underlying that, creating a risk-aware culture in which risk management becomes embedded within the organizational language and methods of working.

Review of Risk Exposures

The control loop is closed when the effectiveness of the risk controls is evaluated through a reporting and review process. This then leads to a new risk identification and evaluation process. This process itself has three main components:

- Review process: This should include a regular review of risk forecasts, a review of the management responses to significant risks, and a review of the organization's risk strategy. It should also include the establishment of an early warning system to indicate material changes to the risks faced by the organization.
- Internal reporting to the board or senior management group: This might include a (a) review of the organization's overall risk management strategy, and (b) reviews of the processes used to identify and respond to risks, and of the methods used to manage them. It should also include an assessment of the costs and benefits of the organization's risk responses, and an assess ment of the impact of the organization's risk management strategy on the risks it faces.
- External reporting: External stakeholders should be informed of the organization's risk management strategy, and be given some indication of how well it is performing.

This basic framework for risk management can now be applied to each of the different categories of financial risk, namely: market, credit, financing, liquidity, and cash flow risks.

References

- Profitability: readyratios.com, Retrieved 03, June 2020
- Npv-vs-irr-362789: xplaind.com, Retrieved 25, April 2020
- Capital-rationing, finance, knowledge: corporatefinanceinstitute.com, Retrieved 07, July 2020
- Financial-risk: cimaglobal.com, Retrieved 11, February 2020

4

Financing Decisions

The decisions concerning the financing-mix of an organization taken by the financial manager are classified as financing decisions. They deal with the borrowing and dispensing of funds necessary for the investment decisions of an organization. The topics elaborated in this chapter will help in gaining a better perspective about financing decisions, cost of capital and capital structure.

Cost of Capital

Cost of capital is the required return necessary to make a capital budgeting project, such as building a new factory, worthwhile. When analysts and investors discuss the cost of capital, they typically mean the weighted average of a firm's cost of debt and cost of equity blended together.

Many companies use a combination of debt and equity to finance their businesses and, for such companies, the overall cost of capital is derived from the weighted average cost of all capital sources, widely known as the weighted average cost of capital (WACC).

Cost of capital represents a hurdle rate that a company must overcome before it can generate value, and it is used extensively in the capital budgeting process to determine whether a company should proceed with a project. The cost of capital concept is also widely used in economics and accounting. Another way to describe the cost of capital is the opportunity cost of making an investment in a business. Wise company management will only invest in initiatives and projects that will provide returns that exceed the cost of their capital.

Cost of capital, from the perspective of an investor, is the return expected by whoever is providing the capital for a business. In other words, it is an assessment of the risk of a company's equity. In doing this, an investor may look at the volatility (beta) of a company's financial results to determine whether a certain stock is too risky or would make a good investment.

Weighted Average Cost of Capital (WACC)

A firm's cost of capital is typically calculated using the weighted average cost of capital formula that consider the cost of both debt and equity capital. Each category of the firm's capital is weighted proportionately to arrive at a blended rate, and the formula consider every type of debt and equity on the company's balance sheet, including common and preferred stock, bonds, and other forms of debt.

Finding the Cost of Debt

Every company has to chart out its financing strategy at an early stage. The cost of capital becomes a critical factor in deciding which financing track to follow: debt, equity, or a combination of the two.

Early-stage companies seldom have sizable assets to pledge as collateral for debt financing, so equity financing becomes the default mode of funding for most of them. Less-established companies with limited operating histories will pay a higher cost for capital than older companies with solid track records since lenders and investors will demand a higher risk premium for the former.

The cost of debt is merely the interest rate paid by the company on its debt. However, since interest expense is tax-deductible, the debt is calculated on an after-tax basis as follows:

$$\text{Cost of debt} = \frac{\text{Interest expense}}{\text{Total Debt}} \times (1 - T)$$

Where,

- Interest expense = Int. paid on the firm's current debt.
- T=The company's marginal tax rate.

The cost of debt can also be estimated by adding a credit spread to the risk-free rate and multiplying the result by (1 - T).

Finding the Cost of Equity

The cost of equity is more complicated since the rate of return demanded by equity investors is not as clearly defined as it is by lenders The cost of equity is approximated by the capital asset pricing model as follows:

$$\text{CAPM(Cost of equity)} = R_f + \beta(R_m - R_f)$$

Where,

R_f = risk-free rate of return.

R_m = market rate of return.

Beta is used in the CAPM formula to estimate risk, and the formula would require a public company's own stock beta. For private companies, a beta is estimated based on the average beta of a group of similar, public firms. Analysts may refine this beta by calculating it on an unlevered, after-tax basis. The assumption is that a private firm's beta will become the same as the industry average beta.

The firm's overall cost of capital is based on the weighted average of these costs. For example, consider an enterprise with a capital structure consisting of 70% equity and 30% debt; its cost of equity is 10% and the after-tax cost of debt is 7%. Therefore, its WACC would be:

$$(0.7 \times 10\%) + (0.3 \times 7\%) = 9.1\%$$

This is the cost of capital that would be used to discount future cash flows from potential projects and other opportunities to estimate their net present value (NPV) and the ability to generate value.

Companies strive to attain the optimal financing mix based on the cost of capital for various funding sources. Debt financing has the advantage of being more tax-efficient than equity financing since interest expenses are tax-deductible and dividends on common shares are paid with after-tax dollar However, too much debt can result in dangerously high leverage, resulting in higher interest rates sought by lender to offset the higher default risk.

The Cost of Capital and Tax Considerations

One element to consider in deciding to finance capital projects via equity or debt is the possibility of any tax savings from taking on debt since the interest expense can lower a firm's taxable income, and thus, its income tax liability.

However, the Modigliani-Miller Theorem (M&M) states that the market value of a company is independent of the way it finances itself and shows that under certain assumptions, the value of leveraged versus non-leveraged firms are equal, in part because other costs offset any tax savings that come from increased debt financing.

The Difference Between Cost of Capital and the Discount Rate

The cost of capital and discount rate are somewhat similar and are often used interchangeably. Cost of capital is often calculated by a company's finance department and used by management to set a discount rate (or hurdle rate) that must be beaten to justify an investment.

That said, a company's management should challenge its internally-generated cost of capital number, as it may be so conservative as to deter investment. Cost of capital may also differ based on the type of project or initiative; a highly innovative but risky initiative should carry a higher cost of capital than a project to update essential equipment or software with proven performance.

Cost of Debt

The cost of debt is the effective interest rate a company pays on its debts. It's the cost of debt, such as bonds and loans, among others The cost of debt often refers to the before-tax cost of debt, which is the company's cost of debt before taking taxes into account. However, the difference in the cost of debt before and after taxes lies in the fact that interest expenses are deductible.

Cost of debt is one part of a company's capital structure, which also includes the cost of equity. Capital structure deals with how a firm finances its overall operations and growth through different sources of funds, which may include debt such as bonds or loans, among other types. The cost of debt measure is helpful in understanding the overall rate being paid by a company to use these types of debt financing. The measure can also give investors an idea of the company's risk level compared to others because riskier companies generally have a higher cost of debt. The cost of debt is generally lower than cost of equity.

Examples of Cost of Debt

To calculate the cost of debt, a company must determine the total amount of interest it is paying on each of its debts for the year. Then it divides this number by the total of all of its debt. The result is the cost of debt.

The cost of debt formula is the effective interest rate multiplied by (1 - tax rate). The effective tax rate is the weighted average interest rate of a company's debt. For example, say a company has a $1 million loan with a 5% interest rate and a $200,000 loan with a 6% rate. The effective interest rate on its debt is 5.2%. The company's tax rate is 30%. Thus, its cost of debt is 3.64%, or 5.2% * (1 - 30%).

The interest on the first two loans is $50,000 and $12,000, respectively, and the interest on the bonds equates to $140,000. The total interest for the year is $202,000. The company's cost of debt is 6.31%, with a total debt of $3.2 million.

Cost of Debt after Taxes

The after-tax cost of debt is the interest paid on debt less any income tax savings due to deductible interest expenses. To calculate the after-tax cost of debt, subtract a company's effective tax rate from 1, and multiply the difference by its cost of debt. The company's marginal tax rate is not used, rather, the company's state and the federal tax rate are added together to ascertain its effective tax rate.

For example, if a company's only debt is a bond it has issued with a 5% rate, its pre-tax cost of debt is 5%. If its tax rate is 40%, the difference between 100% and 40% is 60%, and 60% of the 5% is 3%. The after-tax cost of debt is 3%.

The rationale behind this calculation is based on the tax savings the company receives from claiming its interest as a business expense. Imagine the company has issued $100,000 in bonds at a 5% rate. Its annual interest payments are $5,000. It claims this amount as an expense, and this lowe$the company's income on paper by $5,000. As the company pays a 40% tax rate, it saves $2,000 in taxes by writing off its interest. As a result, the company only pays $3,000 on its debt. This equates to a 3% interest rate on its debt.

Cost of Equity (Ke)

The cost of equity is the rate of return investor requires from the stock before looking into other viable opportunities. Suppose you have the US $1000 to invest! So you look for many opportunities. And you choose the one which, according to you, would yield more returns. Now, as you decided to invest in one particular opportunity, you would let go of others, maybe more profitable opportunities. That loss of other alternatives is called "opportunity cost."

Let's come back to the Ke. If you, as an investor, don't get better returns from company A, you will go ahead and invest in other companies. And company A has to bear the opportunity cost if they don't put their effort to increase the required rate of return. Let's take an example to understand this.

Let's say Mr. A wants to invest in Company B., But as Mr. A is a relatively new investor, he wants a low-risk stock, which can yield him a good return. Company B's current stock price is US $8 per share, and Mr. A expects that the required rate of return for him would be more than 15%. And through the calculation of the cost of equity, he will understand what he will get as a required rate of return. If he gets 15% or more, he will invest in the company; and if not, he will look for other opportunities.

Formula

The cost of equity can be calculated in two ways. First, we will use the usual model, which has been used by the investors over and over again. And then we would look at the other one.

Cost of Equity – Dividend Discount Model

So we need to calculate Ke in the following manner:

> Cost of Equity = (Dividends per share for next year / Current Market Value of Stock) + Growth rate of dividends

Here, it is calculated by taking dividends per share into account. Mr. C wants to invest into Berry Juice Private Limited. Currently, Berry Juice Private Limited has decided to pay the US $2 per share as a dividend. The current market value of the stock is the US $20. And Mr. C expects that the appreciation in the dividend would be around 4% (a guess based on the previous year's data). So, the Ke would be 14%.

How would you calculate the growth rate? We need to remember that the growth rate is the estimated one, and we need to calculate it in the following manner:

Growth Rate = (1 – Payout Ratio) * Return on Equity

If we are not being provided with the Payout Ratio and Return on Equity Ratio, we need to calculate it. Here's how to calculate them:

Dividend Payout Ratio = Dividends / Net Income

We can use another ratio to find out dividend pay-out. Here it is:

Alternative Dividend Payout Ratio = 1 – (Retained Earnings / Net Income)

And also the Return on Equity:

Return on Equity = Net Income / Total Equity

Cost of Equity – Capital Asset Pricing Model (CAPM)

CAPM quantifies the relationship between risk and required return in a well-functioning market.

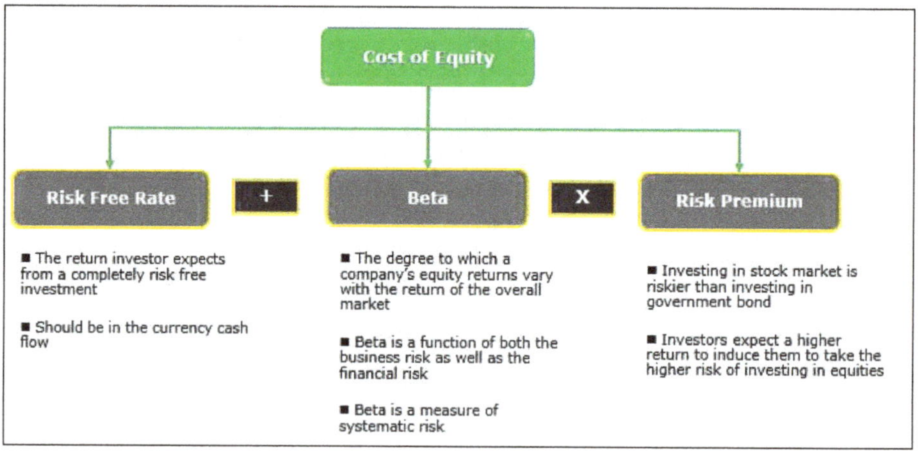

Cost of Equity CAPM

Cost of Equity = Risk-Free Rate of Return + Beta * (Market Rate of Return – Risk-free Rate of Return)

- Risk-free Rate of Return: This is the return of a security that has no default risk, no volatility, and a beta of zero. A ten-year government bond is typically taken as a risk-free rate.
- Beta is a statistical measure percentage of the variability of a company's stock price in relation to the stock market overall. So if the company has high beta, that means the company has more risk, and thus, the company needs to pay more to attract investors Simply put, that means more Ke.

- Risk Premium (Market Rate of Return – Risk-Free Rate): It measures the return that equity investors demand over a risk-free rate in order to compensate them for the volatility/risk of an investment that matches the volatility of the entire market. Risk premium estimates vary from 4.0% to 7.0%.

Let's take an example to understand this. Let's say the beta of Company M is 1, and the risk-free return is 4%. The market rate of return is 6%. We need to calculate the cost of equity using the CAPM model.

- Company M has a beta of 1, which means the stock of Company M will increase or decrease as per the tandem of the market.
- Ke = Risk-Free Rate of Return + Beta * (Market Rate of Return – Risk-free Rate of Return).
- Ke = 0.04 + 1 * (0.06 – 0.04) = 0.06 = 6%.

Interpretation

The Ke is not exactly what we refer to. It's the responsibility of the company. It is the rate which the company needs to generate to allure the investors to invest in their stock at the market price. That's why the Ke is also referred to as the "required rate of return."

So let's say as an investor, you don't have any idea what is the Ke of a company! What would you do?

First, you need to find out the total equity of the company. If you look at the balance sheet of the company, you would find it easily. Then you need to see whether the company has paid any dividends or not. You can check their cash flow statement to be ensured. If they pay a dividend, you need to use the dividend discount model and if not, you need to go ahead and find out the risk-free rate and calculate the cost of equity under the capital asset pricing model (CAPM). Calculating it under CAPM is a tougher job as you need to find out the beta by doing regression analysis.

Cost of Equity Example:

In US $	Company A
Dividends Per Share	12
Market Price of Share	100
Growth in the next year	5%

Now, this is the simplest example of a dividend discount model. The dividend per share is US $30, and the market price per share is US $100. The growth percentage. Let's calculate the cost of equity.

Ke= Dividends per share for next year / Current Market Value of Stock) + Growth rate of dividends.

In US $	Company A
Dividends Per Share (A)	12
Market Price of Share (B)	100
Growth in the next year (C)	5%
Ke[(A/B)+C]	17%

So, Ke of Company A is 17%.

Details	Company MNP
Risk-Free Rate	8%
Market Rate of Return	12%
Beta Coefficient	1.5

Example: MNP Company has the following information.

We need to calculate Ke of MNP Company. Let's look at the formula first, and then we will ascertain the cost of equity using a capital asset pricing model.

Ke = Risk-Free Rate of Return + Beta * (Market Rate of Return – Risk-free Rate of Return)

Details	Company MNP
Risk-Free Rate (A)	8%
Market Rate of Return (B)	12%
[B – A] (C)	4%
Beta Coefficient (D)	1.5
Ke [A+D*C]	14%

To calculate the beta coefficient for a single stock, you need to look at the closing price of the stock every day for a particular period, also the closing level of the market benchmark for the similar period and then use excel in running the regression analysis.

Leverage

Leverage results from using borrowed capital as a funding source when investing to expand the firm's asset base and generate returns on risk capital. Leverage is an investment strategy of using borrowed money—specifically, the use of various financial instruments or borrowed capital—to increase the potential return of an investment. Leverage can also refer to the amount of debt a firm uses to finance assets.

Leverage is the use of debt (borrowed capital) in order to undertake an investment or project. The result is to multiply the potential returns from a project. At the same time, leverage will also multiply the potential downside risk in case the investment does not pan out. When one refers to a company, property, or investment as "highly leveraged," it means that item has more debt than equity.

The concept of leverage is used by both investors and companies. Investors use leverage to significantly increase the returns that can be provided on an investment. They lever their investments by using various instruments, including options, futures, and margin accounts. Companies can use leverage to finance their assets. In other words, instead of issuing stock to raise capital, companies can use debt financing to invest in business operations in an attempt to increase shareholder value.

Investors who are not comfortable using leverage directly have a variety of ways to access leverage indirectly. They can invest in companies that use leverage in the normal course of their business to finance or expand operations—without increasing their outlay. Leverage amplifies possible returns, just like a lever can be used to amplify one's strength when moving a heavy weight.

Special Considerations

Through balance sheet analysis, investors can study the debt and equity on the books of various firms and can invest in companies that put leverage to work on behalf of their businesses. Statistics such as return on equity (ROE), debt to equity (D/E), and return on capital employed (ROCE) help investors determine how companies deploy capital and how much of that capital companies have borrowed.

To properly evaluate these statistics, it is important to keep in mind that leverage comes in several varieties, including operating, financial, and combined leverage. Fundamental analysis uses the degree of operating leverage. One can calculate the degree of operating leverage by dividing the percentage change of a company's earnings per share (EPS) by its percentage change in its earnings before interest and taxes (EBIT) over a period.

Similarly, one could calculate the degree of operating leverage by dividing a company's EBIT by EBIT less interest expense. A higher degree of operating leverage shows a higher level of volatility in a company's EPS. Analysis uses the "equity multiplier" to measure financial leverage. One can calculate the equity multiplier by dividing a firm's total assets by its total equity. Once figured, one multiplies the financial leverage with the total asset turnover and the profit margin to produce the return on equity. For example, if a publicly-traded company has total assets valued at $500 million and shareholder equity valued at $250 million, then the equity multiplier is 2.0 ($500 million / $250 million). This shows the company has financed half its total assets by equity. If reading spreadsheets and conducting fundamental analysis is not your cup of tea, you can purchase mutual funds or exchange-traded funds (ETFs) that use leverage. By using these vehicles, you can delegate the research and investment decisions to experts.

Leverage vs. Margin

Although interconnected—since both involve borrowing—leverage and margin are not the same. Leverage refers to taking on debt, while margin is debt or borrowed money a firm uses to invest in other financial instruments.

A margin account allows you to borrow money from a broker for a fixed interest rate to purchase securities, options, or futures contracts in the anticipation of receiving substantially high returns. You can use margin to create leverage.

Disadvantages of Leverage

Leverage is a multi-faceted, complex tool. The theory sounds great, and in reality, the use of leverage can be profitable, but the reverse is also true. Leverage magnifies both gains and losses. If an investor uses leverage to make an investment and the investment moves against the investor, their loss is much greater than it would've been if they have not leveraged the investment.

For this reason, leverage should often be avoided by first-time investors until they get more experience under their belts. In the business world, a company can use leverage to generate shareholder wealth, but if it fails to do so, the interest expense and credit risk of default destroy shareholder value.

Example of Leverage

A company was formed with a $5 million investment from investors, where the equity in the company is $5 million—this is the money the company can use to operate. If the company uses debt financing by borrowing $20 million, it now has $25 million to invest in business operations and more opportunity to increase value for shareholders.

An automaker, for example, could borrow money to build a new factory. The new factory would enable the automaker to increase the number of cars it produces and increase profits.

Combined Cost of Capital

WACC is a way to calculate the Combined Cost of a company's capital that gives different weight to different components of capital based upon their proportion in the company's capital structure instead of taking the simple average of all costs together. The simple average cost of capital may not be appropriate because there is hardly a firm that employs equal proportion of various sources of finance.

The basis of determining WACC is to determine the specific costs of each of the sources of long term financing for the firm individually, assign weights to these individual sources of finance depending upon the degree to which the firm uses these sources, and then, simply add up the weighted costs, that is the product of individual cost with their respective weights.

Therefore, following are the four steps involved in calculation of WACC:

- Calculate the specific cost of each source of fund.
- Find out the weight or proportion of each source of fund in the total capital structure of the firm.
- Multiply the specific cost of each source of funds with their respective proportion.
- Add the weighted component cost calculated in Step 3 above to get WACC.

For instance, think of a company that makes use of only two sources of financing; debt and equity. Let E be the value of all of the common stock of the firm and D be the value of all of the debt of the firm (We can assign the value to debt and equity either on the basis of their Book Value or Market Value). Thus E+D must be the total value of the firm. Let Kd be the after tax cost of debt financing and let Ke be the costs for equity financing. The WACC for this firm will be:

$$WACC = \left(\frac{E}{E+D}\right)K_e + \left(\frac{D}{E+D}\right)K_d$$

This equation is the same as saying: WACC = (percent of the firm that is equity) times (cost of equity) plus (percent of the firm that is debt) times (cost of debt)

Next step is the assignment of weights. The weights can be assigned on the following three bases:

- Historical Weights: These are based upon existing capital structure. It assumes that additional finance will be raised in the same proportion as the proportion of funds in the existing capital structure. It is based upon the assumption that the existing capital structure is optimum.
- Marginal Weights: These are based upon the proportion of funds in which the new capital will be raised. It is quite logical because it is very unlikely that a company is able to raise additional funds in the same proportion as they are in the existing capital structure.

The concept of Historical weights and Marginal weights can be made clearer with the help of following example: Suppose there is a company with its present capital structure comprised of Equity and Debt. Out of total capital of \$ 50,000; debt component is 20,000 and equity component is 30,000. Now, if the company wants to raise additional finance of \$ 20,000; it has two options: First, it can raise the additional \$ 20,000 in the same proportion of its existing capital structure, i.e., $ 8,000 or 40% through debt and $ 12,000 or 60% through equity. Second, it can raise additional $ 20,000 in any proportion without referring to the existing capital structure. If the company goes for first option, it would have said to use Historical weights, and if the company goes for second option, it would have said to use Marginal weights.

- Target Weights: Target weights are either Book Value or Market value weights based on desired capital structure proportions.

Historical Weights

The historical weights can further be divided into two types:

- Book Value Weights
- Market Value Weights

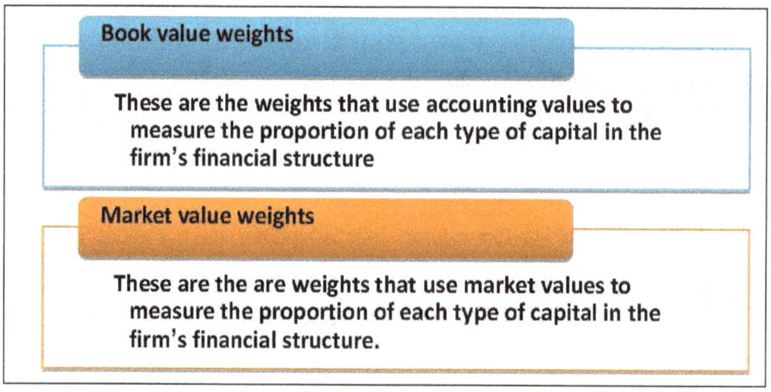

WACC calculated using the Book value weights is generally lower than the WACC calculated on the basis of Market value because the market value of the capital components is usually higher than the book value. For instance, M Ltd. has the following Capital Structure:

	Book Value ($)	Market Value ($)
Equity Share Capital (25,000 shares of $ 10 each)	2,50,000	4,50,000
14% Preference Share Capital (500 shares of $ 100 each)	50,000	45,000
Reserves and Surpluses	1,50,000	-
12% Debentures (1500 Debenture of $100 each)	1,50,000	1,45,000

The expected dividend per share is $1.40 and is expected to grow at 8% forever. The cost of equity is 15.77%. The preference shares are redeemable after 5 years at par and debentures are redeemable after 6 years at par. Cost of preference share is 16.84%. Tax rate is 50% and cost of debentures is 6.66%. The WACC (Ko) can be calculated by using the following formula:

On the basis of Book Value Weights:

K_o = (2,50,000/6,00,000)*15.77 + (1,50,000/6,00,000)*15.77 + (50,000/6,00,000)*16.84 + (1,50,000/6,00,000)*6.66

K_o = (0.417*15.77 + 0.25*15.77 + 0.083*16.84 + 0.25*6.66)

K_o = 6.57 + 3.94 + 1.397 + 1.665

K_o = 13.572%

*Internal cash in hand or retained earnings are part of the equity of the firm. Therefore, cost of retained earnings is taken as equal to the cost of equity except in the presence of floatation cost. There are no flotation costs for the use of retained cash flow, while there are for new issues of stock.

On the Basis of Market Value Weights

K_o = (4,50,000/6,40,000)*15.77 + (45,000/6,40,000)*16.84 + (1,45,000/6,40,000)*6.66

K_o = (0.7031*15.77 + 0.0704*16.84 + 0.2265*6.66)

K_o = 11.0878 + 1.1855 + 1.5085

K_o = 13.782%

Under market value weights, there is no separate cost of retained earnings. It is the same as cost of equity because retained earnings belong to equity shareholders only and therefore, it is included in the market value of equity.

However, the insufficiency of the Retained Earnings to cover the required equity financing, will increase the WACC because a new stock issue will be needed and this involves floatation costs which are now included in the cost of equity. Both Book Value weights and Market value weights have some advantages over the other, but they are also not free from the flaws. There are some drawbacks as well for both of them.

The book value weights are generally preferred by managers for calculating WACC because of the following advantages associated with Book Value weights:

The book value information is easily available from the company's annual report.

- It is simple to use.
- The capital structure targets are usually fixed in terms of book value.
- It is easier to evaluate the performance of a management in procuring funds by comparing on the basis of book values.

However, there are some limitations of Book Value weights as well:

- Book values are based on arbitrary accounting policies and thus, do not reflect the true economic value.
- They cannot be justified on theoretical grounds.

On the other hand, Market Value weights are preferred and considered to be theoretically superior to Book Value weights because they reflect true economic values and are also not affected by the accounting policies. The other points favoring Market Value weights are:

- The sale price of securities is more close to the market value.
- Costs of specific sources of finance which constitute the capital structure of the firm are also calculated using prevalent market prices.

But, Market Value weights are also not free from the limitations. There arises difficulty in using them because:

- Market Value is subject to frequent and wide fluctuations, so they need to be normalized first to calculate the weights.
- Sometimes, current Market Value is not available easily.

Marginal Weights

Marginal weights refer to the proportions in which the firm wants or intends to raise additional funds from different sources without any reference to the proportion of funds in the existing capital structure of the company. The basis of assigning weights is new and hence called marginal weights. Marginal weights are better because it is the new capital being raised for new investment that is important so the weighted cost of new capital is of relevance.

The other features justifying Marginal weights system are:

- The firm may be using some source of finance in its existing capital structure, which may not be available currently. So, there is no use of including its weight for calculating the WACC.
- It is practically very difficult for the firm to raise the additional funds in the same proportion as employed in the existing capital structure, because the current scenario might not favour the same. The reasons can be the firm's poor performance or bad state of capital market, which does not allow firm to raise capital in the existing proportion.
- This will give more freedom to the finance manager to raise funds after analyzing

the costs and benefits associated with different sources of finance. For instance, if the new debt is available at a cheaper interest rate, the manager can finance the additional capital more through debt as compared to equity.

However, the Marginal weights system also suffers from the following limitation:

- The main problem is that if we go by marginal weighting, we may resort to too much borrowing and accept many projects because of lower cost at the moment. But, at a later date, company may have the problem of raising more finance. Marginal weights ignore long term view.

Thus, the fact that today's financing affects tomorrow's costs, is not considered in using marginal weights. Following points should be noted while calculating the overall cost of capital:

- For computational convenience, it is best to convert the weights into decimal form and leave the individual costs in percentage terms.
- The weights must be non-negative and sum to 1.0. In other words, WACC must account for all financing costs within the firm's capital structure.
- The firm's additional equity stock weight, we, is multiplied by either the cost of retained earnings, Kr, or the cost of new common stock, Ke. Now, which cost is used depends on whether the firm's additional equity stock will be financed using retained earnings, Kr, or new common stock, Ke.

Weighted Marginal Cost of Capital

Weighted Marginal Cost of Capital refers to the incremental cost of raising additional amount of capital by the firm. So, while calculating the combined cost of capital, we should take the new cost of different sources of finance instead of taking their existing cost. It is the weighted average of marginal cost of each source of capital.

Capital Structure

Net Income Approach

There exist two schools of thought on the relationship between capital structure and value of firm. One view is on relevance of capital structure i.e. capital structure affects the firm's value. The capital structure theories which support this view are = Net Income approach and Traditional Approach.

The other school of thought (led by Modigliani and Miller) argue for the irrelevance of capital structure i.e. capital structure is irrelevant in determining the value of firm. A firm's value is independent of its capital structure. Theories which support this view include - Net Operating Income approach, MM Hypothesis and Millers Argument.

Net Income Approach: Relevance of Capital Structure

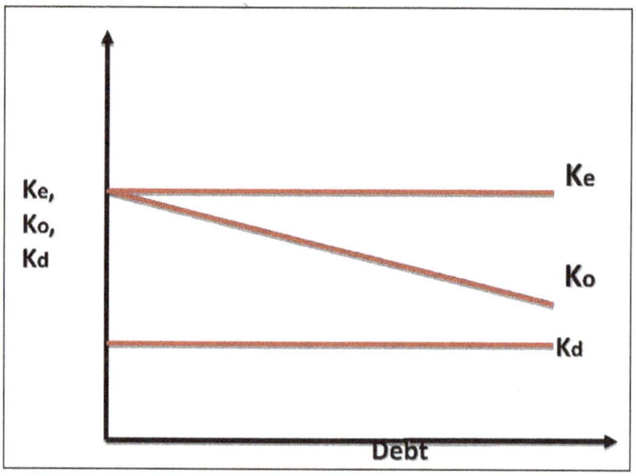

Net Income Approach.

The Net Income approach was developed by David Durand. As per Net Income Approach, there is a relationship between capital structure and value of the firm and therefore firm can affect its value by increasing or decreasing the debt proportion in the overall financing mix. This approach shows that capital structure has relevance in determining the value of firm. Therefore the value of a Levered firm (a firm which uses debt capital) will always be higher than the value of an Unlevered firm (i.e. an all equity firm). Further, the higher the amount of debt capital in the capital structure, the greater will be the firm's value. The Net Income Approach makes the following main assumptions:

- The total capital requirement of the company is given and remains constant.
- Cost of debt (Kd) is less than the cost of equity (Ke).
- Both Kd and Ke remain constant and increase in financial leverage i.e. use of more and more debt financing in the capital structure does not affect the risk discernment of the investors.
- There are no taxes and no transaction costs.
- Firm has perpetual life.

Given these assumptions it can be observed that as the proportion of debt capital increases in the total capital of a firm, its overall cost of capital declines continuously. This happens because cost of debt is lower than the cost of equity and irrespective of the degree of financial leverage, these two cost remain constant. Hence as the proportion of debt capital rises, cheaper debt replaces expensive equity capital and the overall cost of capital declines, resulting in increase in firm's value. In figure, one can observe that as more and more of debt capital is used, the overall cost of capital declines because cheaper debt replaces expensive equity capital. Decline in overall cost implies that the market value of the firm increases with increase in the amount of debt capital.

We will use the following notations in subsequent equations:

Value of firm = VF

Value of Equity = E

Value of Debt = D

Interest amount = I

Earnings before interest and Taxes or Net Operating Income (NOI) = EBIT.

Firm Valuation

Using Net Income approach we can calculate the values of a levered and unlevered.

Value of a Levered Firm

In case of an unlevered firm debt capital is not used. Hence it is called as an all equity firm. In such a firm, the overall cost of capital (Ko) comprises of only cost of equity (Ke), i.e. the two are equal. Further, there is no interest to be paid by the firm. Therefore the entire net operating income or EBIT is provided to equity shareholders In such a case the value of the firm will be the capitalized value (or discounted value) of all the operating earnings of the company, with Ke as the capitalization rate (or appropriate discount rate). Hence,

$$Vu = \frac{EBIT}{Ke}$$

A levered company is one which uses debt capital in its capital structure. Mathematically, a Firm's value is computed by adding value of equity and value of debt.

Value of a levered Firm = Value of Equity + Value of Debt

$$VL = E + D$$

Value of Equity = Discounted Value of Net Income available to equity shareholders.

$$E = \frac{\text{Net Income available to equity shareholders}}{\text{Cost of Equity}} = \frac{EBIT - I}{K_e}$$

Value of Debt = Discounted Value of Interest

$$D = \frac{\text{Interest}}{\text{Cost of Debt}} = \frac{I}{K_d}$$

Hence,

$$VL = \frac{NOI - I}{Ke} + \frac{I}{Kd}$$

Further we can calculate the Weighted average cost of capital (WACC) denoted by Ko as below. Ko is also termed as overall cost of capital.

$$K_o = We * Ke = Wd * Kd$$

Where:

We = proportion of equity capital

Wd = proportion of debt capita

When we are given the Net operating income (NOI or EBIT) of a firm and its market value (V) then the following identity holds true:

$$K_o = \frac{\text{Net Operating Income or EBIT}}{V}$$

As per NI approach the optimum capital structure (i.e. the one having minimum overall cost of capital) is one when 100% debt financing is used. This will enhanced the value of the firm. However NI approach is criticized condemned because of its impracticable suppositions. In real life we cannot have constant cost of equity and debt. Further, presence of taxes and transaction costs also distort the link betwixt capital structure and firm's value.

Calculating Value of a Firm using NI Approach

Example: The expected Earnings before interest and taxes (EBIT) of a firm is $ 2,00,000. It has issued equity share capital and the cost of equity is 10%. It has also issued 6% debt of $ 5,00,000. Find out the value of company and overall cost of capital (WACC).

Solution: Here we are given that EBIT = $ 200,000. Ke = 10%, Kd = 6% and Value of Debt = $ 500,000.

EBIT	2,00,000
Less: Interest (6% of $ 5,00,000)	30,000
Net Profit available for equity shareholders (EBT)	1,70,000

Cost of Equity (Ke)	10%
Value of Equity (1,70,000/0.10)	17,00,000
Value of Debt	5,00,000
Total Value of Firm	22,00,000

Weighted Average Cost of Capital (WACC) = $K_o = \frac{2,00,000}{22,00,000} = 0.09$ or 9% (approx.)

WACC can also be calculated as follows:

WACC = Cost of Equity × Weight of Equity + Cost of Debt × Weight of Debt

$$= Ke \times \frac{E}{V} + K_d \times \frac{D}{V}$$

$$= 0.10 \times \frac{1700000}{2200000} + 0.06 \times \frac{500000}{2200000} = 0.09 \text{ or } 9\%$$

Now if the company had issued 6% debt of $7,00,000 instead of $5,00,000 the position have been as follows:

EBIT	2,00,000
Less: Interest (6% of $7,00,000)	42,000
Net Profit available for equity shareholders (EBT)	1,58,000
Cost of Equity (Ke)	10%
Value of Equity (158,000/0.10)	15,80,000
Value of Debt	7,00,000
Total Value of Firm	22,80,000

Weighted Average Cost of Capital (WACC) = $\frac{2,00,000}{22,80,000} = 0.087$ or 8.7%

So, if 6% debt is increased from $5,00,000 to $7,00,000 the value of firm increases from $22,00,000 to $22,80,000 and WACC decreases from 9% to 8.7%.

Now suppose that the company has issued 6% debt of $2,00,000 only instead of $5,00,000. The position would be as follows:

EBIT	2,00,000
Less: Interest (6% of $2,00,000)	12,000
Net Profit available for equity shareholders(EBT)	1,88,000
Cost of Equity (Ke)	10%
Value of Equity (188,000/0.10)	18,80,000
Value of Debt	2,00,000
Total Value of Firm	20,80,000

$$\text{Weighted Average Cost of Capital (WACC)} = \frac{2,00,000}{20,80,000} = 0.096 \text{ or } 9.6\%$$

So, when the proportion of 6% debt is reduced to \$2,00,000 the value of firm reduces to \$20,80,000 and WACC increases from 9% to 9.6%.

Traditional and NOI Approach

As per the traditional approach, a firm should make judicious use of both the debt and the equity to achieve a capital structure which may be called the optimum capital structure. At this capital structure, the overall cost of capital, WACC of the firm will be minimum and the value of the firm maximum. The traditional view point states that the value of the firm increases with increase in financial leverage but up to a certain limit only. Beyond this limit, the increase in financial leverage will increase its WACC and the value of the firm will decline. The reason for decline in WACC is replacement of expensive equity capital with low cost debt. Due to increasing financial risk of equity shareholders, the cost of equity capital starts rising. It is widely held assertion that employment of debt funds is cheaper than the employment of equity funds.

This assertion has the implication that cost of debt plus the increased cost of equity, together on a weighted basis, will be less than the existed cost of equity before debt financing.

Suppose the cost of capital for totally equity financed company is 10%. Cost of equity and cost of capital will be same as company is totally financed with equity capital. If firm replaces 50% of its equity capital with interest bearing 7% debt capital, the cost of equity will increase slightly because of added financial risk of equity shareholders New cost of equity increases to 11%.

$$\text{WACC} = \text{Cost of Equity} \times \text{Weight of Equity} + \text{Cost of Debt} \times \text{Weight of Debt}$$

$$\text{WACC (Ko)} = \text{Ke} \times \text{We} + \text{Kd} \times \text{Wd}$$

$$= 0.11 \times 0.50 + 0.07 \times 0.50$$

$$= 0.09 \text{ or } 9\%$$

Thus, financial leverage will lower the WACC. But, this decline in WACC will be obtained only up to a point. As leverage will increase further, the risk for equity shareholders will also increase and they will require a higher risk premium and therefore, the cost of equity will increase. This increase in cost of equity will not be able to offset the advantage of lower cost of debt and therefore, after this point WACC will start increasing.

Example: ABC Ltd. having an EBIT of \$1, 50,000 is contemplating to redeem a part of capital by introducing the debt financing. Presently, it is 100% equity from with equity capitalization rate Ke of 16%. The firm is to redeem the capital by introducing debt financing up to $3,00,000 i.e. 30% of total funds or up to $5,00,000 i.e. 50% of total funds. It is expected that for debt financing up to 30%, the rate of interest will be 10% and the cost of equity will increase to 17%. However, if the firm opts for 50% debt financing, then interest will be payable at the rate of 12% and cost of equity will be 20%, find out the value of firm and WACC under different levels of debt financing.

	100% Equity	30% Debt	50% Debt
Total debt	....	3,00,000	5,00,0000
Cost of debt	....	10%	12%
EBIT ($)	1,50,000	1,50,000	1,50,000
Less: Interest	....	30,000	60,000
Profit before tax	1,50,000	1,20,000	90,000
Cost of equity	16%	17%	20%
Value of equity (Profit before tax/Cost of equity)	9,37,500	7,05,882	4,50,000
Value of firm (D+E)	9,37,500	10,05,882	9,50,000
WACC (EBIT/Value of firm)	0.16	0.149	0.158

Value of firm increases and WACC goes down with increase in debt but up to a certain limit only i.e. up to 30% debt. But if we employ more than 30% debt, then value of firm goes down and WACC increases. Therefore, firm should make judicious use of both the debt and equity to maximize firm's value and minimize WACC. The relationship between capital structure and the value of firm can be explained through three stages under traditional approach.

First Stage: Increasing Value

In the first stage, as a company starts moving from all equity to debt financing, the cost of equity (Ke) starts increasing by a very less amount. Thus, this slight increase in cost of equity is not able to set off the advantage of low cost of debt (Kd). The cost of debt also remains constant as the market perceives debt as a reasonable policy. Consequently, the overall cost of capital (WACC or Ko) goes down and thus, the value of the firm increases.

Second Stage: Optimum Value

As the company keeps increasing debt financing, there comes a point which gives optimum value of the firm. In this case, any further increase in debt causes the cost of equity to increase by such an amount which completely off sets the advantage of low cost debt. The result of this is that the WACC shows no change and therefore attains the minimum level. Such a point or range shows the maximum value of the firm due to lowest WACC. At this stage, firm achieves its optimum debt-equity ratio.

Third Stage: Decreasing Value

After reaching the optimum level, any increase in debt results into very large increase in the cost of equity as required by the shareholders for the increased financial risk.

Such a large increase in cost of equity is not able to set off the advantage of low cost debt. Moreover, the cost of debt also increases, as a result of which the WACC increases and thus, value of the firm goes down.

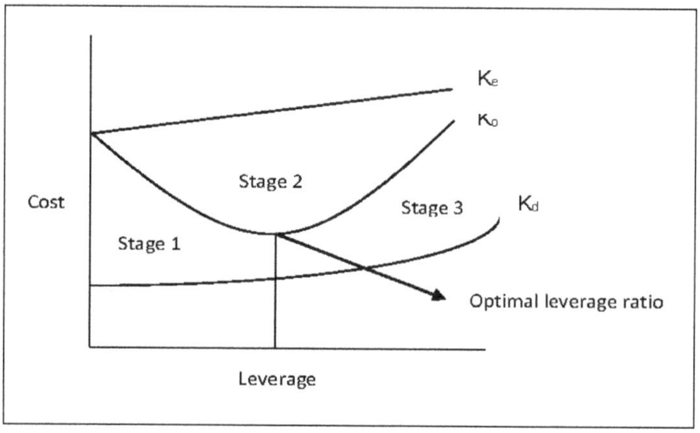

Thus, the three stages show that the value of the firm and WACC depend upon the leverage of the firm. In the initial phase an increase in leverage results into decline in WACC due to the comparative advantage of low cost debt. On further increase in leverage, WACC reaches its minimum point beyond which it starts increasing. Therefore, WACC gets a U-shaped curve which implies that there exist a point where the overall cost of capital is minimum and the value of the firm is maximum. This point signifies the optimal debt-equity ratio.

The main points of traditional approach are:

- It does not assume cost of equity to be constant. Rather, it increases with increase in financial leverage due to the added financial risk for equity shareholders.
- WACC is not continuously declining. It declines but up to certain limit only and after that limit it again starts rising.
- Moderate degree of debt can lower the firm's overall cost of capital and thereby, increase the firm value.
- The initial increase in the cost of equity is more than offset by the lower cost of debt.
- But as debt increases, shareholders perceive higher risk and the cost of equity rise until a point is reached at which the advantage of lower cost of debt is more than offset by more.

Criticism of Traditional Approach

The main criticism of this approach is that its assumption of financial risk premium is not justifiable. The theory explains that increase in risk premium required by equity shareholders is very less up to moderate levels of debt and increases by different amount at different levels of leverage. However, the theory is not able to provide any justification for this.

Net Operating Income Approach

The Net Operating Income Approach is opposite to the Net Income Approach. According to Net Operating Income Approach, the market value of the firm depends upon the net operating profit or EBIT and overall cost of capital, WACC. The financing mix or the capital structure is irrelevant and does not affect the value of the firm.

The Net Operating Income Approach makes the following assumptions:

- The investor sees the firm as a whole and thus capitalizes the total earnings of the firm to find the value of the firm as a whole.
- The overall cost of capital, Ko, of the firm is constant and depends upon the business risk, which also is assumed to be unchanged.
- The cost of debt, Kd, is also taken as constant.
- The use of more and more debt in the capital structure increases the risk of shareholder and thus results in the increase in the cost of equity capital, Ke. The increase in Ke is such as to completely off set the benefits of employing cheaper debt.
- There is no tax.

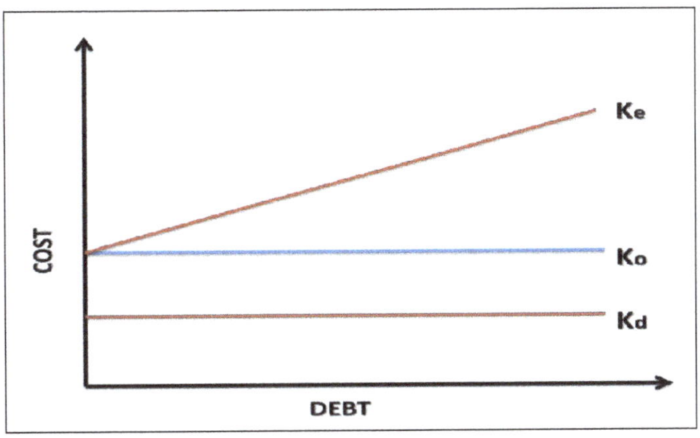

$$\text{Value of the Firm} = \frac{\text{Net Operating Profit}}{\text{WACC}} = \frac{\text{EBIT}}{\text{Ko}}$$

Alternatively, Value of the Firm = Value of Equity + Value of Debt

$$\text{Cost of Equity (Ke)} = \frac{\text{Net Income}}{\text{Value of Equity}}$$

Example: A firm has an EBIT of $2,00,000 and belongs to a risk class of 10%. What is the value of equity capital if it employees 6% debt to the extent of 30%, 40% or 50% of the capital fund of $10,00,000.

	30% Debt	40% Debt	50% Debt
EBIT	2,00,000	2,00,000	2,00,000
Overall cost of capital (Ko)	10%	10%	10%
Value of the firm (V = EBIT/ Ko)	20,00,000	20,00,000	20,00,000
Value of 6% debt (D)	3,00,000	4,00,000	5,00,000
Value of Equity (E = V-D)	17,00,000	16,00,000	15,00,000
Interest on debt	18,000	24,000	30,000
Net profit for equity	1,82,000	1,76,000	1,70,000
Ke (Net profit/E)	10.7%	11%	11.33%

The cost of equity capital (Ke) of 10.7%, 11% and 11.33% can be verified for different proportion of debt by calculating WACC as follows:

For 30% Debt:

$$K_o = 0.107 \times \frac{17,00,000}{20,00,000} + 0.06 \times \frac{3,00,000}{20,00,000} = 0.10 \text{ or } 10\%$$

For 40% Debt:

$$K_o = 0.11 \times \frac{16,00,000}{20,00,000} + 0.06 \times \frac{4,00,000}{20,00,000} = 0.10 \text{ or } 10\%$$

For 50% Debt:

$$K_o = 0.1133 \times \frac{15,00,000}{20,00,000} + 0.06 \times \frac{5,00,000}{20,00,000} = 0.10 \text{ or } 10\%$$

These calculations of WACC testify that the benefit of employment of more and more debt in the capital structure is offset by the increase in equity capitalization rate, Ke.

Modigliani and Miller Approach

It is the best known and most widely discussed model of the Nobel Prize receives in Economics - Franco Modigliani and Merton Howard Miller, also known as MM model. The basic thesis is the argument I: under certain assumptions the total costs of the company capital, and therefore the market value of the company, are independent of capital structure. They depend only on the return on total capital (as considering the perfectly functioning market, all combinations of securities are equally good and investments have the same earnings). The argument can be redefined in a way that the composition of the capital structure of the company has no influence on the value of the company, and it does not make any sense to consider the volume of internal and external sources of the company.

The most important condition is that it is a tax-free environment. Modigliani and Miller later formulated another argument which takes the impact of taxes on the company capital structure into account.

The basic conditions of the model functioning are:

- The capital market is perfect, the information is free and available to all investors, transaction costs are not considered, investors behave rationally.
- All current and future investors expect the same future profits of the company characterized by so called homogeneous expectations of future profits and their risk.
- Companies are funded only by stocks and bonds.
- The debt of the company is not risky, the interest rate is also considered risk-free. But the volume of the debt used by the company is not searched.
- The costs of financial distress are not considered.
- The taxation of profits is not taken into account, i.e. there is no benefit of the tax shield.
- The management of the company tries to maximize shareholders' wealth. When optimizing the capital structure the aspect of the owner is preferred.
- Businesses can be incorporated into several groups. Each group includes companies with the same degree of operational risk and as a consequence of this also with the same return on invested capital. Risk and return on invested capital differs among the groups.
- Net income (profit and interest) does not change over the time and the probability of return is the same for all investors of the same class.
- The possibility of getting the credit and the conditions of its obtaining is the same for all subjects of the capital market (for businesses and individuals).

The context of the argument I of the MM model discuss the simplicity of the idea on which this claim is based (this is called the law of value conservation or the principle of value additively). The value of assets is maintained irrespective of the nature of their demands. The argument I of the MM model says that the company value is determined by real assets on the left side of the balance sheet and not by the ratio between debt and equity. So if there are two flows of cash flows A and B in the company, and one of them is a flow of equity (stocks) and the other of debt (bonds), then the mathematical equation is applied that the sum of the present value of the cash flows A + B must equal to the present value of the cash flow of equity A (issued stocks) plus the present value of the cash flow of debt B (issued bonds). Modigliani and Miller expressed this fact also mathematically:

$$V_j = (S_j + D_j) = \bar{X}_j \mid \rho_k \text{ Or } \frac{\bar{X}_j}{(S_j + D_j)} = \frac{\bar{X}_j}{V_j} = \rho_k$$

For each j- company in the class k where:

V_j Market value of a company (market value of all stocks),

S_j Market value of equity (issued stocks),

D_j Market value of debt (issued bonds),

$\bar{X}_j$ Expected earning of assets (expected earnings before interest),

ρ_k Market realization rate of expected earning made by the company in its class.

Based on these equations, it simply came to the economic conclusion that the average cost of capital of any company is independent of the capital structure (i.e. of the combination of the issued securities).

Based on this argument, the managers do not need to pay attention to the right side of the balance sheet (liability), but only to assets, because the value of the company can be derived from their value.

As reported, the law of value conservation can be also applied to select between the issue of preferred stocks, ordinary stocks or any combinations thereof. According to the valid legislation the choice is not important as long as the capital markets perfect and as this option does not affect the investment or operating policies of the company.

They also claim that the combination and allocation of capital does not affect the value of the company, provided that the combination does not influence the investment choices of investors. That arises from the assumption that companies and individuals can borrow at the same risk-free interest rate. If this is so then individuals can eliminate the effect of any change in the capital structure. But in reality the company debt is not risk-free and the company does not have the same interest rate as the government securities. According to some experts this fact degrades the argument of the MM model because one of the basic preconditions of the argument (all bonds have constant earnings over the time and these earnings are the same regardless of the issuer) is not met. Consider this to be a natural reaction, but they point out that the capital structure does not need to change even if the debt is risky. The company lending the money does not guarantee its repayment in advance; it pays its debt only if its assets are worth more than the liabilities. And thus the company shareholders have limited liability.

The definition of the argument II of the MM theory: The expected rate of return on the common stock equals to the realization rate of return of the class plus premium derived from the financial risk which equals to the ratio of debt to equity multiplied by the difference between the realization rate of return of the given class and the interest rate of the debt. Mathematical expression of this statement is expressed by the following equation:

$$i_j = \rho_k + (\rho_k - \tau) D_j | S_j$$

Where,

i_j Expected rate on return of a common stock of j- Company in k- class,

ρ_k Market realization rate of expected return made by the companies of the given class,

τ Interest rate of the debt,

S_j Market value of equity (issued stocks),

D_j Market value of debt (issued bonds).

The expected rate of return on ordinary stock of the company in debt is directly proportional to the ratio of debt to equity capital expressed by the market value, while at the same time it is dependent on the difference between the expected return of the portfolio and all stocks (capital structure) of a particular company and expected return from the debt.

We can simply reformulate the argument II as follows: the requirements of shareholders for higher return on their capital, increasing the portion of the debt, do not appear until some degree of the debt, but they grow steadily. From a certain degree of the debt the interest rate of the debt increases. Rising demands of shareholders cover the financial benefits of increasing portion of the debt, so that the average costs of the company to get and bind the capital remains the same by any capital structure.

The graphical illustration of the MM model is depicted in the figure.

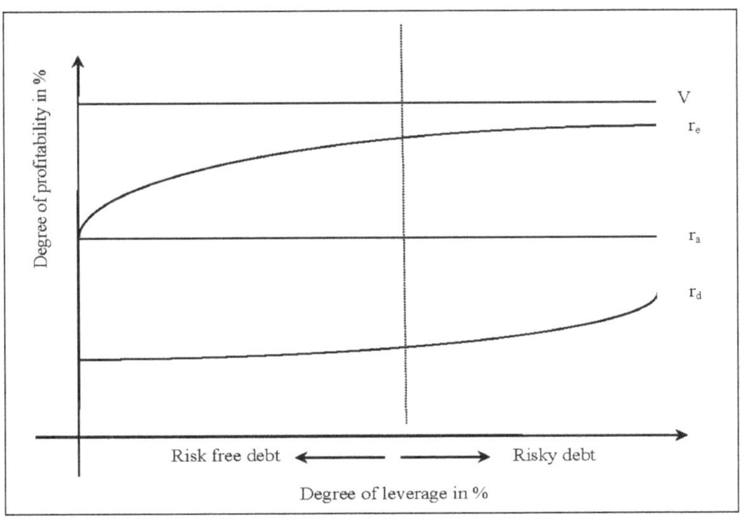

Figure: MM model.

Where,

V company market value in monetary units,

r_e Costs of equity (profit of shareholders in %),

r_d Costs of debt (profit of creditors in %),

r_a Costs on capital (profit of total capital in %),

$\frac{D}{E}$ Ratio of debt to equity (degree of leverage in monetary units).

In the figure we can see that the company bonds are risk-free at low levels of the debt. This explains why the expected return on debt is independent of the ratio of debt to equity in the first phase. It is also true that the expected return on equity increases linearly with increasing proportion of the debt to equity ratio. In a situation where the company borrows more than the safety margin, the owners of bonds (creditors) begin to ask for higher interest rates, leading to an increase in the expected return on the debt because proportionally increases the risk of not meeting the liabilities of the company increases proportionally, too.

In the zone of the risky debt, the return on equity increases more slowly (curve is curving down) because the expected return is less and less sensitive to the further increase of debt. And vice versa, the rate of return on debt increases (curve is curving down). The reason is that the creditors overtake a part of the business risk, i.e. the more the company borrows, the more risk is transferred from shareholders to creditors And so the expected return on debt increases for creditors and this increased risk has to be compensated by the increase of the debt instrument interest rate and it finally leads to the slower pace of growth of the expected return for shareholders Linked to the next fact, and that increases the expected return on the debt to the creditor, which is necessary to compensate for the increased risk of increases in interest rates on debt instruments, but this leads to the reduction in the growth rate of expected return for shareholders.

Then:

$$r_e = r_e + \frac{C_e}{C_d} \cdot (r_a - r_d)$$

Where,

C_d Debt in monetary units,

C_e Equity in monetary units,

r_d Costs of debt in %,

r_e Costs of equity in %,

r_a Total costs of capital in monetary units (costs of company capital funded only by equity).

The relation can be interpreted as follows: The expected rate of return on equity in the company with the participation of the debt increases directly to the ratio of debt to equity expressed by the market value. The rate of this growth depends on the difference between the expected return on the total capital and the return on debt (interest rate).

MM theory is based on the assumptions which do not correspond with real conditions. For this reason, the authors admitted the influence of income taxation on the average cost of capital and the market value of the company. They changed their idea in 1963 in their work "Corporate Income Taxes and the Cost of Capital" A Correction ". According to this work, the growing debt causes that the average cost of capital decreases under the influence of the interest tax shield, the return on equity and market value also increase and therefore the company should increase its debt portion considering its capital structure.

This outcome is mathematically expressed in the following equation:

$$X^{\tau} = (1-\tau)(X-R)+R = (1-\tau)X+\tau R = (1-\tau)\bar{X}Z+\tau R$$

Where,

X^{τ} Earning after taxation in monetary units,

τ Margin tax rate of the company in % multiplied by 1/100,

X Earnings before interest and taxes, can be expressed also by ZX (multiplication of expected earnings and random factor) in monetary units,

R Interest rate of debt in % multiplied by 1/100.

This does not mean that the company has to maximize the amount of its debt at all costs, without consideration of other relevant facts. The authors themselves encourage the financial managers not to seek the maximum debt as in certain circumstances the other forms of funding may be cheaper. They took the impact of personal income tax, the increased requirements of creditors and the other costs associated with the operation of the company into account that cannot be included in the static balanced model.

As the interest tax shield is repeated every year, it is possible to determine its value by the capitalization. Capitalized tax shield increases the market value of the company using the external sources. The interest rate of the debt is used to measure the market capitalization. Then:

$$PV\ TS = \frac{C_d \cdot R \cdot T}{i} = C_d \cdot T$$

Where,

PV TS Present value of the interest tax shield in monetary units,

C_d Debt capital in monetary units,

R Interest rate of debt in % multiplied by 1/100,

T Income tax rate in % multiplied by 1/100.

The market value of the company with debt is mathematically expressed:

$$V_Z = V_N + PV\ TS$$

Where,

V_d Value of the company with debt in monetary units,

V_e Value of the company funded only by equity in monetary units.

Also this equation claims that the theory is the best for the company in the terms of maximizing its value and the use of a high proportion of debt, because it is the way how to maximize the present value of the tax shield and thus to maximize the value of the company.

Taking the income tax into consideration, the equation is then:

$$r_e = r_a + \frac{C_e}{C_d} \cdot (r_a - r_d) \cdot (1 - T)$$

Financial practice did not accept the revised theory of Miller and Modigliani arguing that this conclusion does not take another important factor, costs of financial difficulties, into account. Miller himself wanted to include not only the corporate taxes (corporate income tax) into the theory of the capital structure optimization but also the individual taxes (personal income tax). He presented his idea in Debt and taxes in 1976. After the introduction of personal taxes the main aim of the company is not to minimize the tax shield of the company itself, but to minimize the present value of all taxes which are paid by the company. "All taxes" include personal taxes paid by holders of shares and bonds.

Thus, the aim of the company should be to choose the capital structure that maximizes the total earnings after taxation and minimizes the overall taxation not only of companies but of individuals. This fact can be depicted by the indicator of the relative tax advantage of debt to equity:

$$\text{Relative tax advantage of debt} = \frac{(1 - T_p)}{(1 - T_{pE})(1 - T_c)}$$

Where,

T_p Rate of personal tax of interest in %,

T_{pE} Effective rate of personal tax of stocks profit in %,

T_c Corporate tax rate in %

M&M Hypothesis with Corporate Taxes

Firms do have to pay corporate taxes and the interest paid on debentures is tax deductible. Hence, it becomes more profitable for a firm to have leverage (debt) as it saves taxes and thus the value of such a firm increases. Thus, in the presence of corporate taxes, MM hypothesize that the value of a firm increases as the leverage increases.

How proposition 1 of MM's hypothesis works in the presence of corporate taxes?

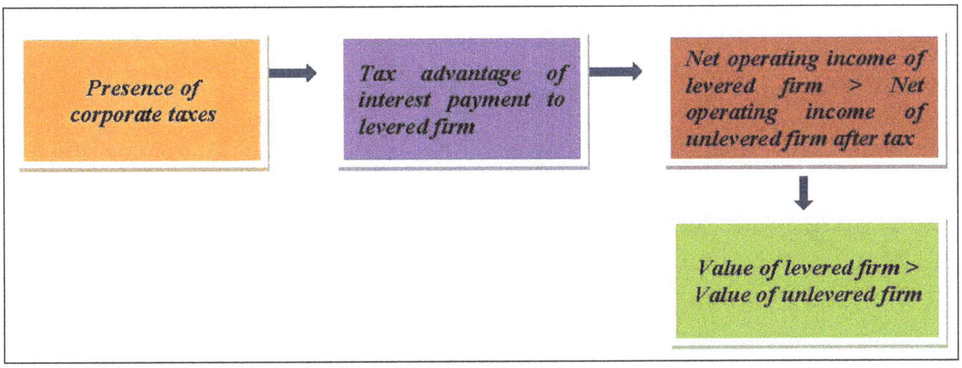

Net Operating Income After Tax (Tax Advantage)

Suppose there are two firms – Firm U and Firm L. Firm U is an unlevered firm with all equity capital. Firm L is a levered firm which has $50,000 debt at 10% interest in its total capital. Net operating income of both the firms is $2,500. Firms are required to pay 50% as corporate taxes and dividend payout is 100%.

Interest payment on debt is tax deductible; the levered firm will get a tax advantage as compared to unlevered firm. This amount of tax advantage is called "Interest Tax Shield (INTS) or Tax advantage of Debt". This advantage will increase the net operating income after tax of the levered firm as compared to unlevered firm. Let's calculate the net operating income after tax of the two firms.

	Firm U	Firm L
Net operating income before tax	2500	2500
Less: Interest (10% of $5,000)	......	500
Taxable Income	2500	2000
Less: Tax @ 50%	1250	1000
Income to shareholders after tax	1250	1000
Add: Interest	......	500
Net operating income after tax	1250	1500

Therefore, Interest tax shield (Tax advantage of debt) = $1500 - $1250 = $250

Relative advantage of debt = 1500/1250 = 1.20.

Thus, it is very clear from the above table that net operating income after tax of levered firm is more than unlevered firm by $250. It is also clear that tax payment of levered firm is less than unlevered firm by the same amount i.e. $250, which is interest tax shield.

Therefore, Interest Tax Shield = Savings in Tax = Tax on Interest

$$\text{INTS} = \text{T} \times \text{Interest}$$

$$\text{INTS} = \text{T} \times \text{K}_d \times \text{D}$$

Value of Firm

As we just discussed that the tax advantage (INTS) increases net operating income after tax of the levered firm as compared to unlevered firm. Now, as the net operating incomes of two firms are different, their value will also be different. Let's first calculate the value of unlevered firm. Suppose the cost of equity is 12.5%, which is same as average cost of capital for unlevered firm.

$$\text{Value of a Firm} = \frac{\text{Net operating income after tax}}{\text{Cost of capital}}$$

$$\text{V}_\text{U} = \frac{\text{Net operating income after tax}}{\text{Cost of capital}(\text{K}_\text{e})} = \frac{1250}{0.125}$$

So, Value of unlevered firm = $10,000.

Now let's consider the value of levered firm. The levered firm has higher operating income than unlevered firm, its value will also be higher. The operating income of levered firm is equal to operating income of unlevered firm plus interest tax shield.

INTS (i.e. 1500 = 1250 + 250). Hence, the value of levered firm will be the value of unlevered firm plus the value of INTS.

So, Value of levered firm = Value of unlevered firm + Value of INTS

$$\text{V}_\text{L} = \text{V}_\text{U} + \text{P.V.of INTS}$$

Value of INTS: As the interest tax shield is an extra income of firm, it has some value. Suppose that the current level of debt of $5,000 will remain permanent and as the tax rate remains same for a long period of time, the INTS will keep on generating over a long period of time on continuous basis. Thus, it forms perpetuity. The value of INTS will be same as value of perpetuity.

$$\text{Value of Perpetuity} = \frac{\text{Installment per period}}{\text{ROI (Discount rate)}}$$

Thus, we need a rate of discount to show riskiness of this INTS. INTS depends on rate of interest on debentures and corporate tax rate. Corporate tax rate remains same and the interest rate depends on rate of earning which is at least equal to rate of borrowing. The INTS is less risky than earnings, thus the discount rate can be taken as at least same as rate of interest on debt (i.e. 10%). Thus, the value of INTS will be:

$$\text{Present value of INTS} = \frac{\text{INTS}}{K_d} = \frac{250}{0.10} = \$\ 2{,}500$$

$$\text{P.V. of INTS} = \frac{T \times K_d \times D}{K_d} = T \times D$$

Thus, the value of INTS does not depend on rate of interest on debt but on amount of debt and tax rate (i.e. 0.5 × 5000 = $2,500). As we know that tax rate remains constant over a period of time, so, if the amount of debt increases the value of INTS also increases and becomes maximum at 100% debt level.

So, $V_L = V_u + T \times D$

Thus, Value of levered firm = $10,000 + $2,500

= $12,500

Hence, it is very clear that the value of levered firm is greater than unlevered firm by the value of INTS. Thus, it can be concluded that the value of levered firm will keep on increasing as the debt portion increases and it will be maximum when debt is 100%. It is shown in the following figure.

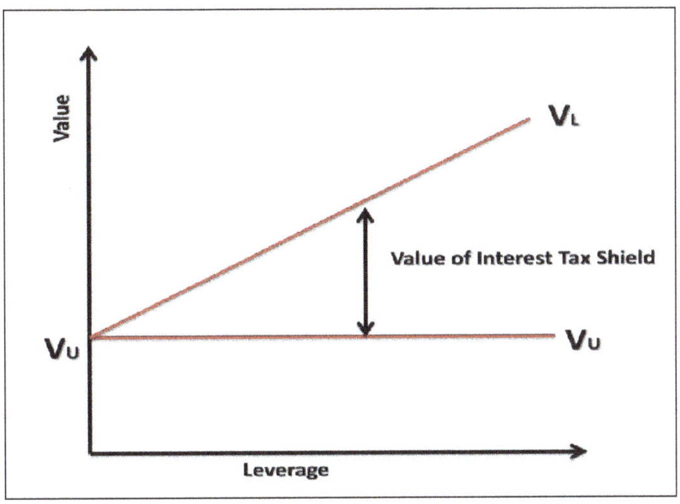

Proposition 2 with Corporate Taxes: Capital Structure Affects Shareholders' Returns

In case of no corporate taxes, the returns to equity holder increases as the leverage increases. The same result holds true in case of existence of corporate taxes as well. With increase in leverage, the risk of shareholders' earnings increases and for this they expect a higher rate of return. However, the amount by which return of shareholders increases on increase in leverage is different when we have corporate taxes. In case of no taxes, the return of shareholders is given as:

$$K_e = K_a + (K_a - K_d)\frac{D}{E}$$

However, with the existence of corporate taxes, the return of equity holders gets reduced by the amount of tax savings. As the firms get interest tax shield, the risk of the shareholders gets reduced by this amount and their expected return is also reduced in the same proportion. Thus, their return is given as:

$$K_e = K_a + (K_a - K_d)(1-T)\frac{D}{E}$$

Hence, it can be concluded that in case of corporate taxes also, shareholders' returns increase on increase in leverage, but this increase is lesser as compared to the case when there are no corporate taxes.

Criticism of MM's Hypothesis with Corporate Taxes

It is proposed by MM in the presence of corporate taxes that the value of firm increases with increase in leverage. Thus, it can be said that a firm can increase its value by increasing its leverage and maximize it by employing 100% debt in capital. But, this proposition is criticized for its practical application. That is in practice, firms do not employ very high levels of debt and lenders also do not lend the money beyond a limit. Therefore, the debt portion never becomes 100% but firms choose an optimum level of debt. The reasons for this are:

- As the debt increases, the savings of corporate taxes also increases and at the same time the amount of personal taxes to be paid also increases. Thus, the liability of personal taxes offsets the advantage of corporate taxes.
- Greater amount of debt also increases financial risk of the firm. Thus, the cost of financial distress also increases which again offsets the advantage of corporate tax savings.

Capital Structure in Practice

Financial distress arises when a firm is not able to meet its obligations to debt holders. For a given level of debt, financial distress occurs of the business risk (operating risk). With higher business risk, the probability of financial distress becomes greater.

Costs of Financial Distress

Financial distress may ultimately force a company to insolvency. Direct costs of financial distress include bankruptcy costs. Specific bankruptcy costs include legal and administrative costs along with the sale of assets at distress prices to meet creditors' claims. The expected cost of bankruptcy raises the lenders' required rate of return, which reduces the market value of equity. Financial distress also has many indirect costs. These costs relate to the actions of employees, managers, customers, suppliers and shareholders:

- Employees: Employees of a financially distressed firm become demoralized, because they are worried about their future. Due to this reason, their efficiency and productivity goes down, which affects the quality of products, which in turn affects the reputation of the firm and sales of its products may also drop.

- Customers: Customers of a financially distressed firm may fear its liquidation, and get concerned about the quality of product/service. They are more concerned about after sale services and maintenance. As a result, the demand for firm's product/service starts falling.

- Suppliers: Suppliers also hesitates at the time of granting credit to firm fearing liquidation of the firm. They force the firm into liquidation to realize their claims.

- Investors: The most important consideration for a financially distressed firm is its inability of raising funds for profitable investments. Either the investors are not willing to supply capital to the firm or they provide funds at high costs & rigid terms & conditions, which in turn negatively affects the operating performance of the company.

- Shareholders: When a firm is under financial distress, but not insolvent, shareholder may be interested in undertaking risky projects by investing the left out cash. If a risky project succeeds, then gain can be substantial but if it fails, creditors will suffer the loss because shareholder have limited liability.

- Managers: When the firm is under financial distress, managers may have greater inducement to pocket firm's resources. Managers start taking decisions on the basis of short term interest of the company. They might reduce costs which affect the quality of products & sell productive assets to enhance the short term liquidity of the company. They don't consider any profitable opportunity to avoid any sort of risk. These decisions will force the company to go into liquidation.

Financial distress reduces the value of the firm. Thus,

Value of levered firm = Value of unlevered firm + P.V. of INTS – P.V. of Financial Distress

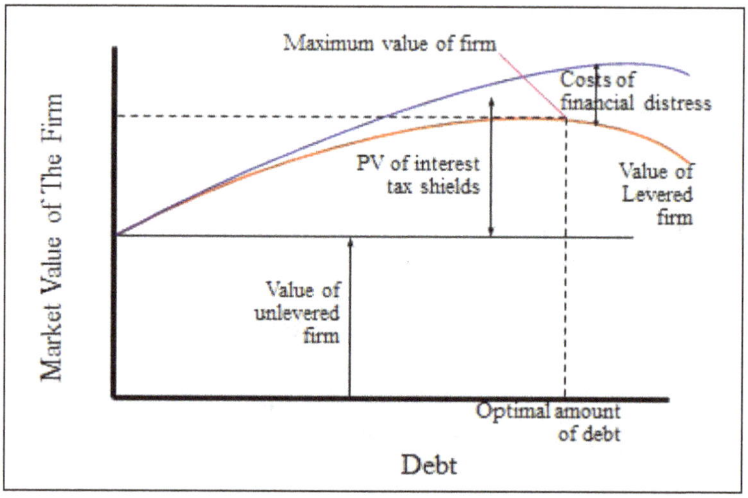

Financial Distress

P.V. of INTS and P.V. of financial distress increases with the borrowing. With the increasing debt, the costs of financial distress rises & thus, the tax benefit reduces. The optimum point is reached where the tax benefit & cost of financial distress becomes equal and the value of firm is highest at this point.

Agency Costs

In practice, there may exist a dispute of interest among shareholders, debt holders & management. These conflicts may raise agency problems, which involve agency costs.

- Shareholders-Debt holders Conflict: Shareholders' value is created either by increasing the value of the firm or by reducing the value of the debt. As we know that, debt holders have a preferential and fixed claim over the assets of the firm, and shareholders have a residual and unlimited claim. Debt holder's risk is very high in case of highly leveraged firm, since shareholders have limited liability. Debt holders are not even compensated for this high risk of default. The conflict between shareholders & debt holders rise since the possibility of shareholder transfers the wealth of debt holders in their favor. The debt holders may provide money to invest in low risk projects while firms may invest in high risk projects, which in turn increases the risk of debt holders.

- Shareholders-Managers Conflict: The conflict between Shareholders& managers may rise on two issues:

    - Manage have a tendency to consume some of the firm's resources for various perquisites.

    - Manage have a tendency to become unduly risk averse and shirk their responsibilities as they have no equity interest and in order to protect their jobs, they may be passing up risky profitable opportunities.

- Monitoring and Agency Costs: Outside investors will discount the prices they are willing to pay for the firm's securities, understanding that managers may not function in their finest comforts. Firms approve for monitoring & obstructive covenants to guarantee the suppliers of capital that they will not operate opposing to their interests. Agency costs are the costs of observing & control mechanisms. Agency costs of debt comprise of the acknowledgement of the possibility of wealth expropriation by Shareholders Agency costs of equity consist of the incentive that management has to enlarge the firm beyond the point at where shareholders' wealth is maximized.

Pecking Order Theory

This theory is based on the assertion that investors have less data about the firm than manage. This is known as asymmetric information. Other things remaining constant, because of asymmetric information, managers will issue debt when they are positive about firm's future prospects, because a commitment to pay a fixed sum of interest & principal to debt holders indicates that company anticipates steady cash flows. And managers will issue equity as soon as they are not very sure about the future prospects because an equity issue would indicate that existing share price is overvalued.

Therefore, it gives a signal to the investors about firm's future scenarios. This implies that firms should always use internal finance (retained earnings) if accessible, & choose debt over an equity issue, if external funds are required. Theory as pecking order theory because there is no properly mentioned debt equity target, and there are two kinds of equity – internal & external, one of which is at the top of pecking order & another at the bottom. Debt is cheaper than the costs of internal & external equity because of interest deductibility. Internal equity (retained earnings) is inexpensive and easier to use than external equity because of no taxes on retained earnings, and no transaction costs.

Managers use retained earnings in preference to debt and equity because it avoids giving adverse signals about their companies. They will issue external equity when they think that shares are overvalued. The announcement of share issue decreases the share price as investors have confidence in managers that they are expected to issue when shares are overpriced. The pecking order theory also predicts that if 2 firms are equally profitable, then the more promptly growing firms will borrow more. The most profitable firm borrows less not because they have lower target debt ratios but since they don't require external finance. So, this theory explains negative relationship among profitability & debt ratio within an industry.

Features of an Appropriate Capital Structure

Capital structure may be evaluated from different perspectives. From shareholders' point of view, risk and return matters a lot. Hence, below mentioned are the characteristics of an appropriate capital structure:

- Return: The capital structure of the company should be most beneficial for Shareholders It should generate maximum returns to the shareholders at minimum possible cost.
- Risk: Risk is variability in return which may be caused due to macro-economic factors, industry factors & firm specific factors. For example, excessive use of debt signifies the variability of shareholders' earnings and threatens the solvency of the company.
- Flexibility: The structure should depend on the debt capacity of the company. The debt capacity depends on the firm's ability to make future cash flows. Firms should have enough cash to pay fixed charges of interest and principal and leave some excess cash to meet future contingencies. The capital structure should be flexible i.e. firm can easily change it if warranted by a changed situation. It should also be easy for the firm to offer funds whenever required profitable projects.
- Control: The capital structure should involve minimum risk of loss of control of the company.

Approaches to Establish Target Capital Structure

Following are the three most common approaches to decide about a firm's capital structure:

- EBIT-EPS Approach for analyzing the impact of debt on shareholders' return and risk.
- Valuation Approach for evaluating the impact of debt on the shareholders' value.
- Cash Flow Approach for determining the firm's ability to service debt and avoid financial distress.

EBIT-EPS Analysis

The firm should contemplate the probable variations in EBIT and impact of EBIT under different financial plans on EPS. If the probability of the rate of return falling below the cost of debt is low, the firm can employ high debt to increase EPS. This may also have a optimistic effect on firm's market value. Alternatively, if the same probability is high, the firm should abstain from retaining too much of debt. Thus, the higher the level of EBIT and lesser the probability of downward fluctuations, the more beneficial it is to employ debt.

However, EBIT-EPS analysis also suffers from certain limitations. In choosing between debt & equity, sometimes considerable focus is paid on EPS. The major shortcomings are:

- EPS is based on arbitrary accounting assumptions and does not reflect the economic profits.
- EPS does not consider the time value of money.
- EPS ignores the risk component.

The conviction of the investors being concerned just with the expected EPS does not have profound base. Investors in valuing the shares of the company consider both expected value and risk.

Valuation Approach

As we know that shareholders undertake a high degree of risk than debt holders Hence, debt is an inexpensive source of finance than equity. But debt causes financial risk which increases the cost of equity. Higher debt raises the costs of financial distress & agency costs. The interest tax shield (INTS) component, adds value to Shareholders Thus, there is a trade-off between the tax benefits and costs of financial distress and agency problems. The firm should use debt up to the point where the marginal benefits & costs are same. This will be the point at which firm's value is maximum and WACC is minimum. The difficulty with this approach is that manage find it difficult to apply in practice. It is not possible for the firm to quantify the effect of debt on firm's value.

Cash Flow Analysis

Cash flow approach focuses on following main areas:

- Cash Adequacy and Solvency In determining a firm's target capital structure, a key issue is the firm's capacity to service its debt. The emphasis of this analysis is also on the risk of cash liquidation—the chance of running out of the cash—given a specific sum of debt in the capital structure. This examination is centered on a comprehensive cash flow analysis & not on rules of thumb based on several coverage ratios.
- Components of Cash Flow Analysis: The expected cash flows can be classified into 3 groups:
    - Operating Cash Flows: It relates to the operations of the firm and can be determined from the projected profit and loss statements. Over the period of time, sales volume, sales price and input price should be cautiously scrutinized.

- Non-Operating Cash Flows: It is the cash flow that company lends or accepts from sources different from its operations. It includes capital expenditures & working capital variations. In the course of recession, the firm may have to particularly spend on advertising for the promotion of its product. Certain expenditures cannot be avoided even during most adverse conditions. They are necessary to maintain the minimum operating efficiency of the firm's resources.

- Financial Flows: It includes interest, dividends, repayment of borrowed capital. It includes two types of obligations: contractual obligations and policy obligations. Former is the matter of contract and should not be defaulted, like interest and lease rent. And latter is at the discretion of board of directors like dividends.

- Reserve Financial Capacity: Reduction in operating & financial flexibility is expensive to firms opposing in charging product & factor markets. Hence firms require sustaining reserve of financial resources in the form of unused debt capacity, huge quantities of liquid assets, additional lines of credit, and access to wide-ranging sources of fund.

- Focus of Cash Flow Analysis:
    - Focus on liquidity and solvency.
    - Identifies discretionary cash flows.
    - Lists reserve financial flows.
    - Goes beyond financial statement analysis.
    - Relates debt policy to the firm value.

Cash Flow Analysis Vs. EBIT-EPS Analysis

The cash flow analysis has the following advantages over EBIT-EPS analysis:

- It focuses on the liquidity and solvency of the firm over a long-period of time, even encompassing adverse circumstances. Thus, it evaluates the firm's ability to meet fixed obligations.

- It goes beyond the analysis of profit and loss statement and also considers changes in the balance sheet items.

- It identifies discretionary cash flows. The firm can therefore formulate an action plan to face unfavorable situations.

- It offers a list of potential financial flows which can be utilized under emergency.

- It is a long-term dynamic analysis and does not remain confined to a single period analysis.

Practical Considerations in Determining Capital Structure

In addition to EBIT-EPS analysis, valuation and cash flow analysis, there are some other practical considerations also which the firm needs to consider while deciding about its capital structure.

- Assets: In deciding about firm's capital structure, form of assets held by a company play a significant role. Tangible fixed assets serve as collateral securities for debt. In case of financial distress, the lenders can use these assets & sell them to raise funds lent by them. Companies having higher tangible fixed assets tend to have less expected costs of financial distress & thus, higher debt ratios. Alternatively, companies with higher intangible assets have greater costs of financial distress because these companies don't have much to lend to debt holders as collateral.

- Growth Opportunities: Firms with high market-to-book value ratios have better growth opportunities mainly in terms of investment opportunities. But there is also a higher cost of insolvency & financial distress if they begin to face financial problems. These firms engage in lower debt ratios to avoid the situation of financial distress. Hence, growth firms would desire to take debt with lower maturity period to retain interest rates down and to preserve the financial flexibility. However, firms with low market-to-book value ratio & constricted growth prospects, face the risk of managers spending free cash flow either in unprofitable businesses or in risky businesses. This conduct of manager can be organized by high leverage because after employing high debt, managers may not have any excess of free cash flows.

- Debt & Non-Debt Tax Shields: Due to interest deductibility, debt decreases the tax liability & upsurges the firm's after tax cash flows. As we have already discussed, in the absence of personal taxes, interest tax shield (INTS) increases the value of the firm. Personal taxes decrease the tax benefit of debt over equity. Firms also have non-debt tax shields accessible to them like depreciation, carry forward losses, etc. This implies that firms with larger non-debt tax shields would involve low debt as they may not have adequate profit at their disposal. However, there is a connection between debt tax shields & non-debt tax shields because companies with larger depreciation would be likely to have higher fixed assets, which assist as collateral securities for debt.

- Financial Flexibility and Operating Strategy: Financial flexibility means a company's ability to adapt its capital structure to the needs of changing conditions. The company should be able to raise funds whenever needed for profitable projects, without undue delay and cost. It should also redeem its debt whenever warranted by the future conditions. So, the financial plan of the company should be flexible enough to change the composition of the capital structure.

- Loan Covenants: Covenants in loan agreements may include restrictions to distribute cash dividends, to incur capital expenditure, to raise additional external finances or to maintain working capital at particular level. Private debt contains both positive and negative covenants while public debt has a lot of negative covenants. Growth firms prefer to take private debt rather than public debt since it is much easier to negotiate terms in time of crisis with few private lenders than several debenture holders A highly levered firm is subject to many constraints under debt covenants that restrict its choice of decisions.
- Financial Slack: Financial flexibility of a firm depends upon financial slack it maintains. Financial slack includes unused debt capacity, excess liquid assets, unutilized lines of credit and access to various untapped sources of funds. If a company borrows to the limit of its debt capacity, it will not be in a position to borrow additional funds for financing of any unforeseen and unpredictable demands. Therefore, company should not borrow to the limit of its debt capacity and keep available some unused capacity to raise funds in future. If a company has the option to repay its debt before maturity, a considerable degree of financial flexibility will be introduced. This will enable management to replace expensive source with cheaper source of finance, whenever warranted by the circumstances.
- Issue Costs: These are incurred when the funds are raised externally. Generally, cost of debt is less than the cost of equity which encourages the companies to use debt more than equity. Retained earnings do not have any floatation costs. Large firms require large amount of funds, and they may plan large issue of securities to economize on the issue costs. And the company should raise only that much funds which it can employ profitably.
- Capacity of Raising Funds: The size of a company also influences its capital structure. The larger companies has comparatively more flexibility in designing its capital structure as compared to the small company that encounter much complications in raising long term loans. If it is able to raise, then rate of interest will be too high and inconvenient terms. It makes the capital structure of the small company very inflexible & management may not be able to carry on its business without interference. Therefore, small companies depend on share capital & retained earnings. It is quite difficult for them to raise share capital in the capital markets because capital base of most of the companies is so small that they cannot be listed on stock exchange. If it is able to get itself listed, then cost of issuing shares is so high for them and their shares are also not widely scattered. But, alternatively, large companies can easily raise funds on favorable terms by issuing equity, preference or debentures. Because of the large size of issues, cost of raising funds is also lower.

References

- Cost-of-capital: investopedia.com, Retrieved 20, August 2020
- Cost-of-debt: investopedia.com, Retrieved 05, January 2020
- Cost-of-equity-capm: wallstreetmojo.com, Retrieved 16, May 2020
- Leverage: investopedia.com, Retrieved 19, July 2020

5

Dividend Decisions

The important decisions taken by the finance manager with respect to the payout to the shareholders are called dividend decisions. A few of the models and theorems studied in relation to dividend decisions are Walter's model, Gordon's model and M&M hypothesis. This chapter discusses in detail these models and theorems connected to dividend decisions as well as dividend policies in practice.

The term dividend usually refers to cash paid out of earnings. If a payment is made from sources other than current or accumulated retained earnings, the term distribution, rather than dividend, is used. However, it is acceptable to refer to a distribution of earnings as a dividend and a distribution from capital as a liquidating dividend. More generally, any direct payment by the corporation to the shareholders may be considered a dividend or a part of dividend policy.

Dividends come in several different forms. The basic types of cash dividends are:

- Regular cash dividends.
- Extra dividends.
- Special dividends.
- Liquidating dividends.

Cash Dividends

The most common type of dividend is a cash dividend. Commonly, public companies pay regular cash dividends four times a year. As the name suggests, these are cash payments made directly to shareholders, and they are made in the regular course of business. In other words, management sees nothing unusual about the dividend and no reason why it won't be continued.

Sometimes firms will pay a regular cash dividend and an extra cash dividend. By calling part of the payment "extra" management is indicating that the "extra" part may or may not be repeated in the future. A special dividend is similar, but the name usually indicates that this dividend is viewed as a truly unusual or one-time event and won't be repeated. Finally, the payment of a liquidating dividend usually means that some or all of the business has been liquidated, that is, sold off. However it is labeled, a cash dividend payment reduces corporate cash and retained earnings, except in the case of a liquidating dividend.

Bonus Shares (Stock Dividend)

An issue of bonus shares is the distribution of shares free of cost to existing shareholder Bonus shares are issued in addition to the cash dividend and not in lieu of cash dividends. Hence, companies may supplement cash dividend by bonus issues. Issuing bonus shares increase the number of outstanding shares of the company. The bonus shares are distributed proportionately to the existing shareholder. Hence there is no dilution of ownership. For example, if a shareholder owns 100 shares at the time when a 10 per cent (ie., 1:10) bonus issue made, he will receive 10 additional shares. The declaration of the bonus shares will increase the paid-up share capital and reduce the reserve and surplus earnings of the company. The total net worth is not affected by the bonus issue.

Stock Split

A stock split is essentially the same thing as a stock dividend, except that a split is expressed as a ratio instead of a percentage. When a split is declared, each share is split up to create additional shares. For example, in a three-for-one stock split, each old share is split into three new shares.

Standard Method of Cash Dividend Payment

The decision to pay a dividend rests in the hands of the board of directors of the corporation. When a dividend has been declared, it becomes a debt of the firm and cannot be rescinded easily. Sometime after it has been declared, a dividend is distributed to all shareholders as of some specific date. Commonly, the amount of the cash dividend is expressed in terms of dollars per share (dividends per share). As we have seen in other chapters, it is also expressed as a percentage of the market price (the dividend yield) or as a percentage of net income or earnings per share (the dividend payout).

Example of procedure for dividend payment.

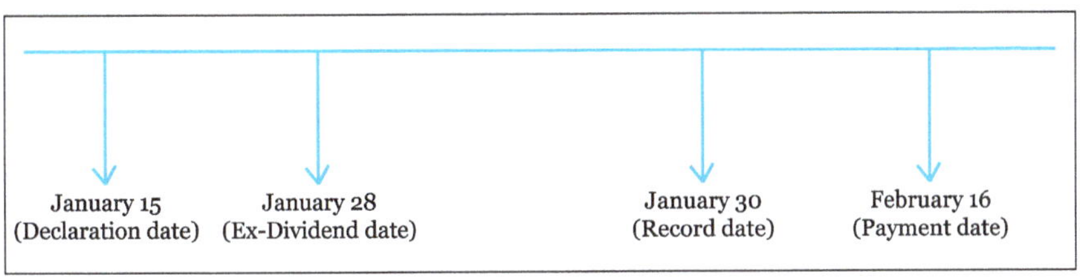

Establishing Dividend Policies and Decisions

How do firms actually determine the level of dividends they will pay at a particular time? As we have seen, there are good reasons for firms to pay high dividends and there are good reasons to pay low dividends. There are three approaches for establishing dividend policy. These are three types of the dividend policy, such as residual dividend approach, dividend stability and a compromise dividend policy.

Residual Dividend Approach

- Firms with higher dividend payouts will have to sell stock more often. Such sales are not very common and they can be very expensive.
- Consistent with this, we will assume that the firm wishes to minimize the need to sell new equity. We will also assume that the firm wishes to maintain its current capital structure.
- If a firm wishes to avoid new equity sales, then it will have to rely on internally generated equity to finance new positive NPV projects. Dividends can only be paid out of what is left over. This leftover is called the residual, and such a dividend policy is called a residual dividend approach.
- With a residual dividend policy, the firm's objective is to meet its investment needs and maintain its desired debt-equity ratio before paying dividends.

Imagine that a firm has $1,000 in earnings and a debt-equity ratio of 0.50. Notice that, because the debt-equity ratio is 0.50, the firm has 50 cents in debt for every $1.50 in total value. The firm's capital structure is thus debt and equity. The first step in implementing a residual dividend policy is to determine the amount of funds that can be generated without selling new equity. If the firm reinvests the entire $1,000 and pays no dividend, then equity will increase by $1,000. To keep the debt-equity ratio of 0.50, the firm must borrow an additional $500. The total amount of funds that can be generated without selling new equity is thus $1,000 + 500 = $1,500.

The second step is to decide whether or not a dividend will be paid. To do this, we compare the total amount that can be generated without selling new equity ($1,500 in this case) to planned capital spending.

- If funds needed exceed funds available, then no dividend will be paid. In addition, the firm will have to sell new equity to raise the needed financing or else postpone some planned capital spending.
- If funds needed are less than funds generated, then a dividend will be paid. The amount of the dividend will be the residual, that is, that portion of the earnings that is not needed to finance new projects.

For example: Suppose we have $900 in planning capital spending. To maintain the firm's capital structure, this $900 must be financed by 2⁄3 equity and 1⁄3debt. So, the firm will actually borrow 1⁄3 X $900 = $300. The firm will spend 2⁄3 X $900 = $600 of the $1,000 in equity available. There is a $1,000 - 600 = $400 residual, so the dividend will be $400. In sum, the firm has after tax earnings of $1,000. Dividends paid are $400. Retained earnings are $600, and new borrowing totals $300. The firm's debt-equity ratio is unchanged at 0.50.

Stability of Dividend

It is considered a desirable policy by the management of most companies in practices. Many surveys have shown that shareholders also seem generally to favor this policy and value stable dividends higher than the fluctuating ones. All other things being the same, the stable dividend policy may have a positive impact on the market price of the share.

It is also meant regularity in paying some dividend annually, even though the amount of the dividend may fluctuate over the years, and may not relate to earnings. There are a number of companies, which have records of paying dividend for a long, unbroken period. More precisely, stability of dividend refers to the amounts paid out regularly. Three forms of such stability may be distinguished:

- Constant dividend per share or dividend rate.
- Constant pay out.
- Constant dividend per share plus extra dividend.

Constant Dividend per Share or Dividend Rate

The companies announce dividend as per cent of the paid-up capital per share. A company follows the policy of paying a fixed rate on paid-up capital as dividend every year, irrespective of fluctuations in the earnings. This policy does not imply that the dividend per share or dividend rate will never be increased. When the company reaches new levels of earnings and expects to maintain them, the annual dividend per share may be increased. The relationship between earnings per shares and the dividend per share under this policy is shown below figure.

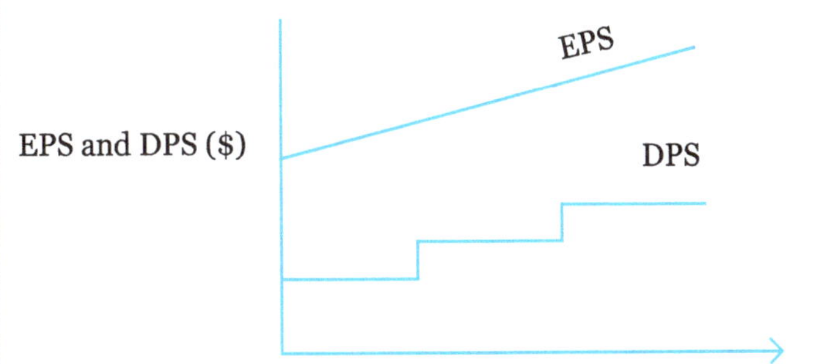

Constant dividend per share policy. Time (Years).

A constant dividend per share policy puts ordinary shareholders at par with preferred shareholders irrespective of the firm's investment opportunities or the preference shareholders Those investors who have dividends as they only sources of their income may prefer the constant dividend policy. They do not accord much importance to the changes in share prices. In the long run, this may help to stabilize the market price of the share.

Constant Payout

The ratio of dividend to earnings is known as payout ratio. Some companies may follow a policy of constant payout ratio i.e., paying a fixed percentage of net earnings every year. With this policy of the amount of the dividend will fluctuate in direct proportion to earnings. If a company adopts a 40 percent payout ratio, then 40 percent of every $ of net earnings will be paid out.

For example, if the company earns, 2 $ per share, the dividend per share will be 0.80 $ and if it earns 1.5 $ per share the dividend per share will be 0.60 $. The relation between the earnings per share and the dividend per share under the policy is exhibited in the below figure:

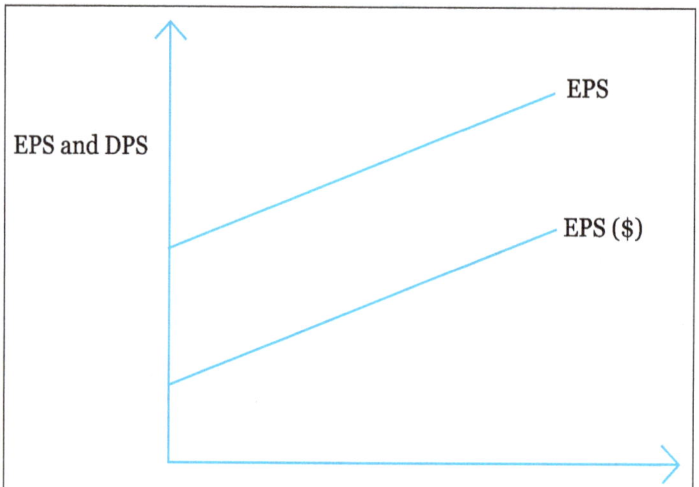

Dividend policy of constant payout ratio.

This policy is related to a company's ability to pay dividends. If the company incurs losses, no dividend shall be paid regardless of the desires of shareholder Internal financing with retained earnings is automatic when this policy is followed. At any given payout ratio, the amount of dividends and the additions to retained earnings increase with increasing earnings and decrease with decrease earnings. This policy does not put any pressure on a company's liquidity since dividends are distributed only when the company has profited.

Constant Dividend Per Share Plus Extra Dividend

The smallest amount of dividend per share is fixed to reduce the possibility of every missing a dividend payment. By paying extra dividend in periods of prosperity, an attempt is made to prevent investors from expecting that the dividend represents an increase in the established dividend amount. This type of policy enables a company to pay a constant amount of dividend regularly without a default and allows a great deal of flexibility for supplementing the income of shareholders only when the company earnings are higher than the usual, without committing itself to make a larger payments as part of the future fixed dividend.

A Compromise Dividend Policy

In practice, many firms appear to follow a compromise dividend policy. Such a policy is based on five main goals:

- Avoid cutting back on positive NPV projects to pay a dividend.
- Avoid dividend cuts.
- Avoid the need to sell equity.
- Maintain a target debt-equity ratio.

Maintain A Target Dividend Payout Ratio

These goals are ranked more or less in order of their importance. In our strict residual approach, we assume that the firm maintains a fixed debt-equity ratio. Under the compromise approach, the debt-equity ratio is viewed as a long-range goal. It is allowed to vary in the short run if necessary to avoid a dividend cut or the need to sell new equity.

In addition to having a strong reluctance to cut dividends, financial managers tend to think of dividend payments in terms of a proportion of income, and they also tend to think investors are entitled to a "fair" share of corporate income. This share is the long-run target payout ratio, and it is the fraction of the earnings the firm expects to pay as dividends under ordinary circumstances. Again, this ratio is viewed as a long-range goal, so it might vary in the short run if this is necessary. As a result, in the long run, earnings growth is followed by dividend increases, but only with a lag.

Factors Determination of Dividend Policies

- Bond Indentures: Debt contracts often limit dividend payments to earnings generated after the loan was granted. Also, debt contracts often stipulate that no dividends can be paid unless the current ratio, times-interest earned ratio, and other safety ratios exceed stated minimums.
- Preferred stock restrictions: Typically, common dividends cannot be paid if the company has omitted its preferred dividend. The preferred average must be satisfied before common dividends can be resumed.
- Impairment of capital rule: Dividend payments cannot exceed the balance sheet item "retained earnings." This legal restriction, known as the impairment of capital rule, is designed to protect creditor Without the rule, a company that is in trouble might distribute most of its assets to stockholders and leave its debt holders out in the cold. (Liquidating dividends can be paid out of capital, but they must be indicated as such, and they must not reduce capital below the limits stated in debt contracts).

- Availability of cash: Cash dividends can be paid only with cash. Thus, a shortage of cash in the bank can restrict dividend payments. However, the ability to borrow can offset this factor.
- Penalty tax on improperly accumulated earnings: To prevent wealthy individuals from using corporations to avoid personal taxes, the Tax Code provides for a special surtax on improperly accumulated income. Thus, if the IRS can demonstrate that a firm's dividend payout ratio is being deliberately held down to help its stockholders avoid personal taxes, the firm is subject to heavy penalties. This factor is generally relevant only to privately owned firms.
- Number of profitable investment opportunities: If a firm typically has a large number of profitable investment opportunities, this will tend to produce a low target payout ratio, and vice versa if the firm's profitable investment opportunities are few in number.
- Possibility of accelerating or delaying projects: The ability to accelerate or postpone projects will permit a firm to adhere more closely to a stable dividend policy.
- Cost of selling new stock: If a firm needs to finance a given level of investment, it can obtain equity by retaining earnings or by issuing new common stock. If flotation costs (including any negative signaling effects of a stock offering) are high, ke will be well above Ks, making it better to set a low payout ratio and to finance through retention rather than through sales of new common stock. On the other hand, a high dividend payout ratio is more feasible for a firm whose flotation costs are low.
- Flotation costs differ among firm For example, the flotation percentage is generally higher for small firms, so they tend to set low payout ratios.
- Ability to substitute debt for equity. A firm can finance a given level of investment with either debt or equity. As noted above, low stock flotation costs permit a more flexible dividend policy because equity can be raised either by retaining earnings or by selling new stock. A similar situation holds for debt policy: If the firm can adjust its debt ratio without raising costs sharply, it can pay the expected dividend, even if earnings fluctuate, by increasing its debt ratio.

Dividend Theories and Behaviour

- Irrelevance of Dividend:
    - MM Approach.
- Relevance of Dividend:
    - Walter's Model.
    - Gordon's Model.

Walter's Model

Professor James E. Walter has developed a theoretical model which shows the relationship between dividend policies and common stocks prices. According to him the dividend policy of a firm is based on the relationship between the internal rate of return (r) earned by it and the cost of capital or required rate of return (Ke).

Assumptions of Model:

- The interval rate of return and the cost of capital (Ke) are constant.
- All new investment opportunities of the firm are to be financed through retained earnings only and no external finance is available to the firm.
- The firm has perpetual or an infinite life.

As per this model, the investment decisions and dividend decisions of a firm are inter related. A firm should retain its earnings if the return on investment exceeds the cost of capital. Such firms are called Growth Firms (r > Ke). Such firms should have zero pay-out and should re-invest their entire earnings. On the other hand, a firm should distribute its earnings to the shareholder if the internal rate of return is less than the cost of capital (r < Ke). Such firms are called declining firms.

Such firms should distribute the entire profits i.e. 100 per cent pay-out ratio. Firms with internal rate of return equal to the cost of capital (r = Ke) are called Normal Firms. In such firms, the shareholders will be indifferent whether the firm pays dividends or retain the profits. The formula to determine the market value of share as suggested by Prof. Walter is as under:

$$P = \frac{D}{K_e} + \frac{r(E-D)/K_0}{K_e}$$

Where,

D = Dividend per share

P= Market price per share
r= Internal rate of return
E= Earnings per share
Ke = Cost of equity capital or capitalization rate.

llustration: Santosh Limited earns $5 per share is capitalized at a rate of 10% and has a rate of return on investments of 18%. According the Walter's Formula:

- What should be the price per share at 25% dividend pay-out ratio?
- Is this optimum pay-out ratio?

Solution: Value per share as per Walter formula

$$P = \frac{D}{K_e} + \frac{r(E-D)/K_O}{K_e}$$

Where; P= Market price per share

D = Dividend per share

R = Internal Rate of return

E = Earnings per share

Ke = Cost of equity capital or capitalization rate.

Substituting the values in the above formula, We get,

$$P = \frac{1.25}{0.10} + \frac{0.18(5-1.25)/0.10}{0.10}$$

$= 12.5 + 67.50$

$= \$\ 80$

As per above calculation at 25% dividend pay-out, the value of share is $80. But, according to Walter's model, it is not an optimum dividend pay-out because, in such case where internal rate of return is more than the cost of capital (r > Ke), he has suggested zero dividend pay-out.

Criticisms of Walter Model

The Walter's model provides a single framework to explain the relationship between dividend policy and value of the firm. If the assumptions underlying the model hold good, the behaviour of the market price of the shares in response to dividend policy of this firm can be explained with the help of this model. But, actually these assumptions are unrealistic and that is why the model is criticised on the following grounds:

- Absence of External Financing: Prof. Walter's main assumption that financing of investment proposals only by retained earnings and no external financing is seldom found in real life. Most of the firms meet their financial requirements by loans or issuing new shares.
- Stable Internal Rate of Return: The rate of return earned by the firm is never stable. Actually, the rate of return changes with the increase in investments.
- Stable Cost of Capital: The assumption of constant cost of capital is also unrealistic, because the risk complexion of the firm is not always uniform. Therefore, cost of capital also changes.

Gordon's Model

Myron Gordon's model explicitly relates the market value of the company to its dividend policy. The determinants of the market value of the share are the perpetual stream of future dividends to be paid, the cost of capital and the expected annual growth rate of the company.

Relation of Dividend Decision and Value of a Firm

The Gordon's theory on dividend policy states that the company's dividend payout policy and the relationship between its rate of return (r) and the cost of capital (k) influence the market price per share of the company.

Relationship between r and k	Increase in Dividend Payout
r>k	Price per share decreases
r<k	Price per share increases
r=k	No change in the price per share

Assumptions of Gordon's Model

Gordon's model is based on the following assumptions:

- No Debt: The model assumes that the company is an all equity company, with no proportion of debt in the capital structure.
- No External Financing: The model assumes that all investment of the company is financed by retained earnings and no external financing is required.
- Constant IRR: The model assumes a constant Internal Rate of Return (r), ignoring the diminishing marginal efficiency of the investment.
- Constant Cost of Capital: The model is based on the assumption of a constant cost of capital (k), implying the business risk of all the investments to be the same.
- Perpetual Earnings: Gordon's model believes in the theory of perpetual earnings for the company.
- Corporate Taxes: Corporate taxes are not accounted for in this model.
- Constant Retention Ratio: The model assumes a constant retention ratio (b) once it is decided by the company. Since the growth rate (g) = b*r, the growth rate is also constant by this logic.
- K>g: Gordon's model assumes that the cost of capital (k) > growth rate (g). This is important for obtaining the meaningful value of the company's share.

Valuation Formula of Gordon's Model and its Denotations

Gordon's formula to calculate the market price per share (P) is P = {EPS * (1-b)} / (k-g)

Where,

P = market price per share

EPS = earnings per share

b= retention ratio of the firm

(1-b) = payout ratio of the firm

k = cost of capital of the firm

g = growth rate of the firm = b*r

Explanation

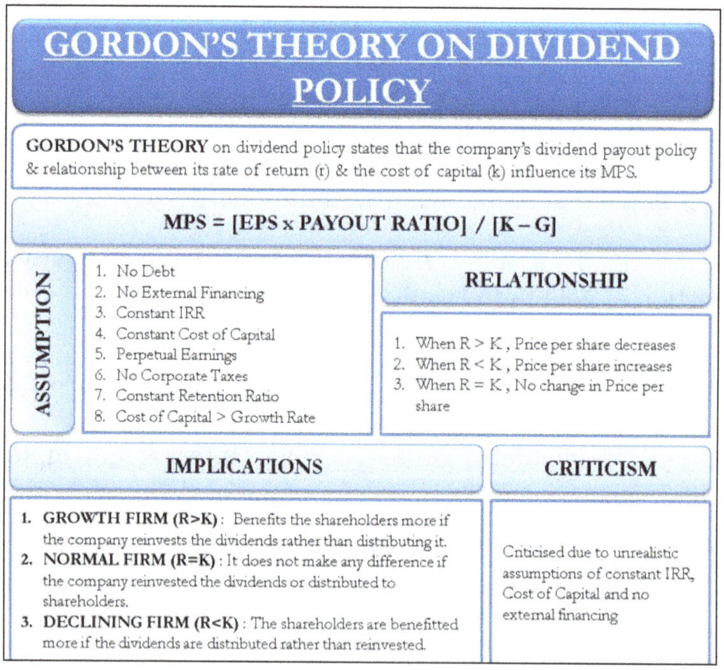

The above model indicates that the market value of the company's share is the sum total of the present values of infinite future dividends to be declared. The Gordon's model can also be used to calculate the cost of equity, if the market value is known and the future dividends can be forecasted.

The EPS of the company is $ 15. The market rate of discount applicable to the company is 12%. The dividends are expected to grow at 10% annually. The company retains 70% of its earnings. Calculate the market value of the share using Gordon's model.

Here, E = 15

b = 70%

k = 12%

g = 10%

Market price of the share = P = {15 * (1-.70)} / (.12-.10) = 15*.30 / .02 = 225

Implications of Gordon's Model

Gordon's model believes that the dividend policy impacts the company in various scenarios as follows:

- Growth Firm: A growth firm's internal rate of return (r) > cost of capital (k). It benefits the shareholders more if the company reinvests the dividends rather than distributing it. So, the optimum payout ratio for growth firms is zero.
- Normal Firm: A normal firm's internal rate of return (r) = cost of the capital (k). So, it does not make any difference if the company reinvested the dividends or distributed to its shareholder So, there is no optimum dividend payout ratio for normal firms.

However, Gordon revised this theory later and stated that the dividend policy of the firm impacts the market value even when r=k. Investors will always prefer a share where more current dividends are paid.

- Declining Firm: The internal rate of return (r) < cost of the capital (k) in the declining firms. The shareholders are benefitted more if the dividends are distributed rather than reinvested. So, the optimum dividend payout ratio for declining firms is 100%.

Criticism of Gordon's Model

Gordon's theory on dividend policy is criticized mainly for the unrealistic assumptions made in the model.

- Constant Internal Rate of Return and Cost of Capital: The model is inaccurate in assuming that r and k always remain constant. A constant r means that the wealth of the shareholders is not optimized. A constant k means the business risks are not accounted for while valuing the firm.
- No External Financing: Gordon's belief of all investments being financed by retained earnings is faulty. This reflects sub-optimum investment and dividend policies.

M&M Hypothesis

Modigliani – Miller theory was proposed by Franco Modigliani and Merton Miller in 1961. They were the pioneers in suggesting that dividends and capital gains are equivalent when an investor considers returns on investment. The only thing that impacts the valuation of a company is its earnings, which is a direct result of the company's investment policy and the future prospects. So, according to this theory, once the investment policy is known to the investor, he will not need any additional input on the dividend history of the company. The investment decision is, thus, dependent on the investment policy of the company and not on the dividend policy.

Modigliani – Miller theory goes a step further and illustrates the practical situations where dividends are not relevant to investor Irrespective of whether a company pays a dividend or not, the investors are capable enough to make their own cash flows from the stocks depending on their Modigliani- Miller Theory on Dividend Policy need for the cash. If the investor needs more money than the dividend he received, he can always sell a part of his investments to make up for the difference. Likewise, if an investor has no present cash requirement, he can always reinvest the received dividend in the stock. Thus, the Modigliani – Miller theory firmly states that the dividend policy of a company has no influence on the investment decisions of the investor.

This theory also believes that dividends are irrelevant by the arbitrage argument. By this logic, the dividends distribution to shareholders is offset by the external financing. Due to the distribution of dividends, the price of the stock decreases and will nullify the gain made by the investors because of the dividends.

Assumptions of the Model

Modigliani – Miller theory is based on the following assumptions:

- Perfect Capital Markets: This theory believes in the existence of 'perfect capital markets'. It assumes that all the investors are rational, they have access to free information, there are no flotation or transaction costs and no large investor to influence the market price of the share.
- No Taxes: There is any existence of taxes. Alternatively, both dividends and capital gains are taxed at the same rate.
- Fixed Investment Policy: The company does not change its existing investment policy. It means whatever may be the dividend payment, the company will make investment as it has already decided upon. If the company is going to pay more amount of dividend, then it will more equity shares and vice versa.
- No Risk of Uncertainty: All the investors are certain about the future market

prices and the dividends. This means that the same discount rate is applicable for all types of stocks in all time periods.

- Investor is indifferent between dividend income and capital gain income: It is assumed that investor is indifferent between dividend income and capital gain income. It means if he requires total return of \$ 500, he may get \$ 200 dividend income and \$ 300 as capital gain income or reverse, in either of the case he gets equal satisfaction.

Valuation Formula and its Denotations

Modigliani – Miller's valuation model is based on the assumption of same discount rate/rate of return applicable to all the stocks.

$$P_1 = P_0 * (1 + k_e) - D_1$$

Where,

P_1 = market price of the share at the end of a period

P_0 = market price of the share at the beginning of a period

k_e = cost of capital

D_1 = dividends received at the end of a period

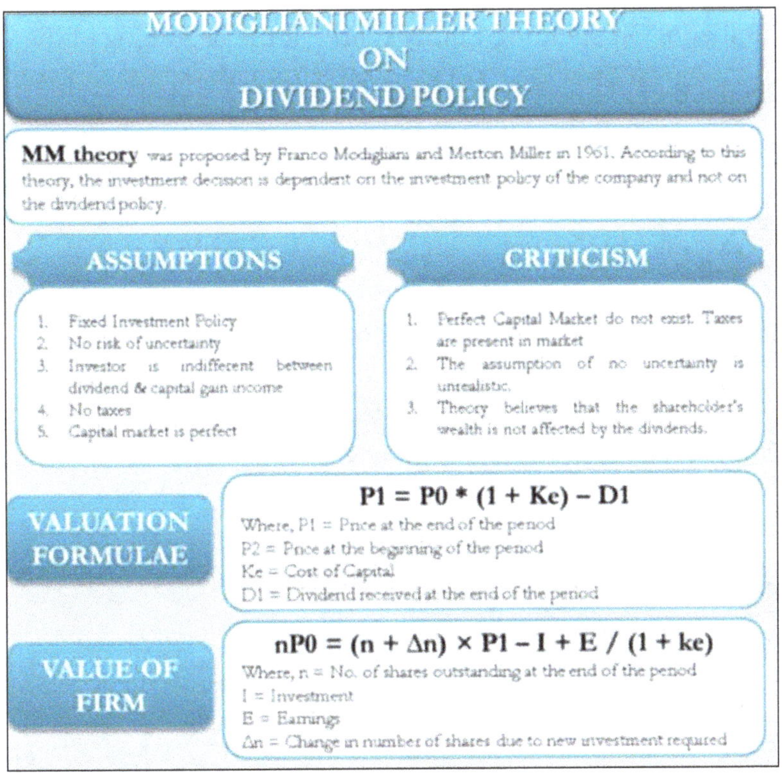

Explanation of Modigliani – Miller's Model

Modigliani – Miller's model can be used to calculate the market price of the share at the end of a period, if the share price at the beginning of the period, dividends and the cost of capital are known. Share price at the beginning of the year is $ 150. The discount rate applicable to the company is 10%. The company declares $ 10 as dividends at the end of a year. Market price of the share at the end of one year using the Modigliani – Miller's model can be found as under.

Here, $P_0 = 150$

$k_e = 10\%$

$D_1 = 10$

Market price of the stock = $P_1 = 150 * (1 + .10) - 10 = 150 * 1.1 - 10 = 155$.

As per M M Approach value of entire firm / company can be found as under:

$$nP_0 = (n + \Delta n) \times P_1 - I + E / (1 + k_e)$$

Explanation of formula:

Retained Earning = $E - n D_1$

E = Earning

n = Number of Outstanding Equity shares at the beginning of the year

D_1= Dividend Paid to existing shareholders at the end of year

New Issue of Equity Share Capital ($) = I – Retained earning

$= I - \{E - n D_1\}$

$= I - E + nD_1$

I = Investment to be made at the end of the year

New Issue of Equity shares at the end of the year (Δn)

New Issue of Equity Shares at the end of year = $\Delta n \times P_1$

So, we can say that

$\Delta n \times P_1$ = New Issue of Equity Share Capital ($)

$\Delta n \times P_1 = I - E + nD_1$

Now, explanation of formula starts,

As we know that for one equity share :

$P_1 = P_0 * (1 + k_e) - D_1$

$P_o = D_1 + P_1 / (1 + k_e)$

Now, in above equation, n is multiplied on both sides, so instead of one share, it will become value of firm:

$nP_o = nD_1 + nP_1 / (1 + k_e)$

In order to derive a formula, $\Delta n \times P_1$ is added and subtracted to right hand side equation:

$nP_o = nD1 + nP_1 + \Delta n \times P_1 - \Delta n \times P_1 / (1 + k_e)$

Now, P_1 is taken common from nP_1 and $\Delta n\ P_1$

$nP_o = nD_1 + (n + \Delta n) \times P_1 - \Delta n \times P_1 / (1 + k_e)$

$\Delta n \times P_1$ is replaced with $I - E + nD_1$

$nP_o = nD_1 + (n + \Delta n) \times P_1 - \{I - E + nD_1\} / (1 + k_e)$

Now, we open bracket of $I - E + nD_1$

$nP_o = nD_1 + (n + \Delta n) \times P_1 - I + E - nD_1 / (1 + k_e)$

nD_1 is cancelled from both sides;

So, now we are left with following formula:

$nP_o = + (n + \Delta n) \times P_1 - I + E / (1 + k_e)$

Criticism of Modigliani Miller's Model

Modigliani – Miller theory on dividend policy suffers from the following limitations:

- Perfect capital markets do not exist. Taxes are present in the capital markets.
- According to this theory, there is no difference between internal and external financing. However, if the flotation costs of new issues are considered, it is false.
- This theory believes that the shareholder's wealth is not affected by the dividends. However, there are transaction costs associated with the selling of shares to make cash inflows. This makes the investors prefer dividends.
- The assumption of no uncertainty is unrealistic. The dividends are relevant under the certain conditions as well.

Dividend and Uncertainty

The argument of uncertainty of dividends is favored by various schools of thought. The reason is that the investors prefer cash dividends in current time rather than in future. The investors preferring current dividends place lower required rate of return and thus value of the stock is high. In this regard, John Emmett Kirshmann made the following concise statement:

> "Of two stocks with identical earnings, records, and prospects, but the one paying a larger dividend than the other, the former will undoubtedly command a higher price merely because stockholders prefer present to future values. Myopic vision plays a part in the price-making process. Stockholders often act upon the principle that a bird in the hand is worth two in the bush and for this reason are willing to pay a premium for the stock with the higher dividend rate, just as they discount the one with the lower rate."

Myron Gordon had earlier given this view that dividend is irrelevant i.e. it has no impact on the value of the share when internal rate of return, r is equal to cost of capital, k. He later modified this assumption and came to a conclusion that dividend policy effects the value of the share when r =k. This argument is known as bird-in-the-hand-argument. The logic behind his argument is that the investors discount the distant dividends at higher required rate of returns than the near dividends. According to him, uncertainty increases as when time progresses. Therefore, the required rate of return cannot be assumed to remain constant. Hence, the investors are reluctant to take risk of future uncertainty prefer current dividends and thus, are willing to pay higher price for such stocks.

Gordon's Model can be expressed in equations as follows:

$$P_0 = \frac{DIV_1}{(1+k_1)} + \frac{DIV_2}{(1+k_2)} + \frac{DIV_3}{(1+k_3)} + \ldots\ldots\ldots\ldots\ldots + \frac{DIV_n}{(1+k_n)}$$

$$= \frac{\sum DIV_t}{(1+k_t)} \ldots\ldots\ldots\ldots\ldots\ldots\ldots\ldots\ldots\ldots$$

Where P_0 = Price of the share when retention rate, b = 0

k = Cost of capital, $k_t > k_{t-1}$

If the firm retains a part b of its earnings, then dividend per share is equal to (1- b) EPS_1 in the first year. Therefore, the growth rate of dividends is g = br when retained earnings are reinvested at rate of return, r. We will get the following equation after incorporating growth in dividends:

$$P_b = \frac{DIV_0(1+g)^1}{(1+k_1)^1} + \frac{DIV_0(1+g)^2}{(1+k_2)^2} + \ldots\ldots\ldots\ldots \frac{DIV_0(1+g)^n}{(1+k_n)^n} + \ldots\ldots\ldots\ldots\ldots$$

Where, P_b = Price of the share when b> 0

If we discount the dividend stream at a uniform rate, k', which is the weighted average of k_t, the value of P_b will be:

$$P_b = \frac{DIV_0(1+g)+}{(1+k)}\frac{DIV_0(1+g)+}{(1+k)}\dots\dots\dots\frac{DIV_0(1+g)^n+}{(1+k)^n}$$

$$= DIV_1 = (1-b)EPS_1 \dots\dots\dots\dots\dots\dots$$

$$k' - gk' - br$$

Through the above derivation Gordon concluded that the increase in the retention of earnings will result in lowering the value of the share. His conclusion is based on the assumption that the investors are risk averters and they consider distant dividends less certain than the near dividends.

Informational Content of Dividends and Signaling Hypothesis

During the times of uncertainty, the investors look for information content of dividends and signaling by the firms. The information content of dividend hypothesis is a firm-specific hypothesis which contends that managers of a firm use the dividend to signal asymmetric information about the firm's future earnings. According to the dividend signaling hypothesis, dividend change announcements trigger share returns because they convey information about management's assessment on firms' future prospects.

Information communicated by dividends about the future prospects of a company can be inferred as an information content of the dividends. By way of announcing the dividends action, the companies signal the investor Usually in the stock market, we see that an increase in stock price happens due to an increase in dividend whereas a decline in dividend leads to a fall in the stock price. The perception of a public shareholder is that a sudden upsurge in dividends is due to improvement of earnings of the firm in future and vice-versa.

This can be explained with an example. XYZ Ltd has been paying a stable dividend of \$ 3 per year with earnings per share as \$ 5. Suppose the current EPS rises from \$5 to \$ 8 and the company does not increase the dividends, then the shareholders may perceive this event as a temporary occurrence. In case, the dividends are increased to \$4 per share, then it may give a signal to the shareholders that the company's earnings are likely to increase in long term. This thought process may instill confidence in the shareholders which may lead to an increase in the share price of the firm. But we should understand that the market value has not raised on account of change in dividends but the information the change of dividends carry.

Public shareholders feel that the directors and managers of the companies have better knowledge about company's prospects. Therefore, shareholders try to gather the scraps of information available from insiders to make sense of it. This is attributed to information asymmetry in the capital markets. Rather than announcing about the expected improvements in future, the managers announce increase in dividends to convince the shareholders about the same.

But the managers have to be cautious too when it comes to signaling the information content of dividends. For example, if firm's long term financial prospects are bright but it is also planning capital expenditures in near future. Therefore, the need of the hour may be to cut the dividends which may send a negative signal in the market by reducing the stock price. The shareholders may think that the company's earnings are likely to fall which is actually false. Hence, the managers should consider the signaling effects while formulating a dividend policy.

Lintner's Model of Corporate Dividend Behavior

The pattern of dividends followed by firms has always been an intriguing topic of research. Various research studies are there on the dividend behavior of firms. One of the earliest works on this area has been done by John Lintner in 1956. Lintner did his study with the firms of USA to study the pattern of dividends.

The findings of his study are as follows:

- Firms set long term target payout ratios.
- Managers are concerned about the change in the dividend rather than the absolute level.
- Managers don't consider investment requirements before amending the pattern of dividend payment behavior.
- Dividend payments depend on earnings.
- Dividends follow a smoother path than earnings.
- Dividends are sticky in nature as managers are reluctant to effect dividend changes that may be reversed.

Let us suppose that a firm has been stringently following a stable payout policy. Assumingly, its expected earnings per share in year 1 are EPS1 and p as the target payout ratio. Its expected dividend per share, DIV_1 will be:

$$DIV_1 =_p EPS1 \ldots\ldots\ldots\ldots\ldots\ldots$$

The dividend change from the previous year will be as follows:

$$DIV_1 - DIV_0 = {}_pEPS_1 - DIV_0 \ldots\ldots\ldots\ldots$$

In reality, the firms don't change dividend per share immediately with the change in earning per share. The dividend change is done slowly and gradually even if the earnings have risen tremendously. In other words, firms manage their dividend payments so as to produce a smooth progression in dividends. The firms adjust the levels of speed with which they progress towards full adjustment of payment to earnings. Let us assume that the speed of adjustment is b. Lintner gave the following formula to incorporate the speed factor of adjustment:

$$DIV_1 \ DIV_0 = b({}_pEPS_1 - DIV_0)$$
$$DIV_1 \ DIV_0 = b_pEPS_1 - bDIV_0 \ldots$$

Where b is the speed of adjustment and p is the target payout ratio.

The equation $\begin{matrix} DIV1 \ DIVo = b({}_pEPS_1 - DIV_0) \\ DIV1 \ DIVo = b_pEPS_1 - bDIV_0 \ldots \end{matrix}$ implies:

- Firms set their dividends as per the level of current earnings.
- The current dividends not only depend on the current earnings but dividends of past year also.

$$DIV_t - DIV_{t-1} = b({}_pEPS_t - bDIV_{t-1})$$

$$DIV_t = b_pEPS_t + (1 - b)DIV_{t-1}$$

Where DIV_t= Dividend per share in year t

p= Target payout ratio

b = Adjustment factor

DIV_{t-1} = Dividend per share in year t-1

Here, we should understand that the adjustment factor, b, will be large in case of aggressive firms where small for conservative firms.

Example: XYZ Ltd. has earnings per share of Rs 5 for the year t. Its dividend per share for year t-1 was Rs 2. Assume the target payout ratio and the adjustment rate for this firm are 0.6 and 0.5 respectively. What would be the dividend per share for XYZ Ltd. for the year t, using Lintner's model?

DPS for year t:

$$DIV_t = b_pEPS_t + (1 - b)DIV_{t-1}$$

= 0.5*0.6*5 + (1-0.5)* 2

= Rs 2.5

Thus, dividend for the current year is $ 2.5 which is partly dependent on previous year's dividend and partly on current earnings.

Dividend Policies in Practice

Even though some theories prove that dividend is irrelevant but relaxing the assumptions make the dividend decision an important decision for the companies. In reality, the firms do follow some kinds of dividend policy. And for deciding the dividend policy, the firm has to consider various concerns like liquidity, shareholder preferences, taxes, etc.

The questions in the minds of the finance manager while formulating a dividend policy can be:

- What are the firm's funds requirements in future?
- What are the future investment opportunities?
- What kind of business risks firm may face in future?
- What are the preferences of the shareholders?
- What are the tax implications by paying dividends?

How much debt repayments in future? There are two important elements before considering the dividend policy.

- Payout Ratio: Decision about Payout ratio i.e. percentage of EPS to be distributed to the shareholders.
- Stability of Dividends: How stable the dividends should be is also an important issue.

Factors Influencing Dividend Policy

- Firm's requirement for Investments and Other Financial Needs: Firms have to consider the future investment projects while deciding about the dividend policies. If the future demands saving for long term projects, it is better to retain earnings rather than distributing the dividends. In case firms distribute its earnings in form of dividends to the shareholders, it will have to raise funds externally and spend floatation costs. In practice, the firms follow this policy of retention of profits. Thus, priority should be to given to retention of earnings over dividends payments. It also depends on the types of firms – Growth firms have large number of investment projects which require them to keep the earnings to be utilized for the same whereas for mature firms the investment projects are few. Hence, these firms can distribute easily to the shareholders. It requires that a firm should have a target payout ratio which matches with the availability of future investment projects. Sometimes, companies' capital structures are also laden with debts which require financial obligations in the form of principal and interest payments. Such financial needs also force companies to plan for a payout which meets the needs of the shareholders and debt holders. Therefore, dividend policy is very much dependent on the companies' long term financial needs.

- Shareholders Expectations: The shareholders have diverse views when it comes to holding shares of a company. There are investors who are interested in capital gains while some want a steady flow of dividends. The reasons are age factor, risk appetite, financial needs, etc. of the investors. A retired elderly investor may prefer for a steady source of income whereas a young investor having a higher risk appetite may be interested in holding a stock for long term in the expectations of high capital gains. Sometimes, the investors plan their portfolios to plan their tax expenses as well. Institutional investors and retail investors too differ when an investing into dividend yielding stocks and stocks yielding capital gains. Therefore, the companies have to consider the conflicting interests of investors preferring capital gains as well as dividends. Also once a dividend policy is put into place; it should be not changed immediately. This can have a negative impact on the shareholders preferring dividends whereby they can shift their preferences to stocks of other companies giving better dividends.
- Constraints on Payment of Dividends: Companies have to undergo various constraints while deciding over their dividend policy which include liquidity, legal pressures etc.

The following are the constraints companies face:

- Liquidity: There is a difference between liquidity and profitability. If the cash flows of the companies are restricted, it will not be able to pay dividends even if it is having very high earnings. This situation is mostly faced by growth companies which enjoy reap in earnings but their liquidity position is tight as their cash is blocked in investment projects. Similarly, the mature companies having lesser investment plans in hand have cash flows available which can be distributed for paying dividends.
- Capital Market: Access to capital market is an important consideration when it comes to deciding dividend policy. Companies with higher cash flows and earnings with a track record are able to raise easily capital from the capital market and hence can pay dividends easily whereas it is vice versa for the firms with tightened liquidity and lower earnings. Also capital market is dependent on overall market conditions like political conditions, world market, etc.

- Inflationary conditions: During the times of inflation, the dividend payout is low. The reason is that the depreciation sinking fund is not sufficient to fund the new equipments available at high costs.

- Financial Leverage: Leverage refers to the amount of debt in the capital structure. If a firm is highly levered with lower profitability, then it is obliged to pay interest and principal amount to the debt holders before preference shareholders and equity shareholders. On the other hand, highly profitable firms even though highly levered can pay dividends easily to its shareholders.

- Legal Restrictions: Companies have to follow legalities before declaring dividends. For example, in India dividend should be paid after providing for depreciation.

- Dilution of Ownership: Shareholders do have concerns over their control over their company. If a company pays dividend, then the firm raises funds by issuing new shares as the cash flow reduces. But it adds to the new shareholder base resulting in dilution of ownership if the existing shareholders don't buy the new shares. In such situations, the company prefers that the dividend payment be avoided and investment plans be financed through existing cash flows only.

Stability of Dividends

Stability of dividends is the most desirable policy favored by companies and investors. It instills confidence in the shareholders to stay invested in the company and has a positive impact on the market price. Stability of dividends means regularity in payment of dividends even though there might be fluctuations in the earnings.

There are following ways by which firms can maintain stability of dividends – Constant Dividend per share, Constant Dividend Payout and Stable Dividend Plus Extra Dividend. we should first know the justification behind dividend stability.

- Investors' needs for current income: There is a class of investors which always prefer dividends over capital gains. The reason is that stable dividends act as current income for them like wages and salaries. These investors include retired, elderly people, widows, etc. For such investors, the expenses remain more or less constant over a time frame. Thus, they prefer the dividend stream should match their expense stream also. In case, the dividend policy changes, they may sell their shares and they have to bear transaction costs. This situation is quite inconvenient to them. Also such investors are ready to pay higher price for dividend paying stocks to avoid the inconveniences of selling the shares.

- Resolves Investors' uncertainty: Dividend decision conveys a good amount of information in the minds of investors. An increase in dividend payment signifies optimistic picture of firm's financial position whereas a decrease in dividends may be perceived as downfall in the future earnings prospects. An erratic dividend policy does not give any information about the company rather investors feel that the company's future is not bright enough. This kind of policy has a negative impact on the market price of its share. Firms should ideally vary dividends gradually when they expect changes in long term prospects.
- Raising Additional Finances: Stability of dividends ensures that a firm will be able to raise additional finance whenever it needs. The reason is that it has provided assurance and confidence to the investors community as they believe that investment in such a company will not result in speculation rather will prove a quality investment. Also a small investor looks forward to issues of such companies due to the reason that they want to supplement their income by stable dividend payments. Even issues of preference shares and debentures of such companies are also favored as the subscribers may feel that if the company is able to satisfy the current needs of the ordinary shareholders, undoubtedly, their interest and principal obligation will be done on time.
- Requirements of Institutional Investors: Institutional investors prefer to invest in companies which have a track record of paying stable dividends. Such investors include financial institutions educational and social institutions. The plausible rationale behind such investment is availability of huge amount of funds with them. Therefore, a stable dividend policy is followed by firms to get funds and satisfy the needs of institutional investors.

On the other hand, a stable dividend policy has drawbacks too. Once a stable dividend policy is set, it cannot be reversed. It tends to have an impact on the investors' attitudes. With a stable dividend policy, the firm is able to create a clientele who prefers dividend and they remain invested in the company. Whereas a dividend cut tends to give a negative impression about a company's financial prospects and the investors may pull out principal amount from the company. Thus, that is the reasoning behind maintaining a stable dividend policy. The solution can be to keep a dividend rate at a conservative figure. The other way out could be to provide extra dividends to signal an improvement in company's earnings. Even if the extra dividends are not paid regularly the investor will not mind but an instance of nonpayment of regular dividends brings a pessimistic reactions.

References

- Dividend-theories-and-policies-333080028: researchgate.net, Retrieved 04, March 2020
- Walter-model-theories-of-dividend: eduncle.com, Retrieved 28, August 2020
- Gordons-theory-on-dividend-policy: efinancemanagement.com, Retrieved 06, February 2020
- Modigliani-miller-theory-on-dividend-policy: efinancemanagement.com, Retrieved 23, June 2020

6

Management of Working Capital

Working capital management is aimed at ensuring the efficient operation of a company by using the present liabilities and assets in an efficient manner. The working capital can be broadly categorized into gross working capital and net working capital. The diverse aspects of working capital management as well as these types of working capital have been thoroughly discussed in this chapter.

Working capital can be understood as a measure of both a company's efficiency and its short-term financial health. For a layman, it simply means the difference between the current assets and current liabilities. It is the firm's holdings of current, or short-term, assets (such as cash).

Working capital is generally divided in two types, viz. gross working capital and net working capital. Gross Working Capital (GWC) is nothing but the total current or circulating assets. Net working capital, NWC (current assets minus current liabilities), provides an accurate assessment of the liquidity position of firm with the liquidity-profitability dilemma solidly authenticated in the financial scheme of obligations which mature within a twelve-month period.

The two main components of the working capital are assets and liabilities. First, short-term, or current liabilities constitute the portion of funds which have been planned for and raised. Since management must be concerned with proper financial structure, these and other funds must be raised judiciously. Short-term or current assets constitute a part of the asset investment decision and require diligent review by the firm's executives. Further, since there exists a close correlation between sales fluctuations and invested amounts in current assets, a careful maintenance of the proper asset and funds should be ensured.

Concept of Working Capital

Working capital typically means the firm's holdings of current, or short-term, assets such as cash, receivables, inventory, and marketable securities. Working capital refers to that part of firm's capital which is required for financing short-term or current assets such as cash, marketable securities, debtors, and inventories. In other words working capital is the amount of funds necessary to cover the cost of operating the enterprise.

Working capital means the funds (i.e.; capital) available and used for day-to-day operations (i.e.; working) of an enterprise. It consists broadly of that portion of assets of a business which are used in or related to its current operations. It refers to funds which are used during an accounting period to generate a current income of a type which is consistent with major purpose of a firm existence.

Working Capital is the money used to make goods and attract sales. The less Working Capital used to attract sales, the higher is likely to be the return on investment. Working Capital management is about the commercial and financial aspects of Inventory, credit, purchasing, marketing, and royalty and investment policy. The higher the profit margin, the lower is likely to be the level of Working Capital tied up in creating and selling titles. The faster that we create and sell the books the higher is likely to be the return on investment. Thus, when we have been using. There are two possible interpretations of working capital concept:

- Balance Sheet Concept
- Operating Cycle Concept

It goes without saying that the pattern of management will be very largely influenced by the approach taken in defining it.

Balance Sheet Concept

There are two interpretations of working capital under the balance sheet concept. It is represented by the excess of current assets over current liabilities and is the amount normally available to finance current operations. But, sometimes working capital is also used as a synonym for gross or total current assets. In that case, the excess of current assets over current liabilities is called the net working capital or net current assets. Economists like Mead, Malott, support the latter view of working capital. They feel that current assets should be considered as working capital as the whole of it helps to earn profits; and the management is more concerned with the total current assets as they constitute the total funds available for operational purposes. On the other hand, economists like Salvers uphold the former view. They argue that:

- In the long run what matters is the surplus of current asserts over current liabilities.
- It is this concept which helps creditors and investors to judge the financial soundness of the enterprise.
- What can always be relied upon to meet the contingencies, is the excess of current assets over the current liabilities since this amount is not to be returned.
- This definition helps to find out the correct financial position of companies having the same amount of current assets.

The conventional definition of working capital in terms of the difference between the current assets and the current liabilities is somewhat confusing. Working capital is really what a part of long-term finance is locked in and used for supporting current activities. Consequently, the larger the amount of working capital so derived, greater the proportion of long-term capital sources siphoned off to short-term activities. It is about tight working capital situation, the logic of the above definition would perhaps indicate diversion to bring in cash, under the conventional method, working capital would evidently remain unchanged. Liquidation of debtors and inventory into cash would also keep the level of working capital unchanged.

A relatively large amount of working capital according to this definition may produce a false sense of security at a time when cash resources may be negligible, or when these may be provided increasingly by long-term fund sources in the absence of adequate profits. Again, under the conventional method, cash enters into the computation of working capital. But it may have been more appropriate to exclude cash from such calculations because one compares cash requirements with current assets less current liabilities. The implication of this in conventional working capital computations is that during the financial period current assets get converted into cash which, after paying off the current liabilities, can be used to meet other operational expenses. The paradox, however, is that such current assets as are relied upon to yield cash must themselves to be supported by long-term funds until are converted into cash.

Importance of Working Capital

Working capital is a daily necessity for businesses, as they require a regular amount of cash to make routine payments, cover unexpected costs, and purchase basic materials used in the production of goods.

Efficient working capital management helps maintain smooth operations and can also help to improve the company's earnings and profitability. Management of working capital includes inventory management and management of accounts receivables and accounts payables. The main objectives of working capital management include maintaining the working capital operating cycle and ensuring its ordered operation, minimizing the cost of capital spent on the working capital, and maximizing the return on current asset investments.

Working capital is an easily understandable concept, as it is linked to an individual's cost of living and, therefore can be understood in a more personal way. Individuals need to collect the money that they are owed and maintain a certain amount on a daily basis to cover day-to-day expenses, bills, and other regular expenditures.

Working capital is a prevalent metric for the efficiency, liquidity and overall health of a company. It is a reflection of the results of various company activities, including revenue collection, debt management, inventory management and payments to suppliers. This is because it includes inventory, accounts payable and receivable, cash, portions of debt due within the period of a year and other short-term accounts.

The needs for working capital vary from industry to industry, and they can even vary among similar companies. This is due to several factors, including differences in collection and payment policies, the timing of asset purchases, the likelihood of a company writing off some of its past-due accounts receivable, and in some instances, capital-raising efforts a company is undertaking.

Working capital management is essentially an accounting strategy with a focus on the maintenance of a sufficient balance between a company's current assets and liabilities. An effective working capital management system helps businesses not only cover their financial obligations but also boost their earnings.

Managing working capital means managing inventories, cash, accounts payable and accounts receivable. An efficient working capital management system often uses key performance ratios, such as the working capital ratio, the inventory turnover ratio and the collection ratio, to help identify areas that require focus in order to maintain liquidity and profitability.

Factors Affecting Working Capital Requirements

The working capital requirement of a concern depends upon a large numbers of factors such as nature and size of business, the character of their operations, the length of production cycles, the rate of stock turnover and the state of economic situation. It is not possible to rank them because all such factors of different importance and the influence of individual factors changes for a firm overtime. However the following are important factors generally influencing the working capital requirement:

- Nature or Character of Business: The working capital requirement of a firm basically depends upon the nature of this business. Public utility undertakings like electricity water supply and railways need very limited working capital because they offer cash sales only and supply services, not products and as such no funds are tied up in inventories and receivables. Generally speaking it may be said that public utility undertakings require small amount of working capital, trading and financial firms require relatively very large amount, whereas manufacturing undertakings require sizable working capital between these two extremes.

- Size of Business/Scale of Operations: The working capital requirement of a concern is directly influenced by the size of its business which may be measured in terms of scale of operations.

- Production Policy: In certain industries the demand is subject to wide fluctuations due to seasonal variations. The requirements of working capital in such cases depend upon the production policy.

- Manufacturing Process/Length of Production Cycle: In manufacturing business the requirement of working capital increases in direct proportion of length of manufacturing process. Longer the process period of manufacture, larger is the amount of working capital required.
- Seasonal Variation: In certain industries raw material is not available throughout the year. They have to buy raw materials in bulk during the season to ensure and uninterrupted flow and process them during the entire year.
- Rate of Stock Turnover: There is a high degree of inverse co-relationship between the quantum of working capital; and the velocity or speed with which the sales are affected. A firm having a high rate of stock turnover will need lower amount of working capital as compared to affirm, having a low rate of turnover.
- Credit Policy: The credit policy of a concern in its dealing with debtors and creditors influence considerably the requirement of working capital. A concern that purchases its requirement on credit and sell its products/services on cash require lesser amount of working capital.
- Business Cycle: Business cycle refers to alternate expansion and contraction in general business activity. In a period of boom i.e., when the business is prosperous, there is a need of larger amount of working capital due to increase in sales, rise in prices, optimistic expansion of business contracts sales decline, difficulties are faced in collection from debtors and firms may have a large amount of working capital lying idle.
- Rate of Growth of Business: The working capital requirement of a concern increase with the growth and expansion of its business activities. Although it is difficulties to determine the relationship between the growth in the volume of business and the growth in the working capital of a business, yet it may be concluded that of normal rate of expansion in the volume of business, we may have retained profits to provide for more working capital but in fast growth in concern, we shall require larger amount of working capital.
- Price Level Changes: Changes in the price level also effect the working capital requirement. Generally the rising prices will require the firm to maintain larger amount of working capital as more funds will be required to maintain the same current assets.

Determinants of Working Capital

The requirements of working capital are not uniform in all enterprises, and therefore, factors responsible for a particular size of working capital in one company are different than in other enterprise. Therefore, a set pattern of factors determining the optimum size of working capital is difficult to suggest.

Nature of Business

It is an important factor for determining the amount of working capital needed by various companies. The trading or manufacturing concerns will require more amount of working capital along-with their fixed investment of stock, raw materials and finished products.

Public utilities and railway companies with huge fixed investment usually have the lowest needs for current assets, partly because of cash, nature of their business and partly due to their selling a service instead of a commodity. Similarly, basic and key industries or those engaged in the manufacture of producer's goods usually have less proportion of working capital to fixed capital than industries producing consumer goods.

Length of Period of Manufacture

The average length of the period of manufacture, i.e., the time which elapses between the commencement and end of the manufacturing process is an important factor in determining the amount of the working capital.

If it takes less time to make the finished product, the working capital required will be less. To give an example, a baker requires one night time to bake his daily quota of bread. His working capital is, therefore, much less than that of a shipbuilding concern which takes three to five years to build a ship. Between these two cases may fall other business concerns with varying periods of manufacture requiring different amounts of working capital.

Volume of Business

Generally, the size of the company has a direct relation with the working capital needs. Big concerns have to keep higher working capital for investment in current assets and for paying current liabilities.

The Proportion of the Cost of Raw Materials to Total Cost

Where the cost of raw materials to be used in manufacturing of a product is very large in proportion to the total cost and its final value, working capital required will also be more.

That is why, in a cotton textile mill or in a sugar mill, huge funds are required for this purpose. A building contractor also needs huge working capital for this reason. If the importance of materials is less, as for example in an oxygen company, the needs of working capital will be naturally not more.

Use of Manual Labour or Mechanisation

In labour intensive industries, larger working capital will be required than in the highly mechanized ones. The latter will have a large proportion of fixed capital. It may be remembered, however, that to some extent the decision to use manual labour or machinery lies with the management. Therefore, it is possible in most cases to reduce the requirements of working capital and increase investments in fixed assets and vice versa.

Need to keep Large Stocks of Raw Materials of Finished Goods

The manufacturing concerns generally have to carry stocks of raw materials and other stores and also finished goods. The larger the stocks (whether of raw materials or finished goods) more will be the needs of working capital. In certain lines of business, e.g., where the materials are bulky and have to be purchased in large quantities, (as in cement manufacturing), stock piling of raw-material is used.

Similarly, in public utilities, which must have adequate supplies of coal to assure regular service, stock piling of coal is necessary. In seasonal industries finished goods stocks have to be stored during off seasons. All these require large working capital.

Turnover of Working Capital

Turnover means the speed with which the working capital is recovered by the sale of goods. In certain businesses, sales are made quickly and the stocks are soon exhausted and new purchases have to be made. In this manner, a small amount of money invested in stocks will result in sales of much larger amount.

Considering the volume of sales, the amount of working capital requirements will be rather small in such type of business. There are other businesses where sales are made irregularly. For example, in case of jewellers, costly jewellery may remain locked up in the show-window for a long period before it catches the fancy of a rich lady.

In such cases, large sums of money have to be kept invested in stocks. But a baker or a news-hawker may be able to dispose of his stocks quickly, and may, therefore, need much smaller amounts by way of working capital.

Terms of Credit

A company purchasing all raw-materials for cash and selling on credit will be requiring more amount of working capital. Contrary to this, if the enterprise is in a position to buy on credit and sell it for cash, it will need less amount of working capital. The length of the period of credit has a direct bearing on working capital.

The essence of this is that the period which elapses between the purchase of materials and sale of finished goods and receipts of sale proceeds, will determine the requirements of working capital.

Seasonal Variations

There are some industries which either produce goods or make sales only seasonally. For example, the woolen textile industry makes its sales generally during winter. In both these cases the needs of working capital will be very large, during few months {i.e., season). The working capital requirements will gradually decrease as and when the sales are made.

Requirements of Cash

The need to have cash in hand to meet various requirements e.g., payment of salaries, rents, rates etc., has an effect on the working capital. The more the cash requirements the higher will be working capital needs of the company and vice versa.

Other Factors

There are also a number of other factors which affect the requirements of working capital. Some of them are given below.

- Degree of co-ordination between production and distribution policies.
- Specialisation in the field of distribution.
- Developments of means of transportation and communications.
- The hazards and contingencies inherent in the type of business.

Types of Working Capital

The concept of Working Capital includes current assets and current liabilities both. There are two concepts of working capital. They are Gross and Net Working Capital.

Gross Working Capital

Gross Working Capital refers to the firm's investment in Current Assets. Current assets are the assets, which can be converted into cash within an accounting year or operating cycle. It includes cash, short-term securities, debtors (account receivables or book debts), bills receivables and stock (inventory).

The concept of Gross Working Capital focuses attention on two aspects of current assets' management. They are:

- Optimizing Investment in Current Assets: Investment in Current Assets should be just adequate i.e., neither in excess nor deficit because excess investment increases liquidity but reduces profitability as idle investment earns nothing and inadequate amount of working capital can threaten the solvency of the firm because of its inability to meet its obligation. It is taken into consideration that the Working Capital needs of the firm may be fluctuating with changing business activities which may cause excess or shortage of Working Capital frequently and prompt management can control the imbalances.

- Way of Financing Current Assets: This aspect points to the need of arranging funds to finance Country Assets. It says whenever a need for working Capital arises; financing arrangement should be made quickly. The financial manager should have the knowledge of sources of the working capital funds as wheel as investment avenues where idle funds can be temporarily invested.

Net Working Capital

Net Working Capital refers to the difference between Current Assets and Current Liabilities are those claims of outsiders, which are expected to mature for payment within an accounting year. It includes creditors or accounts payables, bills payables and outstanding expenses. Net Working Capital can be positive or negative. A positive net working capital will arise when current assets exceed current liabilities and vice versa.

As compared with the gross working capital, net is a qualitative concept. It indicates the liquidity Notes position of and suggests the extent to which working Capital needs may be financed by permanent sources of funds. Current Assets should be optimally more than Current Liabilities. It also covers the point of right combination of long-term and short-term funds for financing current assets. For every firm a particular amount of net Working Capital is permanent. Therefore it can be financed with long-term funds.

Thus both concepts, Gross and Net Working Capital, are equally important for the efficient management of Working Capital. There are no specific rules to determine a firm's Gross and Net Working Capital but it depends on the business activity of the firm.

Every business concern should have neither redundant nor cause excess WC nor it should be short of WC. Both conditions are harmful and unprofitable for any business. But out of these two, the shortage of WC is more dangerous for the well-being of the firms.

Working capital may be of many types, but the most important of them all are equity capital, debt capital, speciality capital and sweat equity. Each of these is a separate category of financial and has its own benefits and characteristics.

Equity Capital

Equity capital can be understood as the invested money that is not repaid to the investors in the normal course of business. It represents the risk capital staked by the owners through purchase of the firm's common stock (ordinary shares). Its value is computed by estimating the current market value of everything owned by the firm from which the total of all liabilities is subtracted. On the balance sheet of the firm, equity capital is listed as stockholders' equity or owners' equity. Equity Capital is also known as equity financing, share capital, net worth and book value.

There are some businesses that are funded entirely with equity capital (cash written by the shareholders or owners into the company that have no offsetting liabilities.) Although it is the favored form for most people because you cannot go bankrupt, it can be extraordinarily expensive and require massive amounts of work to grow your enterprise.

Debt Capital

Debt capital is the capital that a business raises by taking out a loan. It is a loan made to a company that is normally repaid at some future date. Debt capital ranks higher than equity capital for the repayment of annual returns. This means that legally, the interest on debt capital must be repaid in full before any dividends are paid to any suppliers of equity.

Debt capital is that type of capital which is infused into a business with the understanding that it must be paid back at a predetermined future date. In the meantime, the owner of the capital (typically a bank, bondholders, or a wealthy individual), agree to accept interest in exchange for you using their money.

The suppliers of debt capital usually receive a contractually fixed annual percentage return on their loan, and this is known as the coupon rate. Think of interest expense as the cost of "renting" the capital to expand your business; it is often known as the cost of capital. For many young businesses, debt can be the easiest way to expand because it is relatively easy to access. The profits for the owners is the difference between the return on capital and the cost of capital.

Specialty Capital

This is the gold standard. There are a few sources of capital that have almost no economic cost and can take the limits off of growth. They include things such as a negative cash conversion cycle (vendor financing), insurance float, etc.

Negative Cash Conversion Cycle (Vendor Financing)

Imagine you own a retail store. To expand your business, you need ` 1 Million in capital to open a new location. Most of this is the result of needing to go out, buy your inventory, and stock your shelves with merchandise. You wait and hope that one day customers come in and pay you. In the meantime, you have capital (either debt or equity capital) tied up in the business in the form of inventory.

Now, imagine if you could get your customers to pay you before you had to pay for your merchandise. This would allow you to carry far more merchandise than your capitalization structure would otherwise allow.

Typically, vendor financing can be measured in part by looking at the percentage of inventories to accounts payable (the higher the percentage, the better), and analyzing the cash conversion cycle; the more days "negative", the better. Dell Computer was famous for its nearly two or three week negative cash conversion cycle which allowed it to grow from a college dorm room to the largest computer company in the world with little or no debt in less than a single generation.

Insurance Float

Insurance companies that collect money and can generate income by investing the funds before paying it them out in the future in the form of policyholder payouts when a car is damaged, or replacing a home when destroyed in a tornado, are in a very good place.

Float is money that a company holds but does not own. It has all of the benefits of debt but none of the drawbacks; the most important consideration is the cost of capital – that is, how much money it costs the owners of a business to generate float. In exceptional cases, the cost can actually be negative; that is, you are paid to invest other people's money plus you get to keep the income from the investments. Other businesses can develop forms of float but it can be very difficult.

Sweat Equity

There is also a form of capital known as sweat equity which can be explained as equity acquired by a company's executives on favorable terms, to reflect the value the executives have added and will continue to add to the company. This type of equity results when an owner bootstraps operations by putting in long hours at a low rate of pay per hour making up for the lack of capital necessary to hire sufficient employees to do the job well and let them work an ordinarily forty hour workweek.

Although it is largely intangible and does not count as financial capital, it can be estimated as the cost of payroll saved as a result of excess hours worked by the owners. The hope is that the business will grow fast enough to compensate the owner for the low-pay, long-hour sweat equity infused into the enterprise.

Operating Cycle

When the finished goods are sold on credit terms receivables balances will be formed. When the receivables are collected, it is again converted into cash. The need for working capital arises because of time gap between production of goods and their actual realization after sales. This time gap is called technically called as 'operating cycle' or 'working capital cycle'.

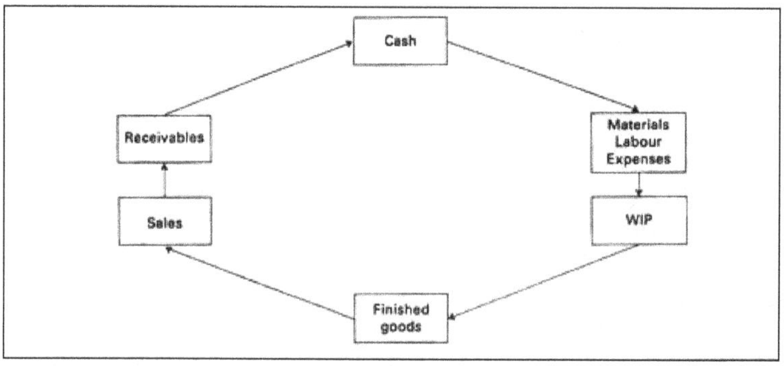

The operating cycle of a company consists of time period between the procurement of inventory and the collection of cash from receivables. The operating cycle is the length of time between the company's outlay on raw materials, wages and other expenses and inflow of cash from sale of goods. Operating cycle is an important concept in management of cash and management of working capital.

The operating cycle reveals the time that elapses between outlay of cash and inflow of cash. Quicker the operating cycle less amount of investment in working capital is needed and it improves the profitability. The duration of the operating cycle depends on the nature of industry and the efficiency in working capital management. The above said periods are ascertained as follows:

- Raw Material Holding Period:

$$\frac{\text{Average raw material stock}}{\text{Average consumption of raw material}/365}$$

- Work-In-Process Period:

$$\frac{\text{Average work}-\text{in}-\text{progress}}{\text{Average cost of goods}/365}$$

- Finished Goods Holding Period:

$$\frac{\text{Average finished goods stock}}{\text{Average cost of goods}/365}$$

- Receivables Collection Period:

$$\frac{\text{Average receivables}}{\text{Average sales}/365}$$

- Creditors Payment Period:

$$\frac{\text{Average creditors}}{\text{Average purchase of raw materials} / 365}$$

The knowledge of operating cycle is essential for smooth running of the business without shortage of working capital. The working capital requirement can be estimated with the help of duration of operating cycle. The longer the operating cycle, the larger the working capital requirements. If depreciation is excluded from expenses in the operating cycle, the net operating cycle represents 'cash conversion cycle'.

The length of operating cycle is the indicator of efficiency in management of short-term funds and working capital. The operating cycle calls for proper monitoring of external environment of the business. Changes in government policies like taxation, import restrictions, credit policy of central bank etc. will have impact on the length of operating cycle.

It is the task of Finance manager to manage the operating cycle effectively and efficiently. Based on the length of operating cycle, the working capital finance is done by the commercial banks. The reduction in operating cycle will improve the cash conversion cycle and ultimately improve the profitability of the firm.

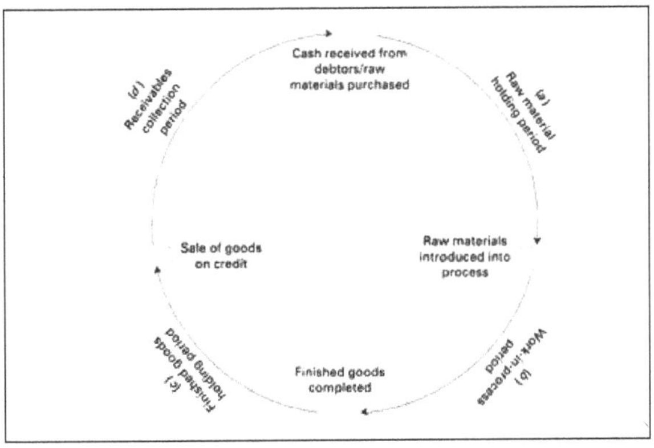

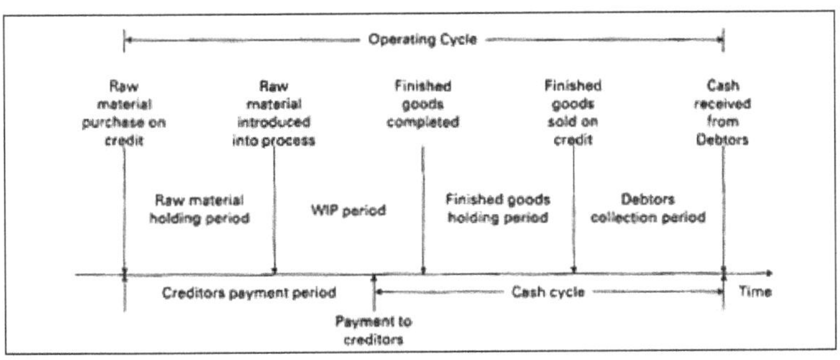

Now, the period of operating cycle can be ascertained as follows:	(Days)
Raw materials holding period	xx
Work-in-progress	xx

Finished goods holding period	xx
Receivables collection period	xx
Gross Operating Cycle	xx
Less: Creditors payment period	xx
Net operating cycle	xx

Reasons for Prolonged Operating Cycle

The following could be the reasons for longer operating cycle period:

- Purchase of materials in excess/short of requirements.
- Buying inferior, defective materials.
- Failure to get trade discount, cash discount.
- Inability to purchase during seasons.
- Defective inventory policy.
- Use of protracted manufacturing cycle.
- Lack of production planning, coordination and control.
- Mismatch between production policy and demand.
- Use of outdated machinery, technology.
- Poor maintenance and upkeep of plant, equipment and infrastructure facilities,
- Defective credit policy and slack collection policy.
- Inability to get credit from suppliers, employees.
- Lack of proper monitoring of external environment etc.

How to Reduce Operating Cycle?

The aim of every management should be to reduce the length of operating cycle or the number of operating cycles in a year, only then the need for working capital decreases. The following remedies may be used in contrasting the length of operation cycle period.

Purchase Management

The purchase manager owes a responsibility in ensuring availability of right type of materials in right quantity of right quality at right price on right time and at right place. These six R's contribute greatly in the improvement of length of operating cycle. Further, streamlining of credit from supplier and inventory policy also help the management.

Production Management

The Production manager affects the length of operating cycle by managing and controlling manufacturing cycle, which is a part of operating cycle and influences directly. Longer the manufacturing cycle, longer will be the operating cycle and higher will be the firm's working capital requirements. The following measures may be taken like:

- Proper maintenance of plant, machinery and other infrastructure facilities.
- Proper planning and coordination at all levels of activity.
- Up-gradation of manufacturing system, technology.
- Selection of the shortest manufacturing cycle out of various alternatives etc.

Marketing Management

The sale and production policies should be synchronized as far as possible. Lack of matching increases the operating cycle period. Production of qualitative products at lower costs enhances sales of the firm and reduces finished goods storage period. Effective advertisement, sales promotion activities, efficient salesmanship, use of appropriate distribution channel etc., reduce the storage period of the finished products.

Credit Collection Policies

Sound credit and collection policies enable the Finance manager in minimizing investment in working capital in the form of book debts. The firm should be discretionary in granting credit terms to its customers.

In order to see that the receivable conversion period is not increased, the firm should follow a rationalized credit policy based on the credit standing of customers and other relevant facts. The firm should be prompt in making collections. Slack collection policies will tie-up funds for long period, increasing length of operating cycle.

External Environment

The length of operating cycle is equally influenced by external environment. Abrupt changes in basic conditions would affect the length of operating cycle. Fluctuations in demand, competitors, production and sales policies, government fiscal and monetary policies, changes on import and export front, price fluctuations, etc., should be evaluated carefully by the management to minimize their adverse impact on the length of operating cycle.

Personnel Management

The Personnel manager by framing sound recruitment, selection, training, placement, promotion, transfer, wages, incentives and appraisal policies can contrast the length of operating cycle.

Use of Human Resources Development technique in the organization enhances the morale and zeal of employees thereby reduces the length of operating cycle. Proper maintenance of plant, machinery, infrastructure facilities, timely replacement, renewals, overhauling etc., will contribute towards the control of operating cycle.

Computation of Working Capital

The two components of Working Capital (WC) are Current Assets (CA) and Current Liabilities (CL). They have a bearing on the cash operating cycle. In order to calculate the working capital needs, what is required is the holding period of various types of inventories, the credit collection period and the credit payment period. Working capital also depends on the budgeted level of activity in terms of production/sales. The calculation of WC is based on the assumption that the production/sales is carried on evenly throughout the year and all costs accrue similarly.

As the working capital requirements are related to the cost excluding depreciation and not to the sale price, WC is computed with reference to cash cost. The cash cost approach is comprehensive and superior to the operating cycle approach based on holding period of debtors and inventories and payment period of creditors. The steps involved in estimating the different items of CA and CL are given below.

Estimation of Current Assets

1. Raw Materials Inventory: The investment in raw materials inventory is estimated on the:

$$\frac{\underset{\text{(in units)}}{\text{Budgeted production}} \times \underset{\text{per unit}}{\text{Cost of raw materials}} \times \underset{\text{(months/days)}}{\text{Average inventory holding period}}}{12\,\text{months}/365\,\text{days}}$$

2. Work-in-Process (W/P) Inventory: The relevant costs to determine work-in-process inventory Notes are the proportionate share of cost of raw materials and conversion costs (labour and manufacturing overhead costs excluding depreciation). In case, full unit of raw material is required in the beginning, the unit cost of work-in-process would be higher, that is, cost of full unit + 50 per cent of conversion cost, compared to the raw material requirement throughout the production cycle; W/P is normally equivalent to 50 per cent of total cost of production. Symbolically,

$$\frac{\underset{\text{(in units)}}{\text{Budgeted production}} \times \underset{\text{per unit inventory}}{\text{Estimated work-in-progress cost}} \times \underset{\text{(months/days)}}{\text{Average time span or work-in-progress}}}{12\,\text{months}/365\,\text{days}}$$

3. Finished Goods Inventory: Working capital required to finance the finished goods inventory is given by factors summed up in 12 months/365 days.

Debtors: The WC tied up in debtors should be estimated in relation to total cost price.

$$\frac{\underset{\text{(in units)}}{\text{Budgeted credit sales}} \times \underset{\text{per unit inventory}}{\text{Cost of sales per unit}} \times \underset{\text{(months/days)}}{\text{Average debt collection period}}}{2\,\text{months} / 365\,\text{days}}$$

4. Cash and Bank Balances: Apart from WC needs for financing inventories and debtors, firms also find it useful to have some minimum cash balances with them. It is difficult to lay down the exact procedure of determining such an amount. This would primarily be based on the motives for holding cash balances of the business firm, attitude of management toward risk, the access to the borrowing sources in times of need and past experience, and so on.

Estimation of Current Liabilities

The working capital needs of business firms are lower to the extent where such needs are met through the current liabilities (other than bank credit) arising in the ordinary course of business. The important current liabilities, in this context are, trade-creditors, wages and overheads:

$$\frac{\text{Trade creditor } \underset{\text{(in units)}}{\text{budgeted yearly production}} \times \underset{\text{per unit}}{\text{Raw material cost}} \times \underset{\text{(months/days)}}{\text{Credit period allowed by creditors}}}{12\,\text{months} / 365\,\text{days}}$$

$$\frac{\text{Directed wages } \underset{\text{(in units)}}{\text{budgeted yearly production}} \times \underset{\text{per unit}}{\text{Direct labor cost}} \times \underset{\text{(months/days)}}{\text{Average time} - \text{lag in payment of wages}}}{12\,\text{months} / 365\,\text{days}}$$

The average credit period for the payment of wages approximates to a half-a-month in the case of monthly wage payment. The first day's monthly wages are paid on the 30th day of the month, extending credit for 29 days, the second day's wages are, again, paid on the 30th, extending credit for 28 days, and so on. Average credit period approximates to half-a-month.

Overheads (Other than Depreciation and Amortisation)

$$\frac{\underset{\text{(in units)}}{\text{Budgeted yearly production}} \times \underset{\text{per unit}}{\text{Overhead cost}} \times \underset{\text{(months/days)}}{\text{Average time} - \text{lag in payment of overheads}}}{12\,\text{months} / 365\,\text{days}}$$

The amount of overheads may be separately calculated for different types of overheads. In the case of selling overheads, the relevant item would be sales volume instead of production volume. The computation of working capital is summarized in format.

1. Estimation of Current Asset: Amount:

- Minimum desired cash and bank balances.
- Inventories, Raw material, Work-in-process, Finished Goods.
- Debtors, Total Current Assets.

2. Estimation of Current Liabilities:

- Creditors
- Wages
- Overheads, Total Current Liabilities

3. Net Working Capital:

- Add: Margin for contingency

4. Net Working Capital Required:

- If payment is received in advance, the item would be listed in CL.
- If advance payment is to be made to creditors, the item would appear under CA. The same would be the treatment for advance payment of wages and overheads.

Management of Cash

Cash generally refers to the coins, currency and cash equivalents like cheques, drafts, demand deposits, marketable securities, time deposits and so on. However, cash as such does not have any earning power but still people hold cash because of the following motives.

Motives of Holding Cash

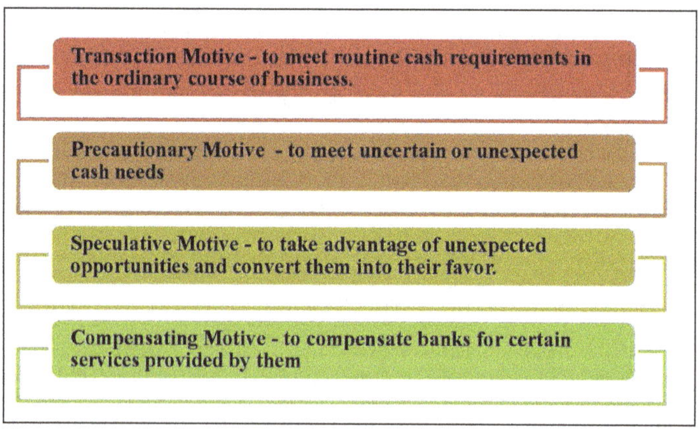

Objectives of Cash Management

There are two main objectives of Cash Management:

- To meet the cash disbursement needs.
- To minimize funds committed to cash balances.

These objectives though contradictory, but have to be achieved in order to manage cash effectively.

To Meet the Cash Disbursement Needs

In the ordinary course of business certain cash payments and cash receipts take place on a regular basis. Thus, businesses need to maintain sufficient cash to meet the cash disbursement needs. Advantages of maintaining sufficient cash can be summarized as below:

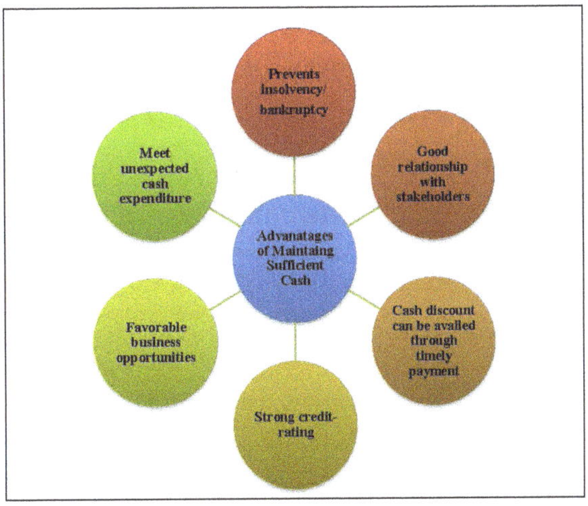

Advantages of Maintaining Sufficient Cash Balance.

To Minimize Funds Committed to Cash Balances

Though it is important to maintain sufficient cash balances as can be seen from the figure above, but at the same time, if large funds are lying idle, firm is losing out the money and not earning anything. Thus, optimal level of cash balances need to be maintained which is neither too high, nor too low.

Factors Determining Cash Needs

Following are the factors which determine the cash needs:

- Synchronization of Cash Flows: Cash balance needs to be maintained as cash receipts and cash payments occur at different times and in different amounts. If they reconcile at all times, the need for maintaining cash balance will be eliminated. Synchronization can be achieved by preparing a cash budget, which will determine the time period when the firm has excess or shortage of cash.
- Short costs: In case there is a cash shortage, the firm may have to bear the burden of extra cost occurring due to the shortfall. Such costs include:
    - Borrowing Costs,

   - Transaction Costs,
   - Loss of cash discounts,
   - Penalty costs,
   - Loss in credit rating leading to higher interest rates in future, etc.

- Excess cash balance costs: If the firm has excess cash, then also it bears the cost in the form of opportunity lost to earn interest on the excess cash, which could otherwise be invested elsewhere.
- Procurement needs: These are costs associated with establishing and operating cash management activities.
- Uncertainty: As the business operates in uncertainty, there are certain costs which crop up suddenly like immediate demand by supplier to make the payment, sudden rise in prices of raw materials, etc.

Cash Management Models

Cash management models aim to minimize the cost and obtain the optimum level of cash balance.

Baumol's Model–Cash Model Under Certainty

According to this model there are two types of costs which need to be minimized:

- Cost of converting marketable securities into cash.
- Lost opportunity cost.

It considers cash management similar to an inventory management problem.

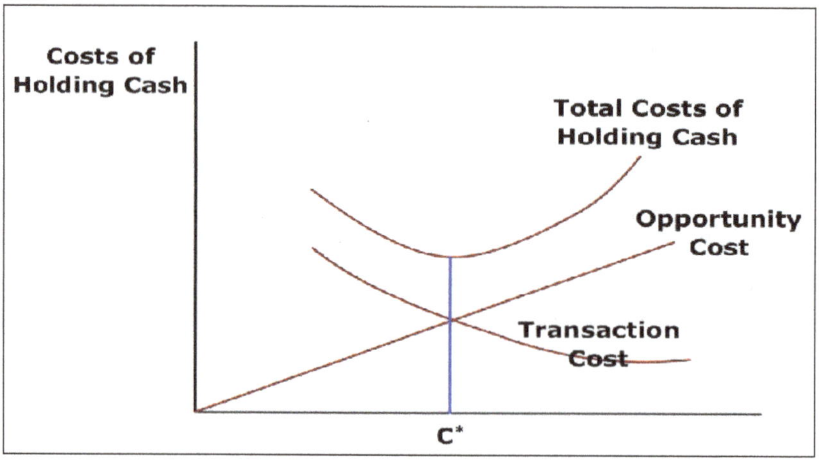

Cost trade-off: Baumol's Model.

The model can be summarized as follows:

$$C = \sqrt{\frac{2bT}{i}}$$

Where,

- C denotes optimal conversion amount per transaction,
- b denotes cost of conversion into cash per transaction,
- T denotes projected cash requirement during the planning period,
- i denotes opportunity interest rate per planning period.

Example: PQR Ltd. requires Rs. 50 lakhs in cash to meet its transaction needs during the next quarter. It holds marketable securities of equal amount. Annual yield on the marketable securities is 15%. The conversion of these securities into cash entails a fixed cost of Rs. 5,000 per transaction. Using Baumol's Model, compute the amount of marketable securities converted into cash per order.

Solution:

$$C = \sqrt{\frac{2bT}{i}} = \sqrt{\frac{2 \times 5\ \text{Rs.}5{,}000 \times \text{Rs.}50{,}00{,}000}{0.0375}} = \text{Rs}\,11{,}54{,}700.54$$

Annual yield @ 15%/4 = 0.0375.

Thus, the amount of marketable securities, which can be converted into cash per order is Rs. 11,54,700.54 as per Baumol's Model.

Miller-Orr Model–Cash Model Under Uncertainty

According to this model, effective cash management helps to determine the optimal cash balance level, which will minimize the cost of cash management. Further, this model assumes that the cash balances randomly fluctuate between an upper bound and a lower bound. The aim of this model is to reach the optimal bound (z) of the cash balance level. Symbolically,

$$z = \sqrt{\frac{3br^2}{4i}}$$

Where,

- z denotes the optimal cash balance or the return point,
- b denotes the fixed cost per conversion,

- r^2 denotes the variance of the daily changes in cash balances,
- i denotes the daily interest rate earned on the marketable securities.

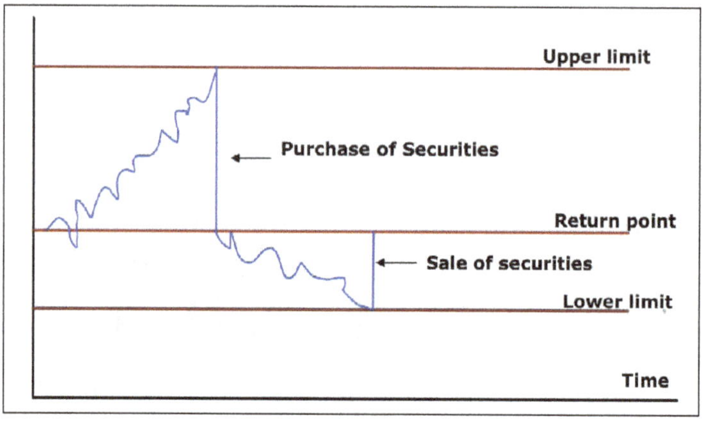

Miller-Orr Model.

In case, the cash balance reaches the upper bound (h), then firm has excess cash, which can be used to buy marketable securities and bring the cash level to the optimal level z. In case, the cash balance reaches the lower bound (o), then firm must sell or convert the marketable securities into cash to reach the optimal cash level by z.

Optimum upper Cash Bound is three times the optimal cash balance or Symbolically, h = 3z.

Example: The management of ABCL Ltd. anticipates Rs. 25 lakhs in cash outlays during the next financial year. The recent experience has been that it costs Rs. 20 to convert marketable securities into cash. The marketable securities currently earn 10% annual return. Also, the variance of daily net cash flows is estimated to be Rs. 30,000. Show the cash balances as per Miller-Orr Model.

Solution:

$$\text{Return point} = z = \sqrt{\frac{3 \times \text{Rs.}20 \times \text{Rs.}30{,}000}{4 \times 0.000278}} = \text{Rs}\,40{,}233.13$$

$$\text{Daily portfolio return} = (10\% \div 360 \text{ days}) = 0.000278$$

$$\text{Upper bound} = 3 \text{ X } 40{,}233.13 = \text{Rs. } 1{,}20{,}699.39$$

Thus, the cash balance of ABCL Ltd. would be allowed to vary between 0 (zero) and Rs. 1,20,699.39. When the upper bound is reached Rs. 80,466.26 (Rs.1,20,699.39 – Rs.40,233.13) would be converted to the marketable securities. And if cash balance falls to zero, Rs.40,233.13 (Rs.40,233.13 – Rs.0) would be converted from marketable securities into cash. This will ensure that the optimum cash balance will be ensured.

Cash Budget

One of the most important tools of effective cash management is the Cash Budget. It is a statement showing the estimated cash inflows and cash outflows during the planning period. Thus, cash budget highlights the net cash position (surplus or deficit) of the firm in the particular planning period undertaken. There are various advantages of preparing a cash budget as shown by the figure below:

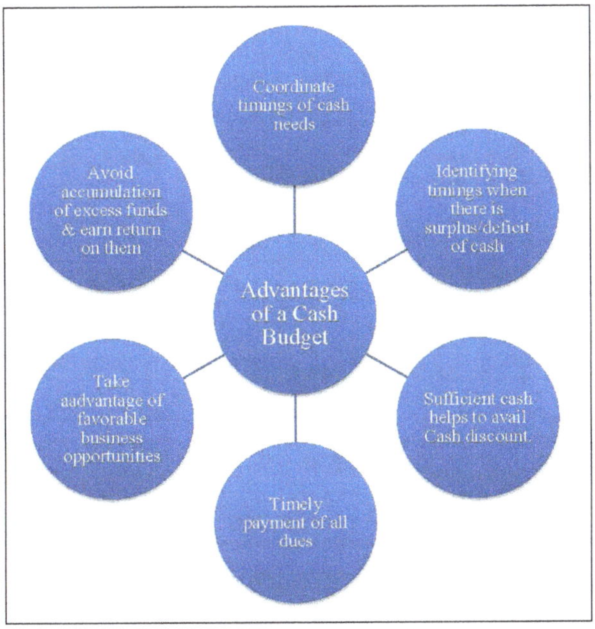

Advantages of a Cash Budget.

Steps undertaken to prepare a cash budget are:

- Step 1: Selection of planning period – The first step to prepare the cash budget is to identify the period for which the cash budget is to be prepared. The planning period differs from firm to firm. It should be neither too long nor too short. The budget can be prepared on a yearly, quarterly, monthly, weekly, daily or seasonal basis depending on the circumstances of the case.
- Step 2: Selection of factors affecting the cash flows –The next step is to identify and select the factors of cash flow. Only cash items are to be included. Generally two types of cash flows can be there: operating cash flows, which are generated by operations of the firm and financial cash flows, which are generated by financial activities of the firm.
    - Operating Cash Flows examples: Cash sales, purchases, salary payments, accounts receivable, accounts payable, etc.
    - Financial Cash Flows examples: Loans/borrowings, income tax payments/ refunds, interest received/paid, dividends received/paid, etc.

- Step 3: Construction of Cash Budget – The final step after deciding the planning period and identifying the operating and financial cash flows is the construction of the cash budget.

Example: Prepare cash budget for Ram Associates for the first three months of 2014:

1. No change in prices and costs.

2. Credit Sales are 80% of total sales.

3. 50% of credit sales are collected after 1 month, 30% after 2 months and 20% after 3 months.

4. Actual and forecast sales are:

Actual	Rs.	Forecast	Rs.
Oct 2013	1,00,000	Jan 2014	70,000
Nov 2013	1,10,000	Feb 2014	90,000
Dec 2013	90,000	Mar 2014	1,00,000
		Apr 2014	1,20,000

5. Company expects a profit margin of 25%.

6. Anticipated sales of each month are purchased and paid in the preceding month.

7. Anticipated operating expenses are as follows:

Forecast	Rs.
Jan 2014	10,000
Feb 2014	15,000
Mar 2014	12,000

8. Interest on 10% bonds, Rs. 1,00,000 is to be paid in each quarter.

9. Company has a cash balance of Rs. 10,000 at 31 Dec 2012, which is the minimum balance to be maintained. Funds can be borrowed in multiples of Rs. 2,000 on a monthly basis at 12% p.a.

10. Interest is payable on first of the month of the borrowing.

11. Rent is Rs.4,000 per month.

Solution: Cash Budget for Ram Associates for the three month period Jan-Mar 2014.

Particulars	Actual 2013				Forecast 2014		
	Oct	Nov	Dec	Jan	Feb	Mar	
A. CASH RECEIPTS (Rs.)							
Total Sales		1,00,000	1,10,000	90,000	70,000	90,000	1,00,000

Credit Sales	80,000	88,000	72,000	56,000	72,000	80,000
Cash sales collection	20,000	22,000	18,000	14,000	18,000	20,000
1 month 50%	-	40,000	44,000	36,000	28,000	36,000
2 months 30%	-	-	24,000	26,400	21,600	16,800
3 months 20%	-	-	-	16,000	17,600	14,400
Total receipts (A)				92,400	85,200	87,200
B. CASH PAYMENTS (Rs.)						
Purchases				67,500	75,000	90,000
Rent				4,000	4,000	4,000
Operating Expenses				10,000	15,000	12,000
Interest				-	-	2,500
Total receipts (A)				81,500	94,000	1,08,500
C. CASH BALANCE (Rs.)						
Net Cash Balance (A-B)				10,900	(8,800)	(21,300)
Previous balance brought forward				10,000	20,900	12,100
Total Cash				20,900	12,100	(9,200)
Beginning of month borrowings				-		20,000
Interest on borrowings				-	-	(200)
Total end of month cash balance				20,900	12,100	10,600

Techniques of Cash Management

Cash management techniques can be divided into two broad heads:

- Speedy collection of receivables.
- Slowing disbursements.

Specific techniques for speedy collections of receivables are:

- Speedy cash collections: Customers should be encouraged to pay as early as possible. This can be done by offering cash discounts if they pay early.
- Early conversion of payments into cash: The payments should be converted into cash at the earliest. There may be a lag time as to when the cheque is prepared and when it is converted into cash. This time needs to be minimized.
- Concentration Banking: This is a collection procedure in which payments are dispersed to collection centers, and then deposited in local banks for quick clearing.
- Lockbox System: This is a collection procedure in which payers send their payments to nearby post-office lock-box. The local banks collect the payments from this lock-box several times during the year and deposit it in the firm's accounts.

Specific techniques for slowing disbursements are:

- Avoidance of early payments: Firm should make the payment as late as possible but before the due date to avoid any penalty and interest charges.
- Centralized disbursements: The payments should be routed through the head office. This will delay the payments and cash can be reserved for several other reasons.
- Float: This refers to the difference in bank balance and book balance of the chequebook. This arises because there is a time gap between when the cheque is written and when it is encashed.
- Accruals: These are current liabilities for a good or service received but not yet paid for. E.g. payroll to employees, rent to be paid, taxes to government, etc. The longer the period, after which the payment is made, greater is the amount of cash with the firm, which can be used elsewhere.

Management of Receivables

Receivables are one of the most important components of current assets. Receivables generally refer to the debt, which the customers owe to the firm from sale of goods or services in the ordinary course of business. When a sale of a good or service takes place in the ordinary course of business and customers do not pay in cash, the firms allow a reasonable period of time for which the credit is extended. This is represented as accounts receivable in the balance sheet of the firm. In today's competitive times, offering credit sales is integral to majority of the businesses. At one end, it helps the business to boost its top line and bottom line, at the other end; it generates risk and cost for the firm.

Costs and Benefits of Receivable Management

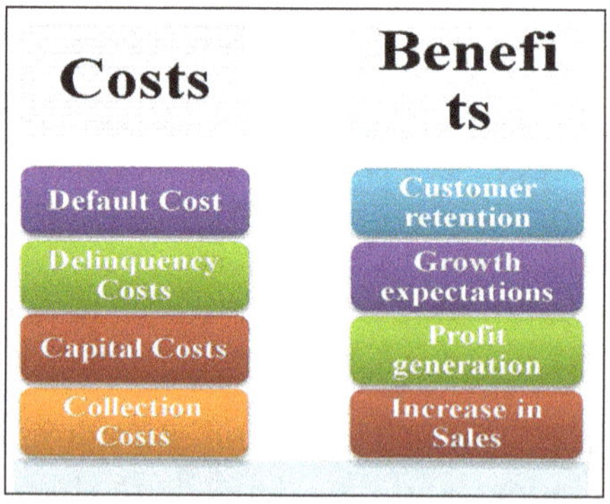

The firms need to do a trade-off between the costs and benefits associated with receivables management. The trade-off between the two helps in determining the optimum level of receivables.

Costs of Receivable Management

- Collection Cost: These are costs incurred in collecting receivables from customers to whom credit sales are made.
- Capital cost: While extending credit, the firms incur additional costs to meet its obligations, when the funds could have been deployed elsewhere. This happens because there is a time gap between when sales are made and when payment is received.
- Delinquency Costs: These refer to the costs, which occur due to failure of the customers to pay within the credit period. Thus, due to failure to receive payment in a timely manner, firms incur additional costs to recover its dues. Examples include reminders, legal notices, etc.
- Default Costs: These represent bad debts, as customers do not pay their dues. Here the firms incur costs as customers fail to make any payment even after repeated reminders.

Benefits of Receivable Management

- Increase in Sales: Firms offer the option of both cash and credit sales to customers in order to boost it sales.
- Profit generation: Credit sales also help in increase in bottom line (profits) along with increase in the top line (sales). Further, it also aids in dealing with competition effectively.
- Growth expectations: With expectations of increase in sales and profits, it provides for further growth and expansion of the firm.
- Customer retention: This also helps in ensuring customer loyalty towards the firm. It is useful for retaining existing customers as well as attracting new customers.

Various Dimensions of Receivables Management

The various aspects of Receivables Management are to decide upon.

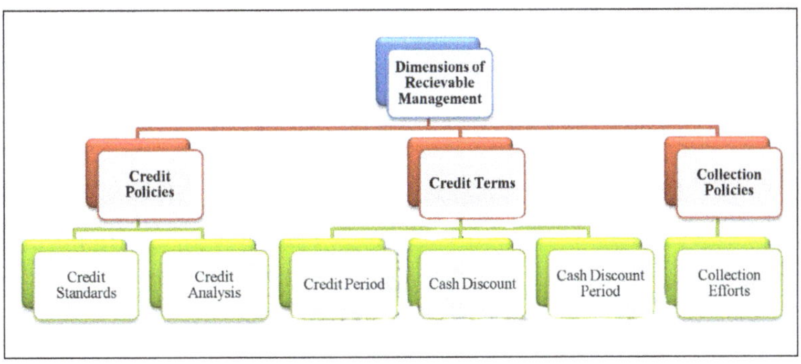

Aspects of Receivables Management.

Credit Policies

The main decision while extending credit includes determining whether the customer should be given credit or not. In case credit is extended, for how much period should the credit be allowed?

Credit Standards

Credit Standards represent the basic conditions for offering credit to customers. These could include credit standing of the customers, credit references, etc. The credit standards can be:

- Tight credit standards: Less credit will be extended.
- Liberal credit standards: More credit can be extended easily.

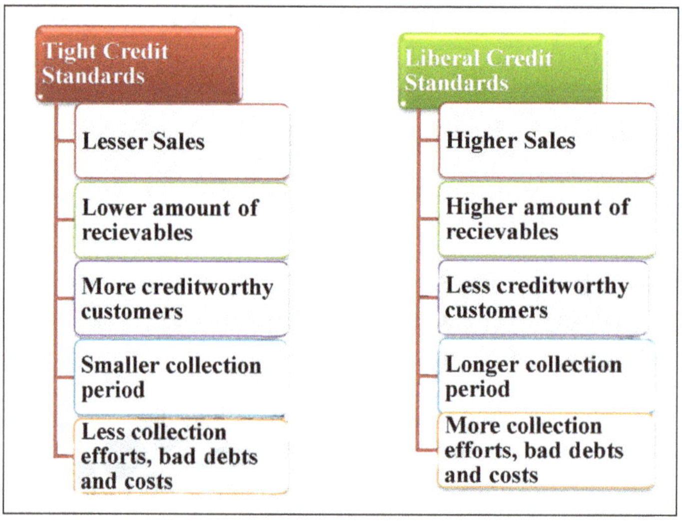

Comparison in types of Credit Standards.

Credit Analysis

Credit Analysis refers to obtaining the information about credit and then analyzing it. Just setting the credit standards is not enough. Based on the credit information analyzed, the decisions for credit policy are undertaken. Credit analysis, thus, helps in knowing the credit worthiness of the customers. Credit information can be obtained through:

- Internal Sources like forms and documents submitted by customers, historical payment pattern, etc.
- External Sources like credit rating, bank references, financial statements, etc. Analyzing of the credit information can be through:
    - Quantitative methods like preparation of Aging Schedules, undertaking ratio analysis, trend analysis, etc.

- Qualitative methods like subjective interpretation of various financial statements, references from suppliers, other creditors, banks, financial institutions, etc.

Credit analysis is done on the following basis:

- Character: This shows the willingness of the customer to make the payment. This can be judged from past payment record of the customers.
- Capacity: This represents the ability of the customer to pay. This can be judged by the amount of capital, financial standing and past payment records of the customer.
- Capital: This determines whether the customer has the necessary cash flows to make the payment as and when it is due.
- Collateral: Sometimes the customer offers certain security to make the payment or generate the cash flows. Such security is known as collateral.
- Conditions: These are the economic circumstances, which might have an effect on the customer's ability to pay.

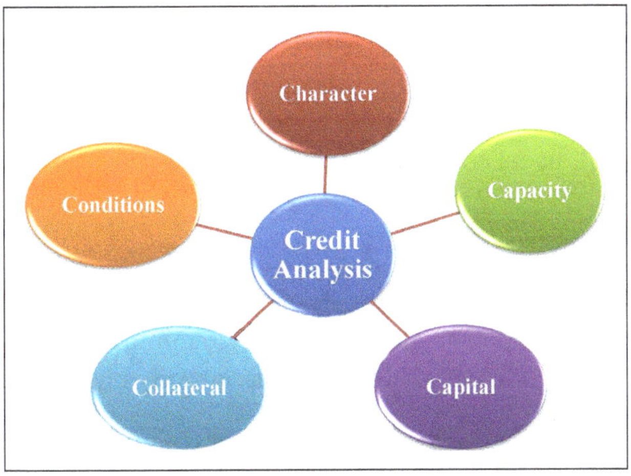

Parameters affecting the Credit analysis.

Credit Terms

Credit Terms refer to the terms and conditions under which the credit will be extended to the customers. Thus, they emphasize on the repayment conditions of the receivables. Its three main components are:

- Cash discount is an advantage available to the customer to pay the overdue amount early and avail the discount. Thus, the total amount to be paid gets reduced by the discount amount. (Change in profits as profits will tend to increase with less bad debts and high sales; and will tend to decrease with decrease in prices).

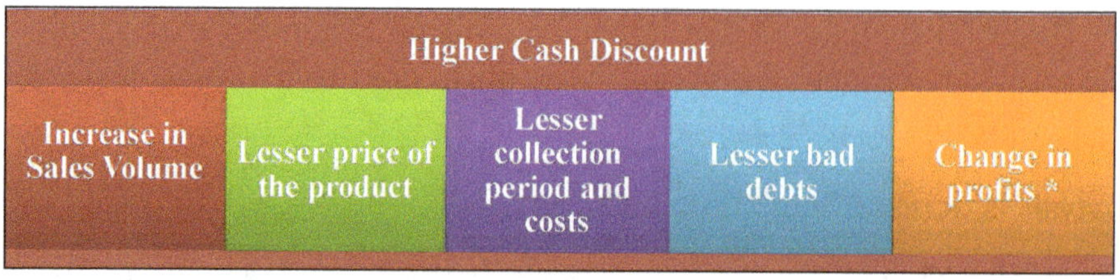

Implications of higher cash discount.

- Cash discount period refers to the period till when the cash discount can be availed.
- Credit period refers to the period till which credit can be extended. The more the average collection period, more the collection effort involved.

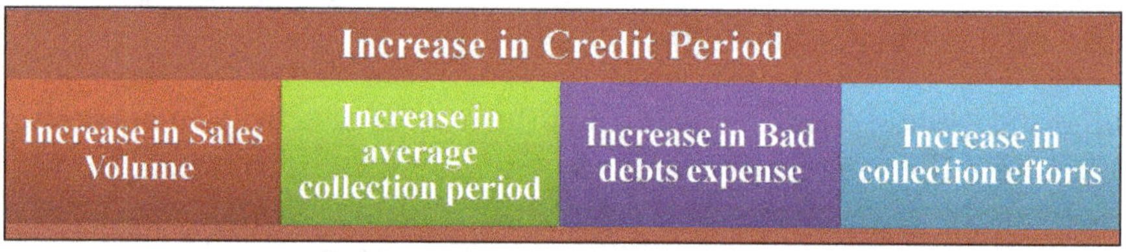

Implications of increasing the credit period.

Example of Credit terms seen in a common policy can be like "3/10 net 30". This means that 3% cash discount is available for a cash discount period of 10 days at the beginning of the credit period of 30 days. If the customer does not want to take the advantage of the cash discount, she should pay within 30 days. If she fails to make the payment within 30 days, she will be assumed to be defaulters.

Collection Policy

Not all customers pay on time. In order to accelerate cash payments from sloppy customers, firms lay down collection policy. The main aim is to minimize the incidents of bad debts and the same time it does not have to be too harsh, or there might be loss of customers.

- Collection policy lays down the procedures to be followed in order to ensure effective collection of the receivables, on the expiry of credit period when receivables become due.
- Collection effort means the total effort (costs) the firm is willing to undertake to recover the credit extended. It will depend on whether the firm offers tight or liberal credit standards. With tight credit standards, the collection efforts can be reduced and vice versa.

Degree of Collection Efforts

- Tight collection policy reduces the default costs and thus leads to lesser collection efforts.

- Liberal collection policy on the other hand, helps in gaining confidence of the customers, increasing the sales volume, but may increase the collection costs and efforts.

Types of Collection Efforts

The firm may undertake various types of collection efforts like letters, reminders, phone calls, personal visits, persuasion through collection agencies and finally the legal action. Legal action should be the last resort undertaken as this may impact the relationships with the customers and ultimately the brand image and goodwill of the firm.

Example: Comprehensive Question - DGC Ltd has been set up as a joint venture between DG Ltd. and GC Ltd. The current sales of DGC Ltd. are Rs. 50 Crores. In the recent board meeting, there has been a proposal to relax the existing credit policy of DGC Ltd. in order to increase the sales volume. The board decided to implement the proposal if relaxation in credit policy will lead to a positive impact on the residual income. The present Credit Policy is as under:

- Credit Standards:
    - DGC Ltd. has 4 categories of customers.
    - Category 1 & 2: Given unlimited credit.
    - Category 3: Given limited credit.
    - Category 4: No credit extended to these customers.
- Credit Period: The Company provides 30 days credit to its customers who are deemed eligible for credit.
- Cash Discount: No such discount is currently provided for.

The following additional information is available:

- Contribution margin ratio is 25%.
- Tax rate – 40%.
- Post-tax cost of capital 10%.
- Average collection period (ACP) of credit sales – 20 days.

If company extends unlimited credit to Category 3 customers & limited credit to Category 4 customers, sales of the company is expected to increase by Rs. 10 Crores, on which the bad debt losses are expected to be 10%. ACP however, will remain unchanged.

If company extends its credit period from 30 to 45 days, its sales will increase by 15 crores. ACP will rise to 40 days and expected proportion of Bad debts on additional sales will be 15%. You are required to examine and suggest the: A. The effect of relaxing credit standards. B. The effect of extending credit period. Solutions both parts independently.

Management of Inventory

One of important components of current assets is inventory. Inventory explains the stock of goods the firm has, either in the form of raw materials, semi-finished goods or finished goods. The raw materials and semi-finished goods are converted into finished goods through its manufacturing process. Finished goods are final goods, which are ready for sale. Effective inventory management would ultimately aim at maximization of the owner's wealth, which is consistent with the overall objective of financial management.

Objectives of Inventory Management

Inventory management deals with the following two conflicting requirements:

- To minimize investments in inventory: Maintaining inventory involves costs, thus, the objective of effective inventory management will be to maintain the minimum possible inventory, in order to lower down the costs.
- To ensure sufficient inventories to meet the production and sales demand: Holding sufficient amounts of inventory ensures smooth functioning of the firm.

Costs and Benefits of Inventory Management

In order to achieve the objective of maintaining optimal levels of inventory, the firms need to undertake cost-benefits trade-off for inventory management.

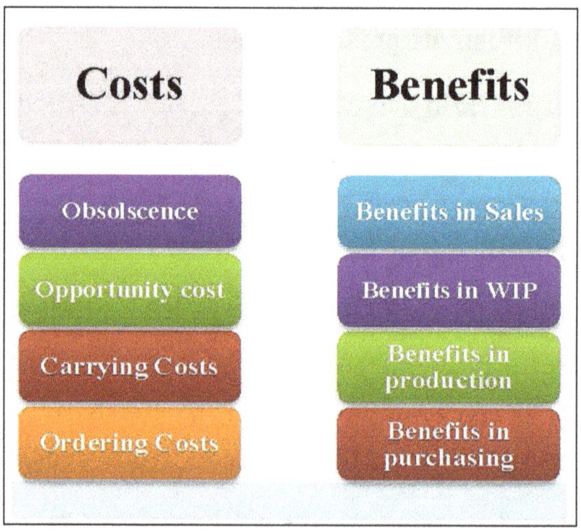

Costs and Benefits Trade-Off for Inventory Management.

Costs of Holding Inventory

- Ordering Costs: These are costs incurred for acquiring or ordering of inventory. For replenishing of stock, firms need to order stock to ensure smooth production. The costs linked with it are the nature of fixed costs like administrative tasks, preparing purchase orders, receiving, inspecting, recording of stock as per the purchase order, etc. These are fixed costs, which necessarily incurred with each order. Higher the number of orders placed, more will be the ordering costs. Thus, ordering costs are inversely related to the size of inventory.
- Carrying cost: These are the costs linked with the maintenance of inventory. These can include storage cost, handling costs, insurance of inventory, etc. Higher the size of inventory, more will be the carrying costs.
- Opportunity Costs: These refer to the expenses to finance the acquisition and maintenance of inventory. Lesser the inventory, less funds would be tied up in inventory and less will be its opportunity costs. If the funds are not tied up in inventory, they can earn a return for the firm.
- Obsolescence: Holding large amounts of inventory over a longer period of time might also lead to obsolescence.

Benefits of Holding Inventory

- Benefits of purchasing: Purchasing raw materials in large quantities will help the firm avail the discounts, which are offered on bulk purchases. This will reduce the cost of acquiring and ordering inventory. Raw materials inventory gives the firm flexibility in purchasing.
- Benefits of production: Finished goods inventory helps in providing flexibility in the production schedule. The firm needs to decide upon the production schedule – whether it has to be continuous (throughout the year) or as per the demand (if seasonal demand) only. Having continuous production lowers down the cost of discontinues in the production process.
- Benefits in Work-in-progress: Shortening of the production process, will lead to reduction in the work-in-progress inventory.
- Benefits of sales: Inventory forms the link between production and sales. Having sufficient inventory helps the firm meet the customers demand. It also helps the firm to gain competitive advantage over its rivals.

Thus, the inventories should be increased only as long as the savings from holding inventories is more than the costs of holding it.

Techniques of Inventory Management

The various problems associated with effective inventory control and the techniques for tackling such problems are:

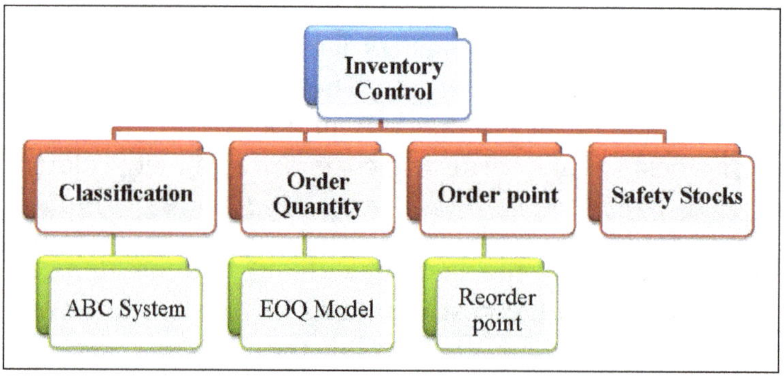

Problems with effective Inventory Control.

Classification Problem: ABC System

Classifying the inventory into various categories determines the type and degree of inventory control required. ABC System is an inventory categorization technique, which suggests that inventories of a firm are not of equal value. Thus, the inventory is grouped into three categories (A, B, and C) in order of their estimated importance.

- 'A' items are very important for an organization. Because of the high value of these 'A' items, frequent value analysis is required. In addition to that, an organization needs to choose an appropriate order pattern (e.g. 'Just- in- time') to avoid excess capacity. For these items, very tight control and accurate records are required.

- 'B' items are important, but of course less important than 'A' items and more important than 'C' items. Therefore 'B' items are intergroup items. For these, very tight control and accurate records are required.

- 'C' items are marginally important. For them, simplest controls possible and minimal records are sufficient.

Examples of ABC class are:

- 'A' items: 20% of the items accounts for 70% of the annual consumption value of the items.

- 'B' items: 30% of the items accounts for 25% of the annual consumption value of the items.

- 'C' items: 50% of the items accounts for 5% of the annual consumption value of the items.

However, sometimes an inventory item in "C Class" although inexpensive, may be critical for the production process and may not be easily available. Thus, in such a case, proper attention needs to be given for its effective management.

Order Quantity Problem

EOQ Model After the classification and identification of the inventory into Class A, B and C, next is the determination of the order quantity. Thus, the management needs to decide upon the following:

- How much inventory should be bought less than one order?
- Should the quantity ordered be large or small?
- Should the inventory be ordered under one lot or in several small lots?

The following figure depicts the impact of holding large and small inventory quantity levels:

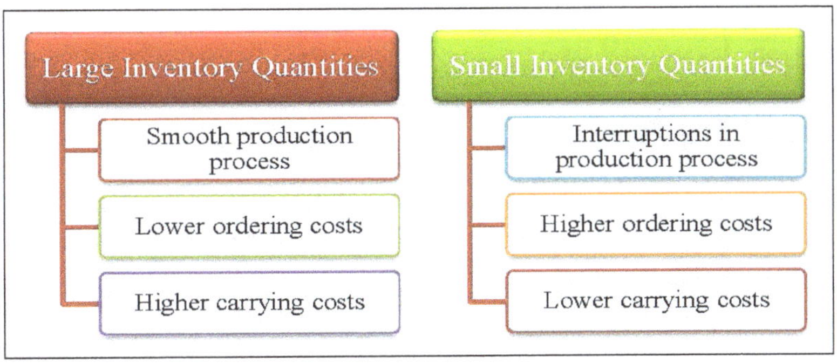

Deciding on the Order Quantity.

Economic Order Quantity (EOQ) Model

The optimum level of inventory can be determined with a popular technique known as Economic Order Quantity (EOQ). EOQ determines the optimum order quantity that minimizes the total cost of inventory management.

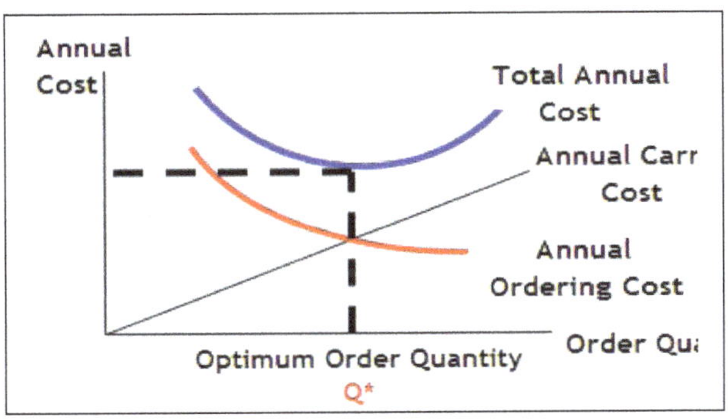

Economic Order Quantity Model.

Q* represents the EOQ level of inventory which leads to minimum total inventory costs. The aim is to find out the order size with lowest total cost (ordering plus carrying).

$$EOQ(Q*) = \sqrt{\frac{2AB}{C}}$$

Where,

- A: Annual usage of inventory.
- B: Buying cost per order.
- C: Carrying cost per unit.

Example: The annual usage for LLC Ltd. is Rs. 2,000 units. The cost per order is Rs. 100 and the carrying costs are Rs. 10 per unit. Thus,

$$EOQ(Q*) = \sqrt{\frac{2(2000)(100)}{10}} = 200\,\text{units}$$

Limitations of EOQ Model

- Assumption of constant consumption and instant replenishment: This may not always happen. The suppliers may take time to deliver inventories, which may take time to refill the stocks.
- Need to maintain additional inventory: There might be unexpected demand for stocks. For the purpose of meeting the contingencies, the company needs to maintain additional safety stocks.
- Assumption of known annual demand: There might be an instability between expected demand and actual demand, which might lead to additional or reduction of inventory levels.

Order Point

EOQ helps to calculate the order size so as to reduce the carrying and the ordering costs.

Reorder Point

Reorder point determines the point at which the order has to be placed to replenish the stocks.

Reorder point = Lead time in days average* Daily usage of inventory

Where, Lead time depicts the time taken in receiving the delivery of the stock, once the order has been placed.

Example: The average daily consumption of stock is 10,000 units. The number of days required to receive the delivery of stock after placing the order is 15 days. Thus, the re-order point will be 10,000 units X 15 days = 1,50,000 units. This means the firm should order for stock for replenishment as soon as the level reaches to 1,50,000 units. The EOQ level, however, will determine the size of the order.

Safety Stock

In the EOQ model, there might be discrepancy in anticipated and actual demand, leading to extra or stock-out situation. Thus, to avoid such a situation, firms tend to keep sufficient safety margin by having additional stock to guard against stock-out situations. Hence, safety stocks represent additional stock, which acts as buffer, or cushion against possible shortage of inventory caused either by increased usage or delayed delivery of stocks.

Costs Related to Safety Stocks

- Stock-out costs: These are costs related with shortage of inventory. The firm may lose out on certain benefits if faced with any stock-out situation. The loss may be in terms of reduced sales, loss of customers, impact on the reputation of the firm, loss in production schedule, etc.
- Carrying costs: These costs would again be the cost of maintaining additional inventory as buffer.

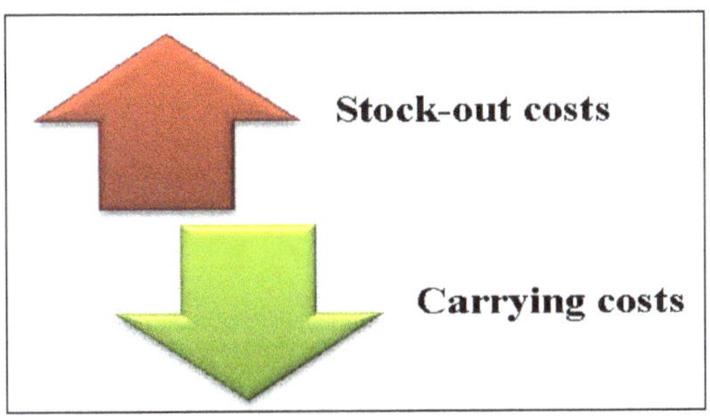

There needs to be a trade-off between the two, as larger safety stock would increase the carrying costs but at the same time, reduce the stock-out costs.

References

- Working-capital-management: lpude.in, Retrieved 27, April 2020
- Why-working-capital-management-important-company-100715: investopedia.com, Retrieved 01, January 2020
- 11-determinants-of-working-capital-financial-management: yourarticlelibrary.com, Retrieved 03, May 2020
- Operating-cycle-and-its-functions-working-capital-11051: accountingnotes.net, Retrieved 10, August 2020

7

Financial Risk Management

The practice associated with the protection of economic value within a firm through the use of financial instruments in order to manage exposure to risk is termed as financial risk management. A few different types of risks considered within this field are operational risk, foreign exchange risk, credit risk and reputational risk. All these diverse types of risks and financial risk management have been carefully analyzed in this chapter.

Financial risk is the possibility of losing money on an investment or business venture. Some more common and distinct financial risks include credit risk, liquidity risk, and operational risk. Financial risk is a type of danger that can result in the loss of capital to interested parties. For governments, this can mean they are unable to control monetary policy and default on bonds or other debt issues. Corporations also face the possibility of default on debt they undertake but may also experience failure in an undertaking the causes a financial burden on the business.

Financial markets face financial risk due to various macroeconomic forces, changes to the market interest rate, and the possibility of default by sectors or large corporations. Individuals face financial risk when they make decisions that may jeopardize their income or ability to pay a debt they have assumed.

Financial risks are everywhere and come in many shapes and sizes, affecting nearly everyone. You should be aware of the presence of financial risks. Knowing the dangers and how to protect yourself will not eliminate the risk, but it can mitigate their harm and reduce the chances of a negative outcome.

Financial Risks for Businesses

It is expensive to build a business from the ground up. At some point in any company's life the business may need to seek outside capital to grow. This need for funding creates a financial risk to both the business and to any investors or stakeholders invested in the company.

Credit risk—also known as default risk—is the danger associated with borrowing money. Should the borrower become unable to repay the loan, they will default. Investors affected by credit risk suffer from decreased income from loan repayments, as well as lost principal and interest. Creditors may also experience a rise in costs for collection of the debt.

When only one or a handful of companies are struggling it is known as a specific risk.

This danger, related to a company or small group of companies, includes issues related to capital structure, financial transactions, and exposure to default. The term is typically used to reflect an investor's uncertainty of collecting returns and the accompanying potential for monetary loss. Businesses can experience operational risk when they have poor management or flawed financial reasoning. Based on internal factors, this is the risk of failing to succeed in its undertakings.

Financial Risks for Governments

Financial risk also refers to the possibility of a government losing control of its monetary policy and being unable or unwilling to control inflation and defaulting on its bonds or other debt issues. Governments issue debt in the form of bonds and note to fund wars, build bridges and other infrastructure, and to pay for its general day-to-day operations. The U.S. government's debt—known as Treasurys—is considered one of the safest investments in the world. The list of governments that have defaulted on debt they issued includes Russia, Argentina, Greece, and Venezuela. Sometimes these entities only delay debt payments or pay less than the agreed-upon amount; either way, it causes financial risk to investors and other stakeholders.

Financial Risks for the Market

Several types of financial risk are tied to financial markets. Many circumstances can impact the financial market. As demonstrated during the 2007 to 2008 global financial crisis, when a critical sector of the market struggles it can impact the monetary well-being of the entire marketplace. During this time, businesses closed, investors lost fortunes, and governments were forced to rethink their monetary policy. However, many other events also impact the market.

Volatility brings uncertainty about the fair value of market assets. Seen as a statistical measure, volatility reflects the confidence of the stakeholders that market returns match the actual valuation of individual assets and the marketplace as a whole. Measured as implied volatility (IV) and represented by a percentage, this statistical value indicates the bullish or bearish—market on the rise versus the market in decline—view of investments. Volatility or equity risk can cause abrupt price swings in shares of stock.

Default and changes in the market interest rate can also pose a financial risk. Defaults happen mainly in the debt or bond market as companies or other issuers fail to pay their debt obligations, harming investors. Changes in the market interest rate can push individual securities into being unprofitable for investors, forcing them into lower-paying debt securities or facing negative returns.

Asset-backed risk is the chance that asset-backed securities—pools of various types of loans—may become volatile if the underlying securities also change in value. Sub-categories of asset-backed risk involve the borrower paying off a debt early, thus ending the income stream from repayments and significant changes in interest rates.

Financial Risks for Individuals

Individuals can face financial risk when they make poor decisions. This hazard can have wide-ranging causes from taking an unnecessary day off of work to investing in highly speculative investments. Every undertaking has exposure to pure risk—dangers that cannot be controlled, but some are done without fully realizing the consequences.

Liquidity risk comes in two flavors for investors to fear. The first involves securities and assets that cannot be purchased or sold quickly enough to cut losses in a volatile market. Known as market liquidity risk this is a situation where there are few buyers but many sellers. The second risk is funding or cash flow liquidity risk. Funding liquidity risk is the possibility that a corporation will not have the capital to pay its debt, forcing it to default, and harming stakeholders.

Speculative risk is one where a profit or gain has an uncertain chance of success. Perhaps the investor did not conduct proper research before investing, reached too far for gains, or invested too large of a portion of their net worth into a single investment.

Investors holding foreign currencies are exposed to currency risk because different factors, such as interest rate changes and monetary policy changes, can alter the calculated worth or the value of their money. Meanwhile, changes in prices because of market differences, political changes, natural calamities, diplomatic changes, or economic conflicts may cause volatile foreign investment conditions that may expose businesses and individuals to foreign investment risk.

Pros and Cons of Financial Risk

Financial risk, in itself, is not inherently good or bad but only exists to different degrees. Of course, "risk" by its very nature has a negative connotation, and financial risk is no exception. A risk can spread from one business to affect an entire sector, market, or even the world. Risk can stem from uncontrollable outside sources or forces, and it is often difficult to overcome.

While it isn't exactly a positive attribute, understanding the possibility of financial risk can lead to better, more informed business or investment decisions. Assessing the degree of financial risk associated with a security or asset helps determine or set that investment's value. Risk is the flip side of the reward. One could argue that no progress or growth can occur, be it in a business or a portfolio, without assuming some risk. Finally, while financial risk usually cannot be controlled, exposure to it can be limited or managed.

Pros	Cons
Encourages more informed decisions.	Can arise from uncontrollable or unpredictable outside forces.

Helps assess value (risk-reward ratio).	Risks can be difficult to overcome.
Can be identified using analysis tools.	Ability to spread and affect entire sectors or markets.

Tools to Control Financial Risk

Luckily there are many tools available to individuals, businesses, and governments that allow them to calculate the amount of financial risk they are taking on. The most common methods that investment professionals use to analyze risks associated with long-term investments—or the stock market as a whole—include:

- Fundamental analysis, the process of measuring a security's intrinsic value by evaluating all aspects of the underlying business including the firm's assets and its earnings.
- Technical analysis, the process of evaluating securities through statistics and looks at historical returns, trade volume, share prices, and other performance data.
- Quantitative analysis, the evaluation of the historical performance of a company using specific financial ratio calculations.

For example, when evaluating businesses, the debt-to-capital ratio measures the proportion of debt used given the total capital structure of the company. A high proportion of debt indicates a risky investment. Another ratio, the capital expenditure ratio, divides cash flow from operations by capital expenditures to see how much money a company will have left to keep the business running after it services its debt.

In terms of action, professional money managers, traders, individual investors, and corporate investment officers use hedging techniques to reduce their exposure to various risks. Hedging against investment risk means strategically using instruments—such as options contracts—to offset the chance of any adverse price movements. In other words, you hedge one investment by making another.

Operational Risk

Operational Risk is a business risk that arises out of day-to-day operations and business activities due to various work-related hazards and uncertain conditions. Such risk may arise from systems, structure, personnel, processes, and products. It is beyond the control of any organization and occurs due to internal failures, breakdowns, or even mismanagement. It does not occur due to external events or factors such as economic turbulence, political uncertainty, etc. Therefore, it is a type of "unsystematic risk" and is unique to a particular company or industry. Operational risk is any risk that may alter or disrupt the regular working process of a business organization. Also, there is a risk of a financial as well as reputations well as reputational loss to the organization.

There is a huge variety of specific operational risks. By their nature, they are often less visible than other risks and are often difficult to pin down precisely. Operational risks range from the very small, for example, the risk of loss due to minor human mistakes, to the very large, such as the risk of bankruptcy due to serious fraud. Operational risk can occur at every level in an organization. The type of risks associated with business and operation risk relate to:

- Business interruption,
- Errors or omissions by employees,
- Product failure,
- Health and safety,
- Failure of it systems,
- Fraud,
- Loss of key people,
- Litigation,
- Loss of suppliers.

Operational risks are generally within the control of the organization through risk assessment and risk management practices, including internal control and insurance.

Application of Operational Risks

Risk Categorization

Risks can be categorized in a number of ways. A popular way is to use one of four main categories, namely operational risk, financial risk, environmental risk and reputational risk. It is important that risks are categorized in a way that is relevant to the needs of the organization. Some of the benefits of categorization include:

- Providing a framework that can be used to define who is responsible, to design appropriate internal controls and to assist in simplified risk reporting.
- Assisting managers to identify how they can use their past experience to categorize risk.
- Helping organizations to identify related risks in the same category.
- Giving assistance in recognizing which risks are inter-related.

Operational Risk Identification

Operational risk sources may be internal or external to the business and are usually generated by people, processes and technology. Identification is one of the most important areas of managing risk. Failure to identify risk will certainly mean that no action is taken to manage that risk.

There are a number of different techniques that can be used to identify risk. A common method used in risk identification is the use of workshops to 'brainstorm'. This can be used at different levels of the organization and can identify a large number of risks in a short time. To keep ideas flowing, it is important to keep identification sessions focused on identifying risks and not to move on to evaluate the risks.

Operational risks are largely based on procedures and processes, so this lends itself to the use of audit for risk identification purposes. Risk based audit can be used as a tool to identify risks, as well as a method of reporting to the board on the effectiveness of the organization's risk management framework. Risk based audit can use the following methods to assess risks:

- Intuitive or judgemental assessment.
- Risk assessment matrix.
- Risk ranking.

Another approach to identifying operational risk is to look for critical dependencies in people, processes, systems and external structures. Once identified, the dependencies can be managed or engineered by adding fail-safes and system redundancies. Other approaches include physical inspection and incident investigation. Once risks have been identified based on a suitable way of categorizing them, it becomes possible to think of tools that may be used to measure and manage them.

Risk Assessment and Measuring

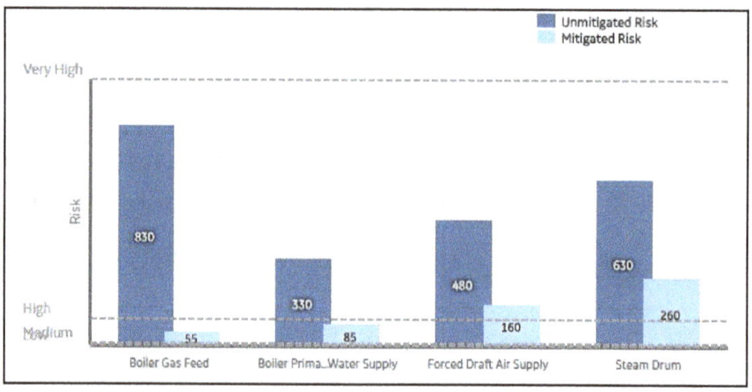

Various methods may be used to assess the severity of each risk once it has been identified. One of the reasons for measuring risk is that it allows the most significant risks to be prioritised. The result or impact of a risk occurring may be financial loss, damage to reputation, process change or a combination of these. One of the simplest ways to measure risks is to apply an impact and likelihood matrix which provides an overall risk rating.

One of the issues with measuring risk is that there are objective or subjective risks. Many risks are subjective and qualitative, rather than objectively identifiable and measurable. For example, the risks of litigation, economic downturn, loss of key employees, natural disasters and loss of reputation are all subjective judgements. There is an important distinction between objective, measurable risks and subjective, perceived risks. Some of the factors that influence this distinction are:

- How recently the risk has occurred.
- How visible the risk is.
- How management perceives the risk.
- How the organization establishes formal or informal ways of dealing with the risk.

The analysis can be either quantitative or qualitative, but it should allow for comparison and trend analysis. One of the issues with risk assessment is that traditional risk assessment techniques often focus on those elements that can be quantified easily. Such techniques fail to address all critical drivers of successful risk management.

Impact of Operational Risks

When considering the impact of operational risk there are three primary areas that affect the business activity.

- Property exposures: These relate to the physical assets belonging to or entrusted to the business.
- Personnel exposures: These relate to the risks faced by all those who work for and with the business, including customers, suppliers and contractors.
- Financial exposures: These relate to all aspects of the company's ability to trade, whether profitability or not, and cover internal and external exposures of all types. Financial exposures also include intellectual property, goodwill and patents.

Managing Operational Risks

Risk evaluation is used to make decisions about the significance of the risks to the organization and whether each specific risk should be accepted or treated. When looking at operational risk management, it is important to align it with the organization's risk appetite. The risk appetite will be influenced by the size and type of organization, its capacity for risk and its ability to exploit opportunities and withstand setbacks. Once the severity of the risk has been established, one or more of the following methods of controlling risk can be applied:

- Accepting the risk,
- Sharing or transferring the risk,
- Risk reduction,
- Risk avoidance.

Insurance is a long established control method for transferring risk. This applies to a number of types of operational risk, for example, damage to buildings. However, more recently there has been an increase in the use of insurance combined with other methods such as business continuity management. One issue with measuring and managing subjective operational risks is that unless the risk occurs, it is not possible to be certain of the impact of the risk. The severity of the risk may be underestimated.

One of the issues with operational risk is the continuously changing business environment. This is stressed in Internal control: guidance for directors on the Combined Code, also known as the Turnbull Report, which states: 'A company's objectives, its internal organization and the environment in which it operates, are continually evolving and, as a result, the risks it faces are continually changing. A sound system of internal control therefore depends on a thorough and regular evaluation of the risks to which it is exposed.'

Once a decision has been made about how to manage or control the risk, it is important to have a process in place to monitor actively and to review and report regularly on the risk management framework. Critical success factors in risk management are:

- Clearly identified senior management to support, own and lead on risk management.
- Existence and adoption of a framework for risk management that is transparent and repeatable.
- Risk is actively monitored and regularly reviewed.
- Management of risk is fully embedded in the management process and consistently applied.
- Clear communication with all staff.
- Management of risks is closely linked to the achievement of objectives.

Foreign Exchange Risk

Foreign exchange risk, also known as exchange rate risk, is the risk of financial impact due to exchange rate fluctuations. In simpler terms, foreign exchange risk is the risk that a business' financial performance or financial position will be impacted by changes in the exchange rates between currencies.

The risk occurs when a company engages in financial transactions or maintains financial statements in a currency other than where it is headquartered. For example, a company based in Canada that does business in China – i.e., receives financial transactions in Chinese yuan – reports its financial statements in Canadian dollars, is exposed to foreign exchange risk.

The financial transactions, which are received in Chinese yuan, must be converted to Canadian dollars to be reported on the company's financial statements. Changes in the exchange rate between the Chinese yuan (foreign currency) and Canadian dollar (domestic currency) would be the risk, hence the term foreign exchange risk.

Foreign exchange risk can be caused by appreciation/depreciation of the base currency, appreciation/depreciation of the foreign currency, or a combination of the two. It is a major risk to consider for exporters/importers and businesses that trade in international markets.

Transaction Risk

Transaction Risk is the exposure to uncertainty factors that may impact the expected return from a deal or transaction. It can include but is not limited to foreign exchange risk, commodity, and time risk. It essentially encompasses all negative events that can prevent a deal from happening. A deal with a high transaction risk will typically require a higher expected return; therefore, it is important to consider such risk when evaluating a prospective investment. In some instances, transaction risk can stop a deal from going through due to potentially negative outcomes associated with the transaction.

Common Transaction Risks

Some of the most common transaction risks that can affect the deal or transaction value include the following:

- Foreign Exchange Risk: Foreign exchange risk is the unforeseen fluctuation of foreign exchange, which can affect the expected transaction value. This risk is especially important to consider for cross-border transactions or deals with countries that have relatively high currency volatility. Foreign Exchange Risk is also called economic exposure.
- Commodity Risk: Similar to foreign exchange, commodity risk considers the unexpected fluctuation of commodity prices. While commodity fluctuation affects all sectors, it is a primary consideration in the Oil & Gas and Mining sectors.
- Interest Rate Risk: Interest rate risk examines how interest rate fluctuation can affect transaction value. Depending on the changes in rates, this risk can affect the ability of the purchasing party to raise the necessary capital for the transaction and can impact the debt obligations of the selling party. For companies that engage in debt covenant agreements with financial institutions, interest rate fluctuation can impact the company's ability to meet its obligations established in the covenant.
- Time Risk: As market conditions and companies change with time, there is a higher probability that the initial transaction agreement conditions will become unfavorable the longer the negotiation process is extended. As a result, deals can fall through due to the favorable conditions no longer being present for both parties. The longer a deal takes to finalize, the longer the transaction is exposed to the other risks.
- Counterparty Risk: When engaging in transactions, there is a risk that the counterparty will not complete their contractual obligations agreed upon in the transaction. In instances where counterparties default on their contractual obligations, it is often due to the effects of the previously stated transaction risks.

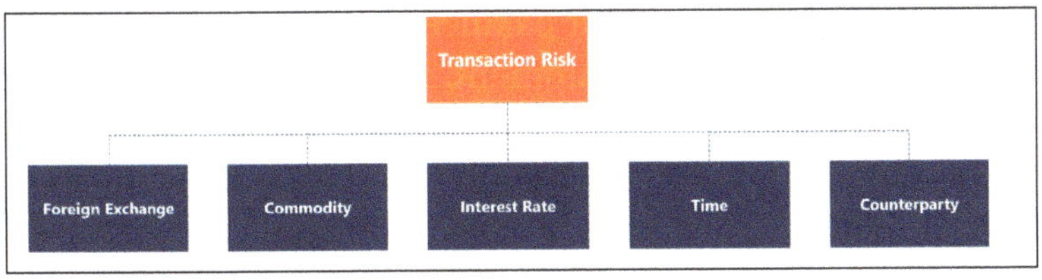

How to Manage Transaction Risk

To mitigate the effects of transaction risk, some precautions each party of the deal can take include the following mitigation techniques. These methods used for transaction risk management are often included in transaction contract clauses or within the deal process.

- Hedging: Companies will engage in hedging arrangements to reduce the level of potential risk from the price movement of various assets. Hedging provides companies with protection against adverse changes to asset prices that can negatively affect investment. Within the context of transactions, companies will often complete hedging arrangements to reduce the effects of Foreign Exchange and Commodity Risk associated with the deal.
- Refinancing: In a fluctuating interest rate environment, companies often look to refinance their debt when interest rates are declining. Debt refinancing allows companies to reduce their debt obligations and to borrow at more attractive rates. To ensure that a party is eligible for refinancing, the borrowing party can include renegotiation clauses in their contracts that allow for refinancing adjustments when notable interest rate changes.
- Due Diligence: To reduce the possibility of the counterparty defaulting on their contractual obligations, parties will undergo an extensive due diligence process to assess various components of the transaction before coming to an agreement. In situations where the counterparty has a higher risk of defaulting, the purchasing party may place a default risk premium into the transaction agreement to create an incentive for taking on more risk.

Including Risks in Financial Models

When including assumptions in a financial model, analysts will often include predictions for commodity prices, interest rates, and other factors associated with transaction risk. Including these assumptions allows analysts to provide comprehensive considerations in their models, leading to better investment decisions. To consider the profitability of an investment in both best and worst-case scenarios, analysts can adjust the prices in these situations according to how they expect market conditions.

Translation Risk

Translation risk is the exchange rate risk associated with companies that deal in foreign currencies and list foreign assets on their balance sheets. Companies that own assets in foreign countries, such as plant and equipment, must convert the value of those assets from the foreign currency to the home country's currency for accounting purposes. In the U.S., this accounting translation is typically done on a quarterly and annual basis. Translation risk results from how many the assets value fluctuate based on exchange rate fluctuations between the two counties involved.

Companies must report their financial performance on a quarterly basis, which involves formulating their financial statements for that quarter. The balance sheet and income statement are two of the financial statements that need to be filed. If a company has assets or revenue in a foreign country, it would likely mean that those assets and revenue would be denominated in the foreign country's local-currency. As a result, the company must translate the value of those assets and revenue into the company's home currency when filing their quarterly financial report. When the exchange rate between the two countries fluctuates, the translation value of those assets and revenue will fluctuate as well.

A financial gain or loss is reported, depending on the extent of the exchange rate movements during the quarter. Any gain a loss would reflect the change in the value of the company's foreign assets based solely on the move in the exchange rate. In actuality, the value of the assets hasn't really changed, but by translating the value of those assets, it provides a clearer picture of what the company owns and its financial performance for that quarter. The risk that the exchange rate could move against the company and depreciate the value of those foreign assets or revenue is called translation risk.

Companies with Translation Risk

Multinational corporations that have international offices have the greatest exposure to translation risk. However, even companies that don't have offices overseas but sell products internationally are exposed to translation risk. If a company earns revenue in a foreign country, it must convert that revenue into the company's home or local currency when they report their financials at the end of the quarter.

If exchange rates have fluctuated by a large amount, this could lead to significant changes in the value of the foreign asset or income stream. This exchange rate volatility or wild fluctuations create risk for the company because it can be challenging to forecast how much exchange rates are going to move relative to each other. The greater the proportion of a company's assets, liabilities, or equities denominated in a foreign currency, the greater the company's translation risk. Translation risk is also sometimes referred to as translation exposure.

Impact of Translation Risk

Exchange rates can change significantly between the reporting of quarterly financial statements, causing variances between the reported figures from quarter to quarter.

This can sometimes cause volatility in the company's stock price. For example, let's say a U.S. company has assets in Europe valued at 1 million euros, and the euro versus the U.S. dollar exchange rate has depreciated by 10% on a quarter-to-quarter basis. The value of the assets, when converted from euros into dollar terms, would also decline by 10%. However, it's not just the assets on the balance sheet that would decline, but revenue and net income (profit) earned in euros would depreciate as well. As a result, a company's reported earnings can be lower due to exchange rate fluctuations leading to a poor quarterly performance and a declining stock price.

Translation risk tends to be higher in developing countries and emerging market economies. Oftentimes, these economies are not fully developed, and the political climate is unstable, which exacerbates the exchange rate volatility of the local currency.

Managing Translation Risk

There are various financial products that companies can use to mitigate or reduce translation risk. One of the most popular products is called a forward contract, which locks in an exchange rate for a period of time. The rate lock allows companies to fix the value of their foreign assets based on the forward contract's exchange rate.

Companies that sell products overseas and earn foreign revenue can request that their foreign clients pay for goods and services in the company's home currency. As a result, the risk associated with local currency fluctuations would not be borne by the company but instead by the client who is responsible for making the currency exchange prior to conducting business with the company. However, the policy of shifting the exchange rate risk onto a foreign customer can backfire, if the customer doesn't want to take on the exchange rate risk, and as a result, finds a local company to do business with instead.

Economic Risk

Economic risk is referred to as the risk exposure of an investment made in a foreign country due to changes in the business conditions or adverse effect of macroeconomic factors like government policies or collapse of the current government and significant swing in the exchange rates.

Types of Economic Risk

Many factors can be a cause of economic risk, although the chances mentioned below are not an exhaustive one. The following are types of Economic Risk:

1. Sovereign Risk: This type of economic risk is one of the most critical risks that can have a direct impact on the investment since the repercussions arising out of these risks can trigger other troubles that are related to the business. Sovereign Risk is the risk that a government cannot repay its debt and default on its payments. When a government

becomes bankrupt, it directly impacts the businesses in the country. Sovereign Risk is not limited to a government defaulting but also includes the political unrest and change in the policies made by the government. A change in government policies can impact the exchange rate, which might affect the business transactions, resulting in a loss where the business was supposed to make a profit.

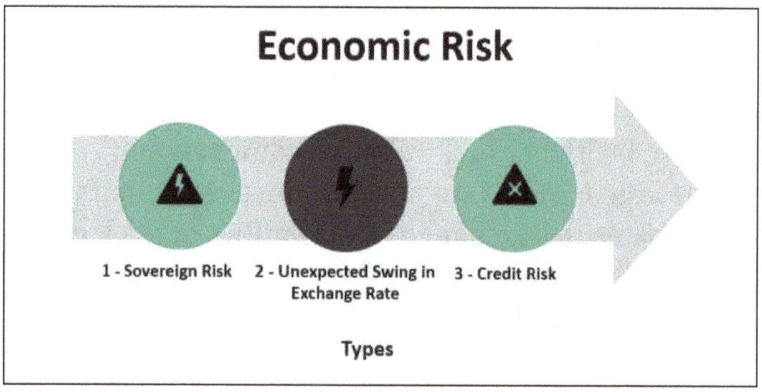

Example: The debt crisis of the Greek government during early 2009 to late 2018, which occurred as an aftermath of the financial crisis of 2007, had occurred because of improper management of funds and lack of flexibility in the monetary policies. The Greek banks could not repay their debts and, as a result, lead to a crisis. The government had to levy increased taxes and reduce the facilities provided to its citizens, which triggered an outrage. The crisis not only disturbed the wellbeing of the local people but also impacted international trade. It brought the turmoil under control by negotiating a 50% haircut for its existing debts owed and by new loans provided by European banks.

2. Unexpected Swing in Exchange Rate: This type of sovereign risk is the risk if the market moves drastically to impact the exchange rate. When the market moves considerably, it affects international trade. This can be due to speculation or the news that can cause a fall in demand for a particular product or currency. Oil prices can significantly impact the market movement of other traded products. Government policies can also result in a dip or hike in the market movement. Change in inflation, interest rates, import-export duties, and taxes also impact the exchange rate. Since this directly impacts trade, exchange rates risk seeming to be a significant economic risk.

Example: A US microchip manufacturer imports electrical circuits from a Chinese manufacturer places an order for CNY 300,000 today, and agrees to pay after 90 days. At the current market price, it would be roughly $43,652, which is CNY 6.87 per dollar. If the market price for yen moves above 6.87, the payment to be made will be above $43,652, whereas if the market price for yen moves below 6.87, the cost to be made will fall below $43,652.

3. Credit Risk: This type of sovereign risk is the risk that the counterparty will default in making the obligation it owes. Credit risk is entirely out of control since it depends on another entity's worthiness to pay its debts. The counterparty's business activities

need to be monitored on a timely basis so that the business transactions are closed at the right time without the risk of counterparty default to make it payments.

Example: In 2016, Invexstar Capital Management failed to make payments for the trades it had done. The company's sole trader only settled those trades which were profitable for his company and refused to make payments for any of the loss-making transactions. This resulted in a chain reaction of losses for the banks dealing with an investor. Market-making banks were impacted economically, which summed up to £120 million. This rogue trading caused regulatory repercussions and also resulted in traders from the banks being sacked for bad KYC checks being done for the clients. The impact of counterparty default might result in a collapse in the whole market, causing market conditions to worsen and stricter trade laws being implemented to curb such payment defaults.

Disadvantages of Economic Risk

- Economic risk can cause the downfall of not just the business but the whole market.
- Although economic risk can be mitigated, it cannot be negated entirely.
- Economic risk impacts international trade and has the potential to create a lasting effect on the business activities of all participants.

Important Points of Economic Risk

- Economic risk is the most challenging risk to foresee, and hence mitigating or formulating plans to control the risk is a challenging task.
- Like all other risks, economic risk can be mitigated by investment options like international mutual funds, which facilitate diversification by allowing investment in various products at a time.
- Economic risk can also be mitigated by investing in insurance, covering the losses arising out of a counterparty defaulting to pay their obligation.
- Hedging activities against exchange rate fluctuation will prove worthwhile to mitigate the risk.

Credit Risk

Credit risk is a measure of the creditworthiness of a borrower. In calculating credit risk, lenders are gauging the likelihood they will recover all of their principal and interest when making a loan. Borrowers considered to be a low credit risk are charged lower interest rates. Lenders, investors, and other counterparties consult ratings agencies to assess the credit risk of doing business with companies.

When determining the credit risk involved in making loans, lenders are judging borrowers' ability to pay back debt. A range of factors go into assessments of credit risk, including credit history and credit score, debt-to-income ratio, and collateral.

- Credit history and credit score: Independent credit bureaus maintain records of borrowers' credit payment history, total debt load, and types of credit taken out to generate credit scores. They sell this data to financial institutions to help them assess credit risks.
- Total debt load: These measures how much existing credit has been extended to a borrower and how much of that credit she has already utilized? The less credit a borrower has used, the more able they should be to pay back a new loan. Creditors like to see how easily a borrower can get credit and judiciously they balance it.
- Debt-to-income ratio: This compares the amount a person makes against their living expenses and debt payments. Lenders use it to decide if a borrower can afford to take on a new debt payment.
- Collateral: This is the assets owned by a borrower that can be used to secure a loan. The more collateral a borrower has, the lower the possible credit risk for a lender.

For companies, credit risk represents the risk that a company may not be able to make payments on its outstanding debt. Ratings agencies – Moody's and Standard & Poor's, for example – analyze bond offerings and issue credit ratings that grade the credit risk of different debt instruments. It's possible to give your creditworthiness a facelift by reviewing your credit report for any mistakes, paying down credit card debt, making all payments on time and cutting expenses wherever possible.

Example: Ignoring credit risks was the major animating factor behind the financial crisis of 2007-2008. In the years leading up to the crisis, banks and other lenders lent vast sums in the form of subprime mortgages to high-risk borrowers. As the economy slowed in 2006-2007, many of these risky borrowers couldn't repay their loans, and the turbulence from this systemic failure to properly account for credit risk nearly wrecked the global financial system in late 2008. Major bank suffered losses because the models they used incorrectly assessed the likelihood of default on mortgage payments.

Reputational Risk

Reputational risk is the risk that some negative circumstance could negatively impact your brand's reputation and image in the marketplace. Damage to a company's reputation can result in decreased revenues, failure to meet key business objectives, loss of market share, reduced shareholder value, and in some cases, financial insolvency or bankruptcy.

Importance of Reputational Risk

A company's reputation affects its ability to do business in the marketplace, appeal to new customers, and drive revenue – activities that are essential for its success and survival. An organization's reputation and brand equity are intangible assets with a real value. They are part of the firm's marketability and should be preserved to ensure its long-term viability. The proliferation of social media means that individuals are empowered to give ratings or write reviews that appear on search engines and impact public perception. The rapid flow of information in the modern world makes it even more crucial for organizations to manage reputational risks.

Potential Sources of Reputational Risk

Reputational risk appears when organizations fail to act ethically, fulfill their duties, and satisfy their customers. There are many situations or circumstances that could negatively impact an entity's reputation, such as:

- Misleading Investors or the Public: Organizations who intentionally mislead investors and the public with fabricated claims of product success and capabilities or falsified financial reports risk doing severe damage to their reputation.
- Poor Working Conditions: An organization's reputation is affected by how its current and former employees reflect on their experiences at work. If an organization offers unfair working conditions and a toxic culture, subjects employees to discrimination, or deals with employee concerns in an unethical way, it may garner a poor reputation as an employer.
- Poor Quality: An organization that delivers poorly performing products and services may see its reputation decline as growing numbers of unhappy customers share their experiences.
- Corruption: Corruption and ethical violations are a significant source of reputational risk. A corruption scandal involving bribery, embezzlement, or antitrust violations could have a significant negative impact on a firm's reputation.
- Poor Data Security and Privacy: Data breaches are a major source of reputational risk in 2021. Organizations whose customer data is stolen by hackers experience significant reputational damage as consumers lose confidence in their competency to safeguard sensitive data.
- Poor Regulatory Compliance: Poor regulatory compliance is a source of reputational risk. An organization with poor compliance could be publicly investigated,

convicted of crimes, and forced to pay hefty fines – all of which negatively impact the brand's perception in the marketplace.

Managing the Risk of Reputational Damage

Companies can manage the risk of reputational damage by implementing internal controls and systems to support regulatory compliance, adequate secure data, detect and prevent corruption, control product quality, maintain safe and healthy working conditions, and deliver timely and accurate information to investors and the public. These objectives can be achieved through the adoption of software technologies that support a comprehensive approach to compliance management.

Market Risk

Risk, whether it be market risk or otherwise, has two components that must both exist for there to be a risk:

- An exposure: In this case the holding of a portfolio of financial instruments.
- An uncertainty: In the case of market risk, the uncertainty lays in the future evolution of the market value of the instruments held. In the event of adverse market developments, the investor is exposed to a loss instead of the expected profit.

Market risk and economic risk should not be confused. Economic risk management is based on long-term investment planning and uses ROI (return on investment) as a fundamental indicator. Market risk management is short-term management (which does not necessarily mean short-termism), in the sense that it aims to avoid substantial losses in the long term by limiting them over a succession of short-term periods.

We immediately notice that risk and result are closely linked. Zero risk does not exist when there is an investment, and as a general rule, the potential gain increases with risk taking. However, there are more or less efficient investment choices in terms of the benefit/risk ratio. The set of portfolios that maximize the potential outcome for a given level of risk (or minimize the level of risk for a given potential outcome) is called the "efficient frontier".

It is closely linked to the valuation of the financial instruments. From this valuation will ultimately result the financial flows generated by the position held, financial flows that directly impact the income statement. This is why risk management is ultimately about asking questions such as:

- What is my position worth today, compared to what it was worth at the time of the acquisition? (Unrealized gain or loss).

- What will my position be worth tomorrow, in a week, in a month, all other things being equal?
- What would my position be worth if this or that market indicator changes?

Valuation of Financial Instruments

Market risk measurement methods therefore require the ability to measure a fair market value (mark-to-market) of the assets held. The calculation of a market value is possible for assets for which there is an active and liquid market. In the absence of such as market, mathematical models (mark-to-model) are used and the question of liquidity risk adds to the management of the market risk itself. Indeed, the market value of the instrument only makes sense if it is actually possible to liquidate the instrument at that price, or if it is certain that the instrument will be held until maturity.

For derivatives, one of the main distinctions with regards to valuation is whether or not the financial instrument is linear. An instrument is said to be linear if its payoff function (result at maturity based on the market value of the underlying) is linear or quasi-linear. Such instruments include spot, forward and futures positions. Non-linear instruments include options, exotic derivatives and bond options (hybrid products).

Market Risk Factors

The market data, which generate market risk for the trading portfolio and on which its valuation depends, are usually classified according to asset classes:

- Rates,
- Foreign exchange,
- Stock,
- Raw materials,
- Credit.

In general, instruments can be categorized by asset class according to the type of market risk to which they are exposed. However, a device is rarely “chemically pure” in terms of the risk factor to which it is exposed. For example, a bond is classically classified as an “interest rate instrument”, but a bond denominated in a currency other than the portfolio’s reference currency also contributes to currency risk. In addition, a corporate bond is exposed to a downgrade risk of the rating of its issuer, which adds a credit component to the risk.

Credit risk is traditionally considered separately. However, in view of the “marketisation” of credit risk, and the existence of instruments specific to this new market such as credit default swaps, the risk of loss related to changes in credit spreads can be considered both a credit risk and a market risk. Market indicators can be imported directly from various sources provided by financial information broadcasters such as Bloomberg or Reuters. The problem with these data is that, however recent they may be, they only provide a picture of a past situation. However, to measure the risk, it is necessary to anticipate the behavior of these indicators in the coming days.

For this, we will have to build a model of the behavior of market indicators, either on the basis of historical data, or on parametric functions, or more often on a combination of the two. For example, the future behavior of a market variable may be based on its past behavior, but with a higher weighting for recent fluctuations.

Measuring Market Risk

To sum up what has just been said, measuring market risk involves market indicator models as well as financial instrument valuation functions. It is then necessary to define a risk metric and calculate this indicator for the portfolio in question. A measure of risk is obtained by the result of this calculation. It is immediately clear that the methodological choices, both in terms of the definition of the indicator chosen and the way it is calculated, have a decisive influence on the measurement of risk. A good indicator is one that gives coherent measures of risks, i.e.:

- If portfolio A consistently produces a lower result than portfolio B, then its risk measure must be higher than that of B.
- If an amount of cash K (risk-free asset) is added to the portfolio, then its risk measure must decrease by the same amount (K).
- If the value of a portfolio is multiplied by an amount M, then its risk measure must be multiplied by the same amount (M).
- If two portfolios A and B are merged, then the risk measure of the resulting portfolio must not be greater than the sum of the initial risk measures of A and B.

Some risk indicators can be more or less well suited and consistent, depending on the nature of the financial instruments held. Risk has two dimensions, a quantitative dimension (how much we risk losing) and a probabilistic dimension (with what probability). Risk indicators can quantify one or the other aspect, or a combination of both.

Moreover, a portfolio rarely consists of single instrument, but as we have just seen, the risk indicator is more or less well suited to the asset class (interest rate, equity, foreign exchange, commodities, credit) and the linearity (or not) of the instrument. Hence the search for synthetic indicators, which led to the concept of Value at Risk, or V@R. These synthetic indicators also need to take into account the correlations between the different markets variables involved in the calculation. The correlation between two variables indicates their tendency to move simultaneously, in the same direction or in opposite directions (correlation does not necessarily mean causality).

Finally, it is important to take into account the use that will be made of the risk measure thus produced. The front office is looking for precise, single-instrument, reactive models. The risk department will adopt a more conservative and comprehensive view of the level of risk and is looking for synthetic indicators, which also have the advantage of facilitating dialogue with the bank's management.

Interest Rate Risk

Interest rate risk is defined as the risk of change in the value of an asset as a result of volatility in interest rates. It either renders the security in question non-competitive or increases its value. Though the risk is said to arise due to an unexpected move, generally, investors are concerned with downside risk. This risk directly affects the fixed-rate security holder. Whenever the interest rate rises, the price of the fixed-income bearing security falls and vice-a-versa.

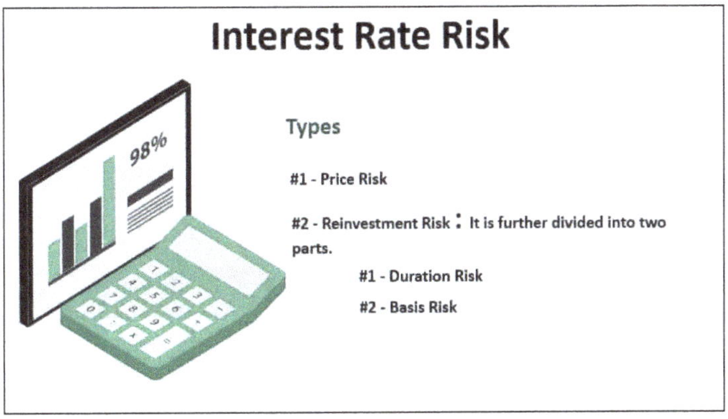

Example of Interest Rate Risk

If an investor has invested some amount in a fixed rate, the bond at the prevailing price, which offers him a coupon rate of 5%, and if thereafter interest rises to 6%, then the price of the bond would decline. This is because the bond is offering a rate of 5% while the market is offering a rate of return of 6%. Hence if the investor wants to sell this bond in the market, the buyer would offer him a lesser amount for the bond as this bond is low-yielding as compared to the market. By doing this, the new investor would try to earn the return similar to the market as the invested amount is less.

In other words, the opportunity cost of getting a better return elsewhere increases with an increase in the interest rate. Hence it results in a decline in bind price. There are various ways of combating the interest rate risk. One can buy interest rate swaps, call or put options for the securities or invest in the negatively correlated securities to hedge the risk.

Impact of Interest Rate Change on Bonds

Interest rate change impacts bonds with different maturities, to a different extent. The correlation between interest rate move and a movement in the price gets stronger with the increase in maturity. This is so because, in case of a rise in interest rate, the bond with a longer maturity will suffer a lower rate of interest for a longer time as compared to a bond with shorter maturity. That's why investing in bonds with different maturities is used as a hedging technique to combat the interest rate risk.

Interest rate change impacts coupon bonds and zero-coupon bonds differently. If we consider both types of bonds with the same maturity, we will be able to experience a sharper decline in the price of zero-coupon bond due to the interest rate rise as compared to the coupon bond. This is because of the fact that the whole amount is to be received at the end of the stipulated period in case of zero-coupon bond and hence, it increases the effective duration whereas the returns are generated periodically in case of coupon bonds, and hence, it reduces the effective duration of repayment.

Interest rate risk is also impacted by the coupon rate. The bond with a lower coupon rate has a higher interest rate risk as compared to a bond with a higher interest rate. This is so, as a small change in the market interest rate can easily outweigh the lower coupon rate and will reduce the market price of that bond.

Types of Interest Rate Risk

There are two types of interest rate risk:

- Price Risk: It is the risk of change in the price of the security, which may result in an unexpected gain or loss when the security is sold.
- Reinvestment Risk: It refers to the risk of change in the interest rate, which may lead to the non-availability of the opportunity to reinvest in the current investment rate. It is further divided into two parts:
    - Duration Risk: It refers to the risk arising from the probability of unwilling pre-payment or extension of the investment beyond the pre-determined time period.
    - Basis Risk: It refers to the risk of not experiencing the exact opposite behavior to interest rate changes in the securities with inverse features.

Calculating Duration and Change in Price Due to the Interest Rate Change

The duration of the security directly relates to the extent to which a change in interest rate will impact the price. It is different from maturity. It calculates the expected change in the price as a result of a 1% change in interest rates. It approximates the price elasticity of demand. It is calculated by adding the product of the time period of cash flow and the respective weights, which are calculated on the basis of the present value of cash flows.

Example: A five-year bond with a face value of $100 is issued with a coupon rate of 6%. It has a semi-annually compounded market yield of 8%. Calculate duration.

Solution: The coupon payment is made on a half-yearly basis. Hence, cash flow after every 6 months would be half of 6%, i.e., $3.

B12 | =-B11*E10*C10

Change in Price = - % Change in Interest Rate * Duration * Current Price

	A	B	C	D	E
1	Years (Time)	Cash Flows ($)	Present Value @ 8% ($)	Weight (PV / Sum of PV)	Duration (Time * Weight)
2	0.5	3	2.88	0.031	0.015
3	1	3	2.77	0.03	0.03
4	1.5	3	2.67	0.029	0.043
5	2	3	2.56	0.028	0.055
6	2.5	3	2.47	0.026	0.066
7	3	3	2.37	0.025	0.076
8	3.5	3	2.28	0.024	0.086
9	4	103	75.26	0.807	3.228
10	**Total**		**93.26**	**1**	**3.599**
11	Interest Rate	0.10%			
12	**Change in Price**	-0.34			
13					

Hence, the duration of this bond is 3.599 years, whereas maturity is 4 years. The price of the bond is the sum total of the present value of all the cash flows, which is $93.27. Change in price is proportional to the change in interest rate, which is calculated by using the following formula:

Change in Price = – % Change in Interest Rate * Duration * Current Price

So, if the % increase in interest rate is 0.1%, then in the above example, the change in the price would be: -0.1% * 3.599 * 93.27 = -$0.34. New price of the bond would be = $93.27 – $0.34 = $92.93.

Advantages:

- Gain from favorable interest rate movements.
- Arbitrage gain by operating in multiple markets.
- Creation of an efficient market platform through the introduction of participants like insurers.

Disadvantages:

- The potential loss from unexpected interest rate movements.
- Increased cost viz. hedging cost, administration cost, etc.

Equity Price Risk

Equity price risk is the risk that the fair value of equities decreases as a result of changes in the levels of equity indices and the value of individual stocks. Each Group subsidiary has in place appropriate strategies, risk management and reporting processes in respect of the risk characteristics of equity investments, including Mudaraba, Musharaka and other investments. Based on Group policies, each subsidiary ensures that its valuation methodologies are appropriate and consistent, and assesses the potential impact of its methods on profit calculations and allocations mutually agreed between that subsidiary and its partners. Further, each subsidiary has defined and established appropriate exit strategies and risk management and reporting processes in respect of its equity investment activities.

Exchange Rate Risk

Exchange rate risk, or foreign exchange (forex) risk, is an unavoidable risk of foreign investment, but it can be mitigated considerably through hedging techniques. To eliminate forex risk, an investor would have to avoid investing in overseas assets altogether. However, exchange rate risk can be mitigated with currency forwards or futures.

- The exchange rate risk is caused by fluctuations in the investor's local currency compared to the foreign-investment currency.
- These risks can be mitigated through the use of a hedged exchange-traded fund or by the individual investor using various investment instruments, such as currency forwards or futures, or options.
- Exchange rate risk isn't completely avoidable but it can be mitigated.

How Exchange Rate Risk Works

For the U.S. investor, hedging exchange rate risk is particularly important when the U.S. dollar is surging since the risk can erode returns from overseas investments. For overseas investors, the reverse is true, particularly when U.S. investments are performing. This is because the depreciation of the local currency against the USD can provide an additional boost to returns. In such situations, since the exchange rate movement is working in the investor's favor, the appropriate course of action is to go unhedged.

The rule-of-thumb, with regard to foreign investments, is to leave the exchange rate risk unhedged when the local currency is depreciating against the foreign-investment currency but to hedge this risk when the local currency is appreciating against the foreign-investment currency.

Two Ways to Mitigate Forex Risk

- Invest in hedged assets: The easiest solution is to invest in hedged overseas assets, such as hedged exchange-traded funds (ETFs). ETFs are available for a wide range of underlying assets traded in most major markets. Many ETF providers offer hedged and unhedged versions of their funds that track popular investment benchmarks or indexes. Although the hedged fund will generally have a slightly higher expense ratio than its unhedged counterpart due to the cost of hedging, large ETFs can hedge currency risk at a fraction of the hedging cost incurred by an individual investor. For example, for the MSCI EAFE index—the primary benchmark for U.S. investors to measure international equity performance—the expense ratio for the iShares MSCI EAFE ETF (EFA) is 0.31%. The expense ratio for the iShares Currency Hedged MSCI EAFE ETF (HEFA) is 0.69.

- Hedge exchange rate risk yourself: Investors most likely have some forex exposure if their portfolio contains foreign-currency stocks or bonds or American depositary receipts (ADRs). A common misconception is that their currency risk is hedged, but that is not the case.

You can hedge currency risk using one or more of the following instruments:

- Currency forwards: Currency forwards can be effectively used to hedge currency risk. For example, assume a U.S. investor has a euro-denominated bond maturing in a year's time and is concerned about the risk of the euro declining against the U.S. dollar in that time frame. The investor can enter into a forward contract to sell euros (in an amount equal to the maturity value of the bond) and buy U.S. dollars at the one-year forward rate. While the advantage of forward contracts is that they can be customized to specific amounts and maturities, a major drawback is that they are not readily accessible to individual investors. An alternative way to hedge currency risk is to construct a synthetic forward contract using the money market hedge.

- Currency futures: Currency futures are used to hedge exchange rate risk because they trade on an exchange and need only a small amount of upfront margin. The disadvantages are that they cannot be customized and are only available for fixed dates.

- Currency ETFs: The availability of ETFs that have a specific currency as the underlying asset means that currency ETFs can be used to hedge exchange rate risk. This is probably not the most effective way to hedge exchange risk for larger amounts. However, for individual investors, their ability to be used for small amounts and the fact that they are margin-eligible and can be traded on the long or short side leads them to provide major benefits.

- Currency Options: Currency options offer another feasible alternative to hedging exchange rate risk. Currency options give an investor or trader the right to buy or sell a specific currency in a specified amount on or before the expiration date at the strike price. For example, currency options traded on the Nasdaq are available in denominations of EUR 10,000, GBP 10,000, CAD 10,000 or JPY 1,000,000, making them well-suited for the individual investor.

Exchange rate risk cannot be avoided altogether when investing overseas, but it can be mitigated considerably through the use of hedging techniques. The easiest solution is to invest in hedged investments such as hedged ETFs. The fund manager of a hedged ETF can hedge forex risk at a relatively lower cost. However, an investor who holds foreign-currency stocks or bonds, or even American depository receipts (ADRs) should consider hedging exchange rate risk using one of the many avenues available such as currency forwards, futures, ETFs or options.

Commodity Price Risk

Commodity price risk refers to financial losses that may occur to both the consumer and the producer when there is a change in commodity prices. A risk for the buyers is that the prices for commodities may be high. Take an example of the carpenters. They have to buy wood to make furniture. If the wood prices go up, it will also mean that the costs of buying furniture will be higher. The producers will have lower profits because there will be few buyers.

Classification of Commodity Price Risk

Generally, producers face the risk of low commodity prices. For instance, if in the first year of planting the prices of crops are high, the farmer plants more hoping for higher profit margins. What will happen when the prices suddenly fall? The farmer makes losses. Commodity price risk does not happen just like that. Factors including weather, technology, politics, market conditions, and seasons affect commodity prices. Financial instruments like futures and options are now in the market to control commodity price risk.

Groups Affected by Commodity Price Risk

- Producers including farmers, mining companies, oil companies, and car manufacturers face price risks on their production inputs.
- Consumers face price risk when the prices go up as this affects their demand for commodities.
- Imposing tariffs on exports causes prices to go up. Exporters also experience hardship in the markets when this happens.
- Governments face price risks, especially when it comes to revenue generation. An increase in prices causes the government to generate more revenue.

Factors Affecting Commodity Prices

- Politics: An increase or decrease in commodity prices can occur due to political factors. In the USA, for example, manufacturers import steel and aluminum from foreign countries. In 2018, President Trump imposed tariffs on the imports. The tariffs' goal was to increase the prices of aluminum, and steel in the USA compared to other countries. China did not take this lightly. They later imposed their tariffs on agricultural products from the US. The low demand for agricultural produce from China meant the crops had to be bought by other countries. As a result, the crop prices in the US market reduced in 2019.

- Weather conditions: Change in seasons and weather conditions largely affect the prices of commodities. Farmers harvest plenty of farm produce towards the end of summer, making prices fall in October. The fluctuation of prices during the major seasons' causes crashes in the stock market. Seasons like drought and floods temporarily lead to a hike in the prices of commodities.

- Transportation and storage costs: The type of commodity will determine its storage mechanism. The commodities that have a physical form need storage spaces before distribution. The cost of storage always affects the overall price of a commodity.

- Technology: Technology has an intense impact on commodity prices. Improvements in technology can cause the prices of a commodity to drop. Take an example of aluminum. It was a valuable metal until new procedures were developed to isolate it. Its value then dropped, and its price in the market decreased.

- Production costs: Capital, labor patterns, raw materials, and production tools have a great influence on the commodity's final price. If the cost of production is high, the commodity price will also be high. However, if the production cost is low, the commodity price will be low. Using hedging futures to control the prices of a commodity Futures markets protect consumers and producers against price fluctuations. A producer faces the risk of prices going down, while consumers face the risk of prices hiking. Hedging protects both parties against financial loss. Futures contracts have periods, and consumers and producers get to choose according to the risks they face. Investors, traders, speculators, and other people in the market can use the futures markets.

References

- Operational-risk, investment-decisions: efinancemanagement.com, Retrieved 10, February 2020
- Foreign-exchange-risk, finance, knowledge: corporatefinanceinstitute.com, Retrieved 30, June 2020
- Economic-risk: wallstreetmojo.com, Retrieved 16, April 2020

- Credit-risk: bankrate.com, Retrieved 23, August 2020
- Equity-price-risk, risk-management, corporate-governance: albaraka.com, Retrieved 17, May 2020
- Commodity-price-risk-definition, investments-trading-financial-markets: thebusinessprofessor.com, Retrieved 11, January 2020

Permissions

All chapters in this book are published with permission under the Creative Commons Attribution Share Alike License or equivalent. Every chapter published in this book has been scrutinized by our experts. Their significance has been extensively debated. The topics covered herein carry significant information for a comprehensive understanding. They may even be implemented as practical applications or may be referred to as a beginning point for further studies.

We would like to thank the editorial team for lending their expertise to make the book truly unique. They have played a crucial role in the development of this book. Without their invaluable contributions this book wouldn't have been possible. They have made vital efforts to compile up to date information on the varied aspects of this subject to make this book a valuable addition to the collection of many professionals and students.

This book was conceptualized with the vision of imparting up-to-date and integrated information in this field. To ensure the same, a matchless editorial board was set up. Every individual on the board went through rigorous rounds of assessment to prove their worth. After which they invested a large part of their time researching and compiling the most relevant data for our readers.

The editorial board has been involved in producing this book since its inception. They have spent rigorous hours researching and exploring the diverse topics which have resulted in the successful publishing of this book. They have passed on their knowledge of decades through this book. To expedite this challenging task, the publisher supported the team at every step. A small team of assistant editors was also appointed to further simplify the editing procedure and attain best results for the readers.

Apart from the editorial board, the designing team has also invested a significant amount of their time in understanding the subject and creating the most relevant covers. They scrutinized every image to scout for the most suitable representation of the subject and create an appropriate cover for the book.

The publishing team has been an ardent support to the editorial, designing and production team. Their endless efforts to recruit the best for this project, has resulted in the accomplishment of this book. They are a veteran in the field of academics and their pool of knowledge is as vast as their experience in printing. Their expertise and guidance has proved useful at every step. Their uncompromising quality standards have made this book an exceptional effort. Their encouragement from time to time has been an inspiration for everyone.

The publisher and the editorial board hope that this book will prove to be a valuable piece of knowledge for students, practitioners and scholars across the globe.

Index

www.ingramcontent.com/pod-product-compliance
Lightning Source LLC
LaVergne TN
LVHW080612210926
848485LV00003B/149